Barcus, Francis Earle, 1927-
    Children's television; an analysis of
programming and advertising / F. Earle Barcus
with Rachel Wolkin. New York, Praeger, 1977.
    xxvii, 218 p. : ill. ; 25 cm. (Praeger
special studies in U.S. economic, social, and
political issues)
    Includes bibliographical references.
    1. Television and children. 2. Television
programs for children--U.S. 3. Television
advertising--U.S. I. Wolkin, Rachel, joint
author.
                                    CIP

Children's Television

F. Earle Barcus
with Rachel Wolkin

The Praeger Special Studies program—
utilizing the most modern and efficient book
production techniques and a selective
worldwide distribution network—makes
available to the academic, government, and
business communities significant, timely
research in U.S. and international economic, social, and political development.

Children's Television

An Analysis
of Programming
and Advertising

PRAEGER SPECIAL STUDIES IN U.S. ECONOMIC, SOCIAL, AND POLITICAL ISSUES

Praeger Publishers   New York   London

Library of Congress Cataloging in Publication Data

Barcus, Francis Earle, 1927–
    Children's television.

    (Praeger special studies in U.S. economic, social,
and political issues)
    Includes bibliographical references.
    1. Television and children. 2. Television programs
for children—United States.   3. Television advertising—
United States.   I. Wolkin, Rachel, joint author.
II. Title.
HQ784.T4B35   791.45'5   76-12843
ISBN 0-275-23210-7

HQ
784
.T4
B35

PRAEGER PUBLISHERS
200 Park Avenue, New York, N.Y. 10017, U.S.A.

Published in the United States of America in 1977
by Praeger Publishers, Inc.

789   038   987654321

This report represents a kind of inventory of the major aspects of programming for children. Because of the broad scope of the study, I was frequently frustrated by not being able to investigate in more depth some areas that deserve a more penetrating examination: the types and nature of violence in the programs; the value structures in program content; interpersonal relationships between characters; questions of racial and sexual roles; and specific advertising techniques employed, among others. It is hoped the data will provide a starting point that will lead to more detailed analysis by the increasing number of young scholars and researchers who are involving themselves in the study of broadcasting to children.

Content analysis, as a research technique, does not provide answers to many of the important issues in children's television. Questions of effects and policy can only be inferred from a description of the content of programming. Nevertheless, such studies are valuable in describing the stimulus; they provide what have been referred to as "cultural indicators" of important aspects of society. Such indicators give us a picture of the overall nature of children's television and point up changes and trends over time. It is in this spirit that the present study was conducted.

ACKNOWLEDGMENTS

The research for this study was supported by a grant from Action for Children's Television (ACT). My thanks to Peggy, Debbie, Rachel, Maureen, Jean, and others on the staff of ACT for their cooperation in providing access to background materials and continued encouragement—and, perhaps more important, for their lack of interference in the conduct of the study, a policy valued by those involved in social research. Needless to say, any errors and misinterpretations are my own.

I also would like to thank Lisa Block, who acted as my chief research assistant throughout all phases of the analysis; Gloria Bersi, who typed the sometimes complex and detailed tables in the original reports; and Meriam Isser, Howard Foxman, Fred Luhman, and Richard Woodward for work in coding, editing, and computer analysis of the data.

CONTENTS

LIST OF TABLES

LIST OF ABBREVIATIONS

ACT   Action for Children's Television

CA   Commercial announcement

FCC   Federal Communications Commission

FTC   Federal Trade Commission

NAB   National Association of Broadcasters

NCA   Noncommercial announcement

INTRODUCTION
Rachel Wolkin

Before television, a child's awareness of the world, of people,
of values, and of ideas was largely filtered through a parent or
other adult. Now, almost from birth, children are exposed to the
influence and expectations of society through the images on a television screen. An American child under the age of 16 has spent more
time watching television than in any other activity except sleep.
Although television's power to affect the thoughts, dreams, attitudes,
and actions of developing children has not been fully measured, its
impact has generated a vast literature recounting the often-conflicting
opinions of broadcasters, advertisers, psychologists, educators,
physicians, consumer groups, and the federal government.

Action for Children's Television (ACT) commissioned a content
analysis of weekend and weekday afternoon commercial children's
television to provide an objective context for scientific research
and a meaningful assessment of the changes occurring in children's
television. This study, prepared by Dr. F. Earle Barcus of Boston
University, includes a breakdown of advertising themes and formats,
a measure of the incidence of aggressive behavior, and descriptions
of racial, cultural, and sexual representations. These data will
give new insight to concerned television critics and perspective to
those engaged in research and in broadcasting decision making.

ACT began in 1968 at Newtonville, Mass., as an informal group
of parents, teachers, and physicians concerned about what children
were seeing on television. Determined to improve children's programming, ACT monitored children's television, studied the structure of the broadcast industry, and examined the process of decision
making that had produced the seemingly endless series of cartoons,
directed at children, that were saturated with violence and excessive
commercialism. Today ACT is a national citizens' organization
with thousands of members, focusing attention on the important
issues of programming and advertising to children.

ACT realized that in order to bring about long-term change,
it was necessary to revise the financial basis of children's television.
It found that advertising on children's television limits the diversity
of programming and encourages a reliance on violence. Programs
peppered with fast action or violence are used to attract a large
audience and therefore can command a higher price to advertisers.
Richard Dodderidge, president of Brewer Advertising, pointed out
that "if the violence gets the ratings, violence will get the adver-

tising." If network executives gave a higher priority to the needs of children than to the interests of advertisers, they would not have to appeal to the entire 2-11-year-old market and could provide programming of high quality designed for children of different ages.

ACT took these messages to Washington in February 1970, when it petitioned the Federal Communications Commission (FCC) to eliminate advertising from children's television. The major principles of the petitions were the following: there shall be no sponsorship and no commercials on children's television; no performer shall be permitted to use or mention brand names during children's programs, nor shall such names be included in any way during children's programs; each station shall provide a minimum of 14 hours per week of age-specific programming for children. One year later, after strong public support for ACT's petition, the FCC made it the essence of a rule-making notice. In the four and one-half years that followed, the FCC held extensive hearings and received more than 100,000 letters and comments, over 95 percent in support of ACT's position—the largest response ever received by the FCC for any rule making prior to that time.

While awaiting action by the FCC, ACT continued to work for change, with some success. According to the National Association of Broadcasters (NAB) Code, vitamins and fireworks can no longer be advertised on children's television; programming for children includes more variety in viewing alternatives; host selling is no longer allowed on children's programs; advertising time has been reduced by 40 percent—from 16 minutes to 9.5 minutes per hour on weekends and from 14 minutes to 12 minutes per hour on weekdays.

These changes are noteworthy, but it is important to recognize that the NAB is a voluntary, self-regulatory association of the television industry and that its members represent only 60 percent of the stations in this country. Further, the code guidelines avoid the issue of the inability of young children to cope with any form of advertising and do not address the basic problem presented by ACT in its FCC rule-making comments: that industry reliance on ratings limits diversity in programming.

Despite the FCC's recognition of children's vulnerability to advertising and the broadcasters' special responsibility toward children, it refused to promulgate a single rule to guarantee that this responsibility be met. Rather, it issued an inconclusive staff report and policy study. Acknowledging the problems of excessive commercialization and current advertising practices, the FCC pointed out the importance of age-specific programming and the responsibility of broadcasters to provide programs that are "designed to educate and inform" children. However, rather than promulgating a rule reflecting the 63 volumes of accumulated evidence, it chose to rely on industry self-regulation.

The results of the Barcus study raise several significant issues. Of primary importance is the question of whether industry self-regulation is an adequate substitute for federal regulation to insure that all children are protected from unfair and misleading advertising practices. The factual data presented in the study strongly point to the necessity for enforceable guidelines that would pertain not only to the NAB Code subscribers but to the industry as a whole.

Although advertising time has been reduced, commercial messages interrupt programs on an average of every 2.9 minutes. Sugared products are featured in more than one-quarter of the ads on weekend commercial television and in almost one-half of the commercials on weekday afternoon programs on independent channels. Especially on the independent stations, programming is mostly entertainment, dominated by out-of-date cartoons that depict an unrealistic picture of a child's world. An examination of character representation demonstrates that women and blacks are rarely portrayed. Violence appears on 60 percent of the independents' programs and continues to play an important role in commercial programming on the weekends.

Diversity of program content, sexual and racial character representation, and advertising practices are key issues to be addressed in children's television.

Advertising forms an integral part of the child's television fare. As a selling vehicle, television provides the young viewer with many of his or her first concepts of what foods to eat and what toys to own. An advertisement directed to children not only sells products; it also sells such sociocultural messages as how to gain peer acceptance and how to evaluate oneself. The advertiser tells children that owning something new is fun. He portrays sweetness as the most desirable quality to be found in food.

Sexual stereotypes are reinforced in these messages by authoritative male announcers and passive female consumers. The representation and participation of minorities in commercials are negligible. In the commercials studied by Dr. Barcus, blacks appeared only in commercials for snack foods. Other minorities were shown only in toy commercials. If young white viewers relied on the advertisers' portrayal of "haves" and "have-nots," of whom to play with or to seek as friends, their perception of the world would be lily-white. Young black viewers see an idealized world in which they have no place.

Independent and government-sponsored research clearly demonstrates that young children and adults have drastically different perceptions of commercial messages. Classic psychological theories have been applied to the study of young viewers' responses to advertising. These studies show that very young children have difficulty perceiving the distinction between fantasy and reality. Scott Ward of Harvard, in his extensive study of advertising and children, found that it is not until a child reaches the fourth grade that he or she develops a clear recognition of commercial motive.[1]

A study in the Harvard Business Review strongly suggests that not until a child is 11 years old does he or she develop a full cognitive ability to evaluate individual commercial messages.[2] It also strongly indicates that children have difficulty understanding the moral justification for false statements made within commercials. However, despite their disappointments, nine- and ten-year-olds continue to have high expectations of the promises made by commercial messages. This response pattern to ads produces frustration and tension. The authors of the study explain, "We recognize that TV advertising is only one way in which society affects the child's growth, but at some point we must decide whether we wish to reduce his exposure to apparently institutionalized hypocrisy, which is what misleading advertising represents to the child until he learns how to interpret it."

Advertising also places stress upon parent-child relationships. This tension, particularly felt within less affluent families, was documented in a study commissioned by ACT. In that study, Daniel Yankelovich, Inc., found that mothers' complaints about television advertising centered around "misrepresentation of the product, manipulation of the child, stress and strain imposed upon low-income mothers by the demands created by the commercials and a generally unhealthful environment."[3] A chief reason for the child's vulnerability to manipulative messages has been expressed by Dr. Richard Feinbloom of the Harvard Medical School, who points out that for a child, an advertisement "has the quality of an order, not a suggestion."[4]

With this understanding of the problems inherent in advertising to children, the question becomes whether advertising should be permitted on children's television. If one does permit advertising, a strong argument exists for the regulation of the kinds of products advertised to children. The Barcus study demonstrates that cereal, candy, snacks, and soft drinks are promoted in roughly half of the ads on children's television. Fruit, milk, meat, and vegetables are virtually nonexistent. There are inherent contradictions between the broadcast industry's purported commitment to serve the needs of its child audience and its insistence on promoting products that are potentially injurious to a child's health.

Dr. Joan Gussow, professor of nutrition at Columbia Teachers College, stated:

The use of expensively produced and appealing television commercials to promote highly sweetened snack-type food to the almost total exclusion of simple foods such as fruits and vegetables, grains, beans, meats, and dairy products is promoting poor nutrition. If the television-watching child ate only the foods she/he is being urged to eat on television, she/he would be malnourished. Since television is now perhaps the single most educative force in the community, occupying more of a child's time than any other single activity except sleep, it is clear something must be done.[5]

These nutritional problems are even more serious for low-income families when their limited financial resources are diverted to the purchase of costly processed snack foods at the expense of diverse, more nutritious, natural food items.

The advertising techniques used to sell these products is another issue subject to scrutiny. Dr. Barcus found various approaches employed to make products particularly appealing to children. Premium offers were common selling mechanisms in cereal commercials. Animated figures, exaggerated audio effects, and visual enlargements were present in both toy and food ads. The themes of action, power, speed, popularity, and sweet taste were frequently emphasized in promoting the product. In addition, there was virtually no information about a product's price, weight, size, durability, or ingredients. A child might not even know that two separate components are necessary to make the advertised toy operate.

Advertising is but one means whereby television transmits social values and helps to structure the perceptions a child develops of himself and others. Character representation is a more subtle, but equally effective, way by which this medium conveys messages about cultural attitudes and life styles. It operates within programming as a statement of what kinds of people merit respect within society; what forms of behavior are rewarded or appreciated by adults and peers; what racial group is socially and economically successful; what occupational roles males and females can and should have. Through the presentation of character roles, children's television has the capacity to expand or contract the young viewer's images of himself and society.

Although television has been termed the child's "window on the world," it more often operates as a periscope to a fantasy land. As the Barcus study demonstrates, most characters are white males whose time is spent resolving personal rivalries or overseeing domestic problems. Given this limited perspective, the child is denied an awareness of the exciting and diverse contributions to society of every ethnic and racial group. Television also has failed to reflect participation by women in all professions and their greater self-determination of their futures.

Television on independent stations is particularly remiss in its afternoon program portrayal of character roles. Because more than a quarter of weekday afternoon programming is composed of dated programs that were initially designed for adults, sexual and racial stereotypes abound. Weekday afternoon programming also attracts a large child audience for cartoon comedy. Within this format, minorities are practically nonexistent, and males constitute 80 percent of the characters portrayed. Sexual and racial representation does not fare any better on weekend commercial television.

In the article "Girls in Cartoons," in Journal of Communication, Helen Streichen describes the results of monitoring animated children's programs: "In general, cartoon females were less numerous than males, made fewer appearances, had fewer lines, played fewer 'lead roles,' were less active, occupied many fewer positions of responsibility, were less noisy, and were preponderantly more juvenile than males. Mothers worked only in the house; males did not participate in housework."6

In the same issue of the Journal, Ann Beuff reports on interviews of children aged three to six years who were questioned about their feelings of sex-role portrayal. She notes that 67 percent of the heavy viewers chose stereotyped careers for themselves. Generally, girls envied male activities and one boy stated, "Oh, if I were a girl I'd grow up to be nothing."7 Intentionally or not, producers seem to be following the advice of Kenneth Roman and Jane Maas, who write in How to Advertise: "Cast children carefully . . . girls emulate boys, but boys don't emulate girls. When in doubt, cast boys."8

When racial character representation is examined, the hidden message seems to be "cast whites." Although adult television has broadened its presentation of minorities, children's television has not been so responsive. On both commercial weekend and weekday afternoon independent programs, 96 percent of the characters were white. Black characters frequently were presented as children or teen-agers, while other minority groups, such as Orientals or Chicanos, were never portrayed on children's television. Since racial minorities constitute 60 percent of the U.S. population, the omission of minority character representation can hardly be deemed an oversight. Young black viewers must be painfully aware they are excluded. Girls are denied professional role models to emulate. All children are presented with an unrealistic image of society.

Leifer, Gordon, and Graves noted the possible impact of these messages in their article "Children's Television: More Than Mere Entertainment," published in Harvard Educational Review. They observed: "At the very least [television] helps to socialize a new generation of children into an already existing pattern. To the extent that television does not reflect reality, it socializes children into a fictitious social system. . . ."[9]

Violence plays a significant role within television's social system. It is a prime means for conflict resolution within dramatic programs, and it is a vehicle for humor within animated shows. The statistics in the Barcus study demonstrate that while there has been some decrease in portrayals of violence on network weekend programming, there is still a high incidence of violence on independent afternoon programming. Even though the overall amount of violence appears to be reduced, the data indicate that overt acts of aggression have been replaced with natural and accidental violence or threats of violence. There is scholarly support for the concept that impending or overwhelming threat to someone or something with whom children can identify is likely to be more frightening than an overt battle scene.

These new data can be applied to the various theoretical assumptions regarding television violence, ranging from Feshbach and Singer's[10] assertion that violence is cathartic to the argument raised by Bandura and Walters that television can help initiate new forms of aggressive behavior.[11] However, regardless of the violence hypothesis one supports or the effects one attributes to portrayal of aggression, the Barcus study indicates that many broadcasters have not chosen to portray alternative forms of problem solving.

Rather, there has been reliance upon the theory that aggressive behavior is the easiest and best way of keeping the child's attention. This adherence to a stylized portrayal of problem solving through aggressive action is consistent with the generally superficial treatment of interpersonal relations. Topics such as love, jealousy, and personal frustration, which could be treated with dramatic sensitivity, are dealt with only in entertainment programs and primarily in cartoon comedy.

Rather than utilizing television as an exciting medium for the presentation of diverse ideas, cultural exchange, and educational growth, broadcasters have chosen, for the most part, the economic security of one-dimensional characters who lack depth of feeling and who offer the child a monotonous litany of clichés.

NOTES

1. S. Ward, G. Reale, and D. Levinson, "Children's Perceptions, Explanations, and Judgements of Television Advertising:

A Further Explanation," in Television in Day-to-Day Life: Patterns of Use, ed. E. A. Rubenstein, G. A. Comstock, and J. P. Murray (Washington, D.C.: U.S. Government Printing Office, 1972), pp. 516-25, vol. 4, Television and Social Behavior.

2. T. G. Bever et al., "Young Viewers' Troubling Response to TV Ads," Harvard Business Review 53, no. 6 (November-December 1975): 109-19.

3. Daniel Yankelovitch, Mother's Attitudes Toward Children's Television Programs and Commercials (Newtonville, Mass.: Action for Children's Television, 1970).

4. Evelyn Kaye, The Family Guide to Children's Television: What to Watch, What to Miss, What to Change and How to Do It (New York: Pantheon, 1974), p. 75.

5. Joan Gussow, "Counternutritional Messages of TV Ads Aimed at Children," Journal of Nutritional Education 4, no. 2 (1972): 48-52.

6. Helen White Streicher, "The Girls in the Cartoons," Journal of Communication 24, no. 2 (Spring 1974): 125-29.

7. Ann Beuff, "Doctor, Lawyer, Household Drudge," Journal of Communication 24, no. 2 (Spring 1974): 142-45.

8. Kenneth Roman and Jane Maas, How to Advertise (New York: St. Martin's, 1976), p. 141.

9. Aimee Dorr Leifer, Neal J. Gordon, and Sherryl Browne Graves, "Children's Television: More Than Mere Entertainment," Harvard Educational Review 44, no. 2 (1974): 221.

10. Seymour Feshbach and Robert D. Singer, Television and Aggression (San Francisco: Jossey-Bass, 1971).

11. Albert Bandura and Richard Walters, Social Learning and Personality Development (New York: Holt, Rinehart and Winston, 1963).

Children's Television

CHILDREN'S COMMERCIAL
TELEVISION ON THE WEEKENDS

METHODOLOGY

The studies reported here are content analyses of two separate samples of children's television. The first is an analysis of programming and advertising on Saturday and Sunday mornings in Boston, Massachusetts, during April 1975. The second is a study of programming in the after-school hours (3:00-6:00 pm) on weekdays for a sample of ten independent television stations across the United States.

The studies are treated separately because they represent two distinct varieties of children's television. Traditionally, Saturday and Sunday mornings have been the prime period for programming addressed to children. All the major networks program exclusively for children during the bulk of this time period. Although a good deal is known about the nature of weekend children's television, there has been no previous systematic analysis of the after-school programming. Such programming is broadcast, to a large extent, by nonnetwork independent stations. It draws large child audiences and therefore deserves careful study.

The basic procedures in the studies were similar to those used in a study of Saturday children's programming in 1971.* However, the current studies are expanded in scope to include additional analyses that will shed light on current issues and concerns in children's television.

---

*F. Earle Barcus, Saturday Children's Television (Newtonville, Mass.: Action for Children's Television, 1971).

Briefly, the procedures included live monitoring and concurrent video-tape recording of all programming matter; playback and coding of each individual unit of programming (program segments, commercial announcements, program promotion, and noncommercial public-service announcements); and detailed analysis of these separate programming elements. (Study codes are included as Appendix A.)

Monitoring, coding, and editing were done by paid graduate students in communication research, broadcasting, and media technology under the direct supervision of F. Earle Barcus. Analysis was carried out with the statistical packages at the Boston University computing center.

The above procedures yielded a total of 25.5 hours of weekend and 30 hours of after-school weekday programming. The sample of weekend programming was distributed as shown below.

			Total Minutes	Hours
Saturday, April 12, 1975				
WBZ–TV Ch. 4 (NBC)	7:00am–11:30am, 12 noon– 1:30pm	360	6.0
WCVB–TV Ch. 5 (ABC)	7:00am–11:30am	270	4.5
WNAC–TV Ch. 7 (CBS)	7:00am– 1:30pm	390	6.5
Sunday, April 27, 1975				
WBZ–TV Ch. 4 (NBC)	10:30am–11:00am	30	0.5
WCVB–TV Ch. 5 (ABC)	7:00am– 9:30am	150	2.5
WSBK–TV Ch. 38 (ind.),	8:00am–11:30am	210	3.5
WLVI–TV Ch. 56 (ind.),	10:00am–12:00 noon	120	2.0
Total time monitored		1,530	25.5

For the after-school program sample, ten stations were selected by compiling a list of all independent television stations from Broadcasting Yearbook (1975 edition). TV Guide and other program sources were then obtained for these stations, as were data on the size of the child audiences for the programs. The period covered is represented by the Nielsen Station Index reports for February-March 1975.

Code sheets were completed for each program appearing between 3:00 and 6:00 pm for 68 of 73 independent television stations in 43 markets.* Distribution of these stations is given below by market size.

------

*Data were not available for five stations. Appendix B lists individual stations, by market.

Market Size	Type of Station		
	VHF	UHF	Total
Large market (825,000 or more television households)	13	27	40
Medium market (550,000 to 825,000 television households)	5	12	17
Small market (550,000 or fewer television households)	4	12	16
Totals	22	51	73

In this preliminary analysis more than 200 hours of programming was classified. The largest amount is represented by large market stations (nearly 55 percent of the total) and by UHF stations (67 percent). The number and total time of programs, by type of station and market size, is given in Table 1.1.

TABLE 1.1

Independent Station Programs, by Type of
Station and Market Size

Type of Station/ Market Size	Number of Programs Studied	Time (minutes)	Percent of Total Time
VHF stations			
Small market	20	720	5.9
Medium market	28	900	7.4
Large market	66	2,340	19.3
Total VHF	114	3,960	32.6
UHF stations			
Small market	55	1,860	15.3
Medium market	61	2,040	16.8
Large market	120	4,290	35.3
Total UHF	236	8,190	67.4
All stations			
Small market	75	2,580	21.2
Medium market	89	2,940	24.2
Large market	186	6,630	54.6
Total VHF and UHF	350	12,150 (202.5 hours)	100.0

To select the sample of stations for detailed study, all 43 markets with independent stations were classified according to market size:

Small   = 100,000 to 599,000 television households
Medium = 600,000 to 849,000 television households
Large   = 850,000 or more television households

There also were three categories of child audience ratings for programs broadcast between 3:00 and 6:00 pm. Stations that had no data available, that were outrated by network-affiliated stations carrying competing nonnetwork programming, and that had average child audience ratings of less than 7 were excluded from further consideration. These procedures eliminated 11 of the 43 markets, and resulted in a matrix of 32 markets from which to sample.

Median 2-11-Year-Old Program Ratings	Size of Market		
	Large Market	Medium Market	Small Market
20 and over	New York* Dallas-Fort Worth Minneapolis-St. Paul	Seattle* Indianapolis Cincinnati Kansas City, Mo. Milwaukee*	Louisville* Las Vegas San Diego
14 to 19	Los Angeles Washington, D.C.* Cleveland St. Louis	Houston Miami Atlanta* Portland, Ore.	Norfolk* South Bend Denver
7 to 13	Chicago Boston San Francisco Detroit*	Tampa Sacramento*	Phoenix Orlando Buffalo* Charlotte, N.C.

*Market selected for study.

Funds permitted a sample of 10 stations from the 32 markets. One station was selected from each cell with four or fewer markets listed and two stations from the one cell with five markets. These were chosen to provide geographic spread and to obtain an approximate proportion of VHF and UHF stations as they exist in the total population of independent stations (roughly 70 percent UHF). For markets with more than one independent station, the one with the larger average child audience rating was selected. The resulting sample, therefore, represents stations from ten markets selected according to market size, average child audience ratings for their programs, geography, and VHF-UHF balance. The ten markets and stations selected for the final sample are listed below.

City	Station	Chan-nel	Day	Date	Time	Total Min-utes
New York	WNEW	5	Friday	6/13/75	3:00-6:00pm	180
Washing-ton, D.C.	WDCA	20	Monday	6/16/75	3:00-6:00pm	180
Buffalo	WUTV	29	Monday	6/16/75	3:00-6:00pm	180
Detroit	WKBD	50	Tuesday	6/17/75	3:00-6:00pm	180
Milwaukee	WVTV	18	Wednesday	6/18/75	3:00-6:00pm	180
Louisville	WDRB	41	Thursday	6/19/75	3:00-6:00pm	180
Norfolk-Portsmouth	WYAH	27	Tuesday	6/17/75	3:00-6:00pm	180
Atlanta	WTCG	17	Wednesday	6/18/75	3:00-6:00pm	180
Seattle-Tacoma	KSTW	11	Thursday	6/19/75	3:00-6:00pm	180
Sacramento-Stockton	KXTL	40	Tuesday	7/1/75	3:00-6:00pm	180

1,800
(30 hrs.)

PROGRAMS

All program time, including commercial announcements (CAs), program promotion (promos), noncommercial, public-service announcements (NCAs), other miscellaneous time (such as station identification), and program segments, was tabulated to obtain an overall picture of the distribution of broadcast time.

A breakdown of total time studied is given in Table 1.2, by station. For all stations combined, approximately 16 percent was devoted to commercial announcements (CAs and promos) and about 1 percent to NCAs. Almost 80 percent was devoted to actual program content. The stations varied somewhat in the amount of commercial and noncommercial minutes. Channel 56 (ind.) had the greatest proportion of commercial announcement time (20 percent, or 24 minutes out of two hours of Sunday morning programming), followed by Channel 7 (CBS) with almost 18 percent. Channel 38 (ind.) devoted proportionately more time to program promos; and Channels 4, 5, and 38 were highest in time devoted to NCAs. Channel 7 (CBS) devoted less than one minute in 6.5 hours of Saturday morning programs to NCAs.

TABLE 1.2

Total Time Studied, by Station and Type
of Material

Type of Material	Ch. 4 (NBC)	Ch. 5 (ABC)	Ch. 7 (CBS)	Ch. 38 (ind.)	Ch. 56 (ind.)	All Stations
			Minutes			
Program time	306.93	340.62	319.08	162.76	93.08	1,222.47
CAs	52.33	40.42	61.50	24.50	21.68	200.43
Promos	4.97	16.66	8.26	10.50	2.50	42.89
Total CAs	57.30	57.08	69.76	35.00	24.18	243.32
NCAs	18.10	17.92	.75	9.17	2.50	48.44
Other*	7.67	4.38	.41	3.07	.24	15.77
Total time (mins.)	390.00	420.00	390.00	210.00	120.00	1,530.00
Total time (hrs.)	(6.5)	(7.0)	(6.5)	(3.5)	(2.0)	(25.5)
			Percent			
Program time	78.7	81.1	81.8	77.5	77.5	79.9
CAs	13.4	9.6	15.8	11.7	18.1	13.1
Promos	1.3	4.0	2.1	5.0	2.1	2.8
Total CAs	14.7	13.6	17.9	16.7	20.2	15.9
NCAs	4.6	4.3	0.2	4.4	2.1	3.2
Other*	2.0	1.0	0.1	1.4	0.2	1.0
Totals	100.0	100.0	100.0	100.0	100.0	100.0

*Station identification announcements, dead air, and miscellaneous transitional material not included above.

Program segments were coded as to station, length, origin, use of animation, program type, subject matter, and time and place settings. In addition, up to five major characters in each segment were classified according to age group, sex, and ethnic status.

Program Origin and Use of Animation

Of all program material studied, about half was of network origin, one-third was recorded-syndicated material, and the remainder was locally produced (Table 1.3).

Channels 4 and 5 both produced more than one hour of local children's programs—almost one-fourth of total program time on each station. This contrasts with Channel 7, which depended entirely on direct or delayed network material, and with the UHF channels, which broadcast only recorded programs.

Overall, more than half of all time used traditional cel animation, about one-third was nonanimated, and the remainder mixed format or 3-D animation. Again, however, there were great differences by station, with Channel 38 using only cel animated programming, Channels 5 and 7 about half, Channel 4 about one-third, and Channel 56 one-quarter.

TABLE 1.3

Program Origin and Use of Animation,
by Station
(percent)

	Ch. 4 (NBC)	Ch. 5 (ABC)	Ch. 7 (CBS)	Ch. 38 (ind.)	Ch. 56 (ind.)	All Stations
Program origin						
Local	26	22	—	—	—	13
Recorded-syndicated	15	37	—	100	100	35
Network	59	41	100	—	—	52
Use of animation						
Cel animation	36	49	57	100	24	53
3-D animation (puppets)	—	9	—	—	27	4
Nonanimated	64	36	22	—	49	36
Mixed	—	6	21	—	—	7
Total minutes	(307)	(341)	(319)	(163)	(93)	(1,223)

Program Format

Twenty-five format classifications were used to classify the program segments in detail. Overall, about 80 percent of the time was devoted to entertainment programming, and more than half of this was cartoon comedy. (See Table 1.4.)

Channels 4 and 5 provided the most varied children's fare, with approximately one-third of programming devoted to information for children; Channel 7 broadcast about half as much informational programming. The two UHF channels were strictly entertainment channels: Channel 38 was devoted solely to cartoon comedy and Channel 56 to other types of comedy. Detailed format categories allow us to see what is not being broadcast, as well as what is. CBS provided the only light children's variety programming, but

TABLE 1.4

Program Format, by Station
(percent)

Program Format	Ch. 4 (NBC)	Ch. 5 (ABC)	Ch. 7 (CBS)	Ch. 38 (ind.)	Ch. 56 (ind.)	All Stations
Situation comedy (I Love Lucy, Gilligan's Island)	–	–	–	–	49	4
Family drama (Leave It to Beaver)	–	8	–	–	–	2
Cartoon comedy (Bugs Bunny, Pink Panther, Flintstones)	29	32	42	100	24	42
Other comedy drama (Little Rascals, Addams Family)	7	–	–	–	27	4
Animal adventure (Lassie's Rescue Rangers, Run Joe Run)	8	6	–	–	–	4
Crime/mystery/detective	–	–	–	–	–	–
Action/adventure (Emergency Plus Four, Devlin, Shazam)	7	7	29	–	–	11
Western	–	–	–	–	–	–
Fantasy/science fiction (Star Trek, Land of the Lost)	15	–	–	–	–	4
Other drama (Davey and Goliath)	–	15	–	–	–	4
Movies	–	–	–	–	–	–
Variety (Hudson Bros., Harlem Globe Trotters)	–	–	14	–	–	4
Quiz	–	–	–	–	–	–
Sports events	–	–	–	–	–	–
Other entertainment	–	–	–	–	–	–
Total entertainment programs	66	68	85	100	100	79
Children's news (In the News)	–	–	7	–	–	2
Documentary/travel (Go, What's the Senate All About?)	7	–	8	–	–	4
Animal/nature films	–	–	–	–	–	–
Interviews/panels (For Kids Only)	18	–	–	–	–	4
Discussion/debate	–	–	–	–	–	–
Music and fine arts	–	–	–	–	–	–
Foreign-language programs	–	–	–	–	–	–
Other informational (Vision on, Make a Wish, Jabberwocky, Captain Bob)	9	32	–	–	–	11
Total informational programs	34	32	15	–	–	21
(Total minutes)	(307)	(341)	(319)	(163)	(93)	(1,223)

8

otherwise concentrated on either cartoon comedy or action-adventure stories. No channel carried strictly crime/mystery formats, western drama, movies, quiz shows, or sports events. Nor were there any films dealing with animals or nature, programs of music and fine arts, or foreign-language programs.*

Because of the diversity of format categories used, they are collapsed into six categories: cartoon comedy, other comedy drama, action-adventure drama, variety, quiz, other entertainment, and information (Table 1.5).

TABLE 1.5

Collapsed Format Categories, by Station
(percent)

Format	Ch. 4 (NBC)	Ch. 5 (ABC)	Ch. 7 (CBS)	Ch. 38 (ind.)	Ch. 56 (ind.)	All Stations
Cartoon comedy	28	32	42	100	24	42
Other comedy drama	7	8	–	–	76	10
Action-adventure drama	31	28	29	–	–	23
Variety/quiz	–	–	14	–	–	4
Other entertainment	–	–	–	–	–	–
Information	34	32	15	–	–	21
Total minutes	(307)	(341)	(319)	(163)	(93)	(1,223)

Origins of the Formats

It was noted earlier that approximately half of all program time studied was network-originated. Such programming provided all children's variety, and the bulk of action-adventure drama, whereas other comedy programs were primarily recorded (Table 1.6). Through the local efforts of Channels 4 and 5, half of information program time was local and about one-third was network-originated.

———

*This is not to say that these subjects were neglected altogether, only that there were no total program formats devoted to them. Later, programs are classified by subject regardless of the traditional format categories in which the topics appear—for instance, a cartoon comedy may deal with a historical event.

TABLE 1.6

Format by Program Origin, All Stations
(percent)

Format	Local	Recorded	Net-work	Total	Total Minutes
Cartoon comedy	—	45	55	100	(518)
Other comedy drama	—	81	19	100	(119)
Action-adventure drama	8	19	73	100	(281)
Variety/quiz	—	—	100	100	(45)
Information	50	19	31	100	(260)
All formats	13	35	52	100	(1,223)

Time and Place Settings of Dramatic
Format Programs

Some interesting images are conveyed through the basic time
and place settings of television drama. First, current or contemporary settings account for approximately 70 percent of the time,
and U.S. settings for more than 80 percent (Table 1.7). In addition,
it is interesting to note that whereas U.S. settings are about evenly
divided between city and rural locales, when the action takes place
in foreign settings, it is in a rural context 80 percent of the time.

TABLE 1.7

Time and Place Settings of Dramatic
Format Programs

	Minutes	Percent
Time settings		
Distant past	144	17
Recent past	71	8
Contemporary	578	69
Future	48	6
Total drama time classified	841	100
Place settings		
U.S., city	352	41
U.S., rural	369	43
Foreign, city	21	2
Foreign, rural	68	8
Outer space	48	6
Total drama time classified	858	100

The Use of Violence

It was not among the main purposes of this study to investigate in detail the portrayal of violence in children's television; that has been done elsewhere. We did, however, attempt to obtain an overall index of the use of violence by classifying each program segment according to the extent of violence (Table 1.8).

In 30 of 70 program segments (42 percent) representing 545 of 918 minutes (59 percent of drama time), there was either no violence or only small acts that were quite incidental and minor. On the other hand, 29 percent of the segments representing 16 percent of drama time were classified as "saturated" with violence. (These were the cases in which the violence was so frequent and recurring that, without it, there would be little to sustain the dramatic segment.) Although it was subordinate to the overall plot (the violence could have been eliminated without seriously affecting the story line), another 29 percent of the segments, representing 25 percent of total drama time, contained observable acts of violence.

Violence was most frequently found in comedy formats, with one-third of the stories "saturated" (22 percent of total time); yet 40 percent (63 percent of time) had no violence or only incidental violence. Action-adventure programs avoided direct and repeated violence in the plots. In 54 percent there was none, or violence only incidental to the plot. Violence was still present, however, in

TABLE 1.8

The Extent of Violence

Extent of Violence	Comedy Formats	Other Dramatic Formats	Total Drama
Percent of segments			
With no violence	14	39	18
With incidental violence	26	15	24
With violence subordinate	25	46	29
Saturated with violence	35	—	29
Total segments	(57)	(13)	(70)
Percent of time			
With no violence	21	35	25
With incidental violence	42	17	34
With violence subordinate	15	48	25
Saturated with violence	22	—	16
Total time	(637)	(281)	(918)

TABLE 1.9

The Nature of Violence

	Number of Segments		Percent of Total Segments*		
	Comedy Drama	Other Drama	Comedy Drama	Other Drama	All Drama
Segments with					
Chase scenes	30	5	53	39	50
Deaths	—	1	—	8	1
Injuries	13	6	23	46	27
Human violence with weapons	33	2	58	15	50
Human violence without weapons	20	2	35	15	31
Natural and accidental violence	7	4	12	31	16
Death or injury as a result of violence	11	5	19	39	23
Violence directed at humans	16	5	28	39	30
Frightening situations	6	10	11	77	24
Total segments	(57)	(13)			

*Percent of segments in which chase scenes, deaths, injuries, and so on occur one or more times.

the more serious drama as well as comedy drama. In 6 out of 13 action-adventure drama segments there were violent acts portrayed, although they were classified as subordinate to the story.

In addition to this overall classification, there were several questions related to the nature of the violence. The most popular form of violence (in 50 percent of drama segments) was that involving weapons (Table 1.9).

About one-third contained violence without weapons (fists, kicking, and so on), and more than 10 percent of the segments contained natural or accidental violence (floods, storms, accidents). In about 25 percent, violence resulted in injuries to others. Although violence was directed at humans in about 30 percent of the segments, it resulted in injury in only about 20 percent.

There is considerable difference in the nature and extent of violence in comedy versus the more serious action-adventure formats.

Traditionally, cartoon comedy has employed chase scenes and attacks with and without weapons as humorous devices. Many segments are based on interpersonal rivalry in which violent actions predominate. (For example, in the Bugs Bunny cartoon "Shis-Ka-Bugs," the plot revolves around attempts by the cook to kill and cook Bugs Bunny.)

There has been a change in the action-adventure programs currently being produced. What seems to be happening is that instead of portraying overt acts of violence (such as, for example, in the older Speed Racer series and similar programs), there is greater reliance on the possibility of violence through threatening situations and on natural or accidental violence to maintain the atmosphere of excitement.

Compared with comedy drama, action-adventure segments contain less human violence with and without weapons, more natural and accidental violence, more threatening situations, and violence more frequently resulting in death or injury. The variety of forms in which aggressive and violent acts take place—often in a humorous context—are summarized in Appendix D.

Program Subject Matter

The basic question asked here is "What kinds of subjects are being treated in children's weekend television and in what contexts are the subjects most likely to occur?" In this analysis, the coding scheme allowed for classification of each program segment into 2 of 19 major subject classifications (Table 1.10).

Overall, more than half of the program time (57 percent) was concentrated in five subject areas: interpersonal rivalry (the effort of one character to "win" over another, 14 percent), the entertainment world (13 percent), domestic topics (home, family), crime, and the supernatural (10 percent each). The remaining 43 percent of time was distributed widely over 14 other subject categories.

Different formats focus on different subjects. Cartoon comedy emphasizes interpersonal rivalry, the supernatural, and crime, whereas other comedy uses primarily domestic subjects and business as topics for humor. Other drama uses more diverse subjects—crime, the supernatural, nature and animals, religion, the entertainment world, and domestic subjects. Informational programming offers the only time devoted to government and public affairs, race and nationality, literature, crafts, and language. The latter format devotes considerably more time to other topics as well.

When considering subject categories, there is the basic question of the effect of format upon certain subjects. For example, love and romance, the supernatural, education, war, and interpersonal

TABLE 1.10

Program Subject Matter, by Format

(percent)

Subject Matter	Cartoon Comedy	Other Comedy	Action-Adventure	Variety	Information	All Types
Domestic (marriage, home, family)	9	34	8	–	5	10
Crime (robberies, police, crime detection)	12	10	19	–	–	10
Historical (association with historical events)	4	–	10	–	6	6
Religion (church, clergy, religious customs)	–	–	6	–	a	2
Love and romance (relations between sexes)	5	–	–	–	–	2
Supernatural (magic, the occult)	14	11	15	–	–	10
Nature and animals (hunting, exploring)	3	4	15	–	6	6
Race/nationality (minorities, foreign)	1	–	–	–	14	4
Education (schools, teachers, training)	3	–	–	–	a	1
Business and industry (labor, private business)	–	22	–	–	1	3
Government/public affairs (law, politics, government)	–	–	–	–	18	4
Science and scientists (medicine, technology)	4	–	4	–	–	3
Entertainment world (sports, show business)	9	11	8	100	16	13
War/armed forces	2	–	–	–	1	1
Literature/fine arts	1	–	–	–	5	1
Interpersonal rivalry (jealousy, conflict)	32	–	5	–	–	14
Crafts/hobbies	–	–	–	–	10	2
Language (words, spelling)	–	–	–	–	6	2
Other, not classifiable above	1	8	10	–	11	6
Totals	100	100	100	100	100	100
(Minutes)b	(787)	(213)	(470)	(45)	(503)	(2,018)

aLess than 0.50 percent.

bTotal minutes coded for subject. Each program segment was coded for one or two subject categories.

rivalry are dealt with only in entertainment programs—primarily in cartoon comedy. Is there a need for a balance in which education, love, and interpersonal relations might be more seriously treated?

In the opposite view, is it not possible that topics such as race, government, literature, and language could be treated in an entertaining manner through drama or other formats, as well as in straight informational contexts?

Program Popularity

Nielsen rating data for February–March 1975 were obtained to determine the basic popularity of different program formats.* Basic program ratings (percent of total children aged 2-11 viewing) and the percent of the total audience who were 2-11 years old were obtained to find an index of program popularity (Table 1.11). Cartoon comedy had the highest average rating—51 cartoon segments drew 11.5 percent of children and the highest percent child audience (73 percent). Although second highest in ratings (11.0), variety programs had the lowest child audience, on the average (51.5 percent). Least popular among children were other comedy programs (average 7.7 rating and 60 percent child audience). (See Table 1.12.)

Characters in the Programs

Up to five major characters in the programs were classified as to sex, age group, and ethnic status. This provided a picture of the "population" of children's television and the resulting sexual and social images that are reinforced. A total of 400 major characters were classified in 97 program segments studied, an average of 4.1 characters per program segment or story.†

Children's television hardly gives a representative picture of society. Of 400 characters, 301 were male and 88 female. The remainder were animal or other characters for which sex could not

---

*Since data were not available for the April period monitored, these should be regarded as the best available estimates of the child audience. Almost all of the same programs were broadcast in the Nielsen rating period.

†"Character" was defined to include all persons, animals, or other anthropomorphic beings that played a major role in the story— or, on information programs, who acted as hosts, panelists, or guests.

TABLE 1.11

Popularity of Children's Television Programs, Boston
(ratings and percent child audience ranked by program format)

Format and Program Title	Channel	2-11 Child Rating	Percent Child Audience
Cartoon comedy			
Bugs Bunny Show	5	21	70
New Adventures of Gilligan	5	21	69
Hong Kong Phooey	5	18	76
Pebbles and Bamm Bamm	7	15	83
Wally Gator and Friends	38	15	78
Bugs Bunny and Friends	38	14	70
Porky Pig and Friends	38	13	73
I Dream of Jeannie	7	13	77
New Pink Panther Show	4	12	60
Addams Family	4	12	82
Fat Albert and the Cosby Kids	7	12	62
Yogi's Gang	5	12	86
Mel-O-Tunes	38	11	76
Bailey's Comets	7	11	86
My Favorite Martian	7	10	79
Goober	5	10	82
Wheelie and the Chopper Bunch	4	8	82
Jetsons	4	8	51
U. S. of Archie	7	8	87
Rocky and His Friends	38	8	61
The Flintstones	56	8	75
Mr. Magoo and Friends	38	8	77
Nutty Squirrels	38	4	72
Other comedy drama			
Sigmund and the Sea Monsters	4	10	73
Gilligan's Island	56	9	56
Leave It to Beaver	5	8	44
Little Rascals	56	7	69
I Love Lucy	56	5	46
Action adventure			
Scooby Doo Where Are You?	7	16	74
Shazam	7	14	64
Land of the Lost	4	12	69
Emergency Plus Four	4	11	83
Devlin	5	10	68
Lassie's Rescue Rangers	5	10	73
Speed Buggy	7	10	89
Valley of the Dinosaurs	7	9	69
Davey and Goliath	5	8	83
Run Joe Run	4	5	68
Jabberwocky (story segment)	5	4	85
Star Trek	4	1	10
Variety and quiz			
Hudson Brothers Razzle Dazzle Show	7	13	52
Harlem Globe Trotters Popcorn Machine	7	9	51
Information			
What's the Senate All About?	7	10	53
Nature World of Captain Bob	5	7	80
Vision on	5	3	78
Jabberwocky	5	2	84
Something Else	4	2	55
For Kids Only (Sunday)	4	1	44
Go	4	1	38
Make a Wish	5	0	80
For Kids Only (Saturday)	4	0	15
Grammar Rock (3 segments)	5	*	*
Mayflower (1 segment)	5	*	*
In the News (12 segments)	7	*	*

*These programs' ratings and percent child audience statistics vary according to the half-hour program segment aired.

TABLE 1.12

Average Ratings and Percent Child Audience,
by Program Format

Program Format	Average Rating	Average Percent Child Audience	Number of Program Segments
Cartoon comedy	11.5	73.2	51
Other comedy drama	7.7	59.5	6
Action-adventure	9.1	70.6	13
Variety/quiz	11.0	51.5	2
Information	8.2	68.6	25

be determined (Table 1.13). By age distribution, 17 percent were children, 12 percent teens, and 61 percent adults, with the remainder animals and others with age indeterminable. Thus, for every female there were 3.4 males. For children the female-male ratio was 1:2.8; for teens, 1:1.6; and for adults, 1:3.9. When others (animals or other anthropomorphic characters for which age was not determinable) were portrayed, the ratio was 1:2.6.

Sex distributions were relatively constant for all categories of programs except informational formats (Table 1.14). In cartoon comedy, the ratio of females to males was 1:4.3; in other comedy, 1:3.8; in action-adventure drama, 1:3.1. In informational programming it was 1:1.8.

One would expect a greater number of child characters in children's television than was found. Only in "other" (nonanimated) comedy was there a substantial proportion of children (15 of 29 characters). All other program types, except for informational programs, in which 28 percent of 67 characters were children, had less than 20 percent children.

Ethnic status was coded for 72 percent (288) of 400 major characters. Of these, 89 percent were white, 7 percent black, and 4 percent of other minority or ethnic group. In addition to having better balance in the sex and age distribution of characters, informational programs contained proportionately more black and other minorities than did dramatic formats. In drama 94 percent of all characters were white, 4 percent black, and 2 percent other minorities, whereas in informational programs 78 percent were white, 9 percent black, and 13 percent other minorities (Table 1.15).

Blacks were disproportionately portrayed as children. Whereas overall, only 7 percent of all characters were black, they constituted

TABLE 1.13

Sex, Age Group, and Ethnic Status of the Characters

	Number	Percent
Male children		
White	34	8.5
Black	7	1.7
Other ethnic	2	.5
Unknown ethnic status, animals, others	8	2.0
Total male children	51	12.7
Male teens		
White	27	6.8
Black	1	.2
Other ethnic	2	.5
Unknown ethnic status, animals, others	—	—
Total male teens	30	7.5
Male adults		
White	125	31.3
Black	8	2.0
Other ethnic	6	1.5
Unknown ethnic status, animals, others	55	13.8
Total male adults	194	48.6
Male, age and race unknown	26	6.5
Total males	301	75.3
Female children		
White	17	4.3
Black	1	.2
Other ethnic	—	—
Unknown ethnic status, animals, others	—	—
Total female children	18	4.5
Female teens		
White	17	4.3
Black	—	—
Other ethnic	1	.2
Unknown ethnic status, animals, others	1	.2
Total female teens	19	4.7
Female adults		
White	36	9.0
Black	2	.5
Other ethnic	1	.2
Unknown ethnic status, animals, others	11	2.8
Total female adults	50	12.5
Female, age and race unknown	1	.2
Total females	88	21.9
Other characters, age, sex, race unknown	11	2.8
Total all characters	400	100.0

TABLE 1.14

Age and Sex of Characters, by
Program Format
(percent)

Sex and Age Group	Cartoon Comedy	Other Comedy	Other Drama	Variety	Information	Total
Male children	8.1	51.7	11.5	10.0	14.9	13.1
Male teens	6.8	–	16.4	–	7.5	7.7
Male adults	56.7	24.1	42.6	70.0	41.8	49.9
Male animals	9.5	3.5	4.9	10.0	–	6.7
Total males	81.1	79.3	75.4	90.0	64.2	77.4
Female children	1.8	–	8.2	–	13.4	4.6
Female teens	4.5	–	8.2	–	6.0	4.9
Female adults	12.2	20.7	8.2	10.0	16.4	12.8
Female animals	.4	–	–	–	–	.3
Total females	18.9	20.7	24.6	10.0	35.8	22.6
Total children	9.9	51.7	19.7	10.0	28.3	17.7
Total teens	11.3	–	24.6	–	13.5	12.6
Total adults	68.9	44.8	50.8	80.0	58.2	62.7
Total animals	9.9	3.5	4.9	10.0	–	7.0
Total characters classified	(222)	(29)	(61)	(10)	(67)	(389)
Sex unknown	(4)	(1)	(3)	–	(3)	(11)
Total characters	(226)	(30)	(64)	(10)	(70)	(400)

TABLE 1.15

Ethnic Status of Characters, by Format

	Percent White	Percent Black	Percent Other Ethnic	Number of Characters
Characters in:				
Cartoon comedy	93.7	4.7	1.6	128
Other comedy	93.2	3.4	3.4	29
Action-adventure	96.4	3.6	–	56
Variety	50.0	50.0	–	8
Information	77.6	9.0	13.4	67
All characters	89.2	6.6	4.2	288

TABLE 1.16

Age Group of Characters, by Race

| Age Group | Race | | | Total Characters |
	Percent White	Percent Black	Percent Other Minorities	
Children	84	13	3	61
Teens	92	2	6	48
Adults	90	6	4	178
Totals	89	7	4	287

only 2 percent of teens and 6 percent of adult characters. However, 13 percent of children were black (Table 1.16).

ADVERTISING

Overall, there were 614 different announcements in the 25.5 hours of programming studied: 66 percent were product commercials, 19 percent program promos, and 15 percent NCAs (Table 1.17). This amounts to an average of one announcement every 2.5 minutes—and a commercial message every 2.9 minutes.* NCAs appear less frequently—an average of one every 16.6 minutes of time. Each announcement averages almost 30 seconds, although NCAs tend to be longer than CAs, and promos are considerably shorter. Major differences by station are in the longer promos and NCAs on Channel 38; for CAs, programs on Channels 7 and 56 are the most heavily saturated and those on Channel 5 the least. CAs appeared an average of every 2.6 minutes on the independent Channel 56, but only every 5.2 minutes on Channel 5.

Several elements of CAs were analyzed. The CAs were coded by product type, use of animation, form, type of product display, time and place settings, and audience appeal. Announcers or charac-

---

*This is not to say that programs are "interrupted" every 2.9 minutes for a CA, but that if one were to average them out over the total time period, there would be a commercial every 2.9 minutes. A separate analysis of program interruptions by nonprogram material showed that stations were following current NAB guidelines, which call for a maximum of two interrupting breaks for announcements during any half-hour program.

TABLE 1.17

Number and Type of Announcements, by Station

Station and Type of Announcement	Number	Time	Average Length	Total Time	Number per "x" mins.
Channel 4 (NBC)					
CAs	102	52.33	.51	390	3.8
Promos	15	4.97	.33	390	26.0
Total comm'ls.	117	57.30	.49	390	3.3
NCAs	41	18.10	.44	390	9.5
Total Channel 4	158	75.40	.48	390	2.5
Channel 5 (ABC)					
CAs	81	40.42	.50	420	5.2
Promos	44	16.66	.38	420	9.5
Total comm'ls.	125	47.08	.48	420	3.4
NCAs	30	17.92	.60	420	14.0
Total Channel 5	155	74.00	.48	420	2.7
Channel 7 (CBS)					
CAs	124	61.40	.50	390	3.1
Promos	36	8.26	.23	390	10.8
Total comm'ls.	160	69.76	.44	390	2.4
NCAs	3	.75	.25	390	130.0
Total Channel 7	163	70.51	.44	390	2.4
Channel 38 (ind.)					
CAs	50	24.50	.49	210	4.2
Promos	17	10.50	.61	210	12.4
Total comm'ls.	67	35.00	.53	210	3.1
NCAs	14	9.17	.66	210	15.0
Total Channel 38	81	44.17	.55	210	2.6
Channel 56 (ind.)					
CAs	46	21.68	.47	120	2.6
Promos	7	2.50	.36	120	17.1
Total comm'ls.	53	24.18	.46	120	2.3
NCAs	4	2.50	.62	120	30.0
Total Channel 56	57	26.68	.47	120	2.1
All stations					
CAs	403	200.43	.50	1530	3.8
Promos	119	42.89	.36	1530	12.9
Total comm'ls.	522	243.32	.47	1530	2.9
NCAs	92	48.44	.53	1530	16.6
Total all stations	614	291.76	.48	1530	2.5

ters associated with products also were classified as to who "speaks for" the product. In addition, all characters who could be identified were classified by age group, sex, and ethnic status.

The Ten-Minute Rule

Through pressures from ACT and others, the NAB Code Authority has issued guidelines on the number of nonprogram minutes per hour permissible on children's programs. From 16 minutes per hour on Saturday and Sunday programming, this was reduced to 12, then to 10 minutes per hour on January 1, 1975. It was further reduced to 9.5 minutes on January 1, 1976.

Currently, on a per-hour basis, most of the Saturday-Sunday children's hours contain slightly more than the maximum ten minutes. All stations exceed the ten-minute maximum during one or more full-hour periods, and some consistently exceed the maximum (see Table 1.18). Commercial minutes were highest on Channel 56 (12.09 per hour, on the average), followed by Channel 7 (CBS) with 10.73, Channel 38 with 10.0, and Channels 4 and 5 with 8.82 and 8.15 minutes, respectively, on the average.

Types of Products Advertised

A total of 403 CAs were studied. This figure represents 403 exposures of 137 different versions of CAs for 119 products on behalf of 65 companies or sponsors.* Since 98 percent of all CAs were 30 seconds in length, they are analyzed by the total number of CAs broadcast, rather than in minutes of time.

Ten major product categories were utilized. Almost half of all CAs were for cereals and candies or other sweets (25 percent each), followed by toys (18 percent), eating places (10 percent), and other miscellaneous products and services (10 percent). There were no vitamin or medicine CAs broadcast. The basic distribution is given in Table 1.19.

Different stations seemed to specialize in certain types of advertising. (See Table 1.20.) Cereal commercials were most frequent on Channel 7, which has a strong lineup of CBS Saturday programs, and Channel 38, which has an all-cartoon format. The independent channels 38 and 56 were strong in CAs for eating places such as McDonald's and Burger King, and Channel 5 in snack foods.

---

*Figures are approximate. A few CAs could not be identified as to company.

TABLE 1.18

Number of Commercial Minutes per Hour, by Station

	Ch. 4 (NBC)	Ch. 5 (ABC)	Ch. 7 (CBS)	Ch. 38 (ind.)	Ch. 56 (ind.)
Saturday					
7:00- 8:00am	6.58	5.50	12.50	—	—
8:00- 9:00am	10.41	11.33	10.42	—	—
9:00-10:00am	6.66	11.08	10.34	—	—
10:00-11:00am	10.41	10.09	10.58	—	—
11:00am-12 noon	5.66[a]	2.75[a]	10.50	—	—
12 noon- 1:00pm	10.75	—	10.42	—	—
1:00- 2:00pm	5.33[b]	—	5.00[b]	—	—
Sunday					
7:00- 8:00am	—	5.66	—	—	—
8:00- 9:00am	—	6.92	—	8.83	—
9:00-10:00am	—	3.75[c]	—	9.50	—
10:00-11:00am	1.50[d]	—	—	10.50	11.50
11:00am-12 noon	—	—	—	6.17[a]	12.67
Total minutes monitored	390	420	390	210	120
Average commercial minutes per hour	8.82	8.15	10.73	10.00	12.09

[a]11:00-11:30 am.
[b]1:00-1:30 pm.
[c]9:00-9:30 am.
[d]10:30-11:00 am.

TABLE 1.19

Number of Commercial Announcements, by Major Product Type

Product Type	Number of CAs	Percent
Toys	73	18.1
Cereals	100	24.8
Candies/sweets	100	24.8
Snack foods	16	4.0
Other foods	16	4.0
Eating places, meals	42	10.4
Vitamins/medicine	—	—
Household products	5	1.2
Personal care products	13	3.2
Other miscellaneous products	38	9.5
Totals	403	100.0

TABLE 1.20

Major Product Type, by Station
(percent)

Product Type	Ch. 4	Ch. 5	Ch. 7	Ch. 38	Ch. 56	All Stations
Toys	20	15	17	14	28	18
Cereals	23	14	30	32	26	25
Candies/sweets	24	32	26	22	11	25
Snack foods	2	10	5	–	–	4
Other foods	4	2	4	8	2	4
Eating places, meals	7	10	3	22	26	10
Household products	1	2	2	–	–	1
Personal care products	1	4	6	–	5	3
Other misc. products	18	11	7	2	2	10
Total CAs	(102)	(81)	(124)	(50)	(46)	(403)

Specific Products Advertised

Table 1.21 gives a detailed breakdown of all CAs by detailed product category. A further listing of all CAs is given in Appendix E.

Toy products were primarily cars and dolls. Sugared cereal CAs outnumbered those for unsugared cereals by 3:1, and candy bars or drops, cakes and cookies, and fruit drinks constituted the bulk of sweets. Only a few CAs were broadcast for other foods individually (such as milk, bread, fruits), although many were aired for quick meals and eating places. Of the miscellaneous products, movies were by far the most frequently advertised.

Basic Structure of the CAs

Style, use of animation, and other characteristics of CAs are given in Table 1.22. Overall, about 16 percent of CAs used animation solely, and about 40 percent used some form of animation. The forms of the commercials were mixed, with the off-stage announcer most frequent, dramatic skits second, and musical forms third.

Sixty percent of CAs showed the product being used, whereas 20 percent showed only pictures or drawings of the product. Two-thirds were classified as appealing directly to children* and about

---

*Some judgments had to be made here. The most obvious cue was the use of words such as "hey kids," or other language indicating the CA was addressed primarily to children. Other cues included the use of animated animals or other types of characters that appeal to children.

TABLE 1.21

Number and Percent of CAs, by
Specific Product Type

Product Types	Number	Percent
Toys		
Cars, planes, trains	20	5.0
Dolls and doll play sets	27	6.7
Indoor games, puzzles	2	0.5
Outdoor games and toys	6	1.5
Toy stores	—	—
Other toys, hobbies, crafts	18	4.4
Total toys	73	18.1
Cereals		
General—cereal company	1	0.2
Sugared cereals	76	18.9
Unsugared cereals	23	5.7
Total cereals	100	24.8
Candies/sweets		
Candy bars, packaged candies	47	11.7
Chewing gum (sugarless)	—	—
Chewing gum (regular)	2	0.5
Cakes and cookies	22	5.4
Ice cream, puddings, desserts	9	2.2
Soft drinks (carbonated)	—	—
Fruit drinks and ices	20	5.0
Juice drinks (orange, grape)	—	—
Other candies, sweets	—	—
Total candies/sweets	100	24.8
Snacks		
Chips—potato, corn, other	5	1.3
Peanut butter and spreads	11	2.7
Other snacks	—	—
Total snacks	16	4.0
Other foods		
Canned, prepared packaged foods	3	0.8
Fruits and fruit juice	5	1.2
Vegetables	—	—

(continued)

(Table 1.21 continued)

Product Types	Number	Percent
Meats	–	–
Bread	2	0.5
Milk, dairy products	6	1.5
Other foods	–	–
Total other foods	16	4.0
Eating places		
Restaurants, meals	40	9.9
Grocery stores, supermarkets	2	0.5
Other	–	–
Total eating places	42	10.4
Vitamins/medicines		
Vitamins	–	–
Medicines, analgesics	–	–
Other	–	–
Total vitamins/medicines	–	–
Household products		
Cleansers, detergents	1	0.2
Appliances	–	–
Tools, hardware	–	–
Other household products (Dixie Cups)	4	1.0
Total household products	5	1.2
Personal care products		
Shampoos, deodorants, soaps	7	1.7
Health (sauna suit, exerciser)	–	–
Clothing (shoes, other)	6	1.5
Total personal care	13	3.2
Other miscellaneous products		
Motion pictures	30	7.4
Recreation/amusements	1	0.3
Books/magazines	1	0.3
Record offers	2	0.5
Automobiles (repair, parts)	–	–
Airlines (travel offers)	4	1.0
Schools	–	–
Hi-fi and stereo stores	–	–
Other miscellaneous products	–	–
Total miscellaneous	38	9.5
Total all products	403	100.0

TABLE 1.22

Commercial Announcements: Style of Presentation

	Number of CAs	Percent
Type of CA		
Animated	63	16
Nonanimated	233	58
Mixed	107	26
Form		
Off-stage voice	144	36
On-stage announcer	52	13
Musical structure	97	24
Dramatic skit	109	27
Other	1	*
Display style		
Product display only	87	21
Product shown in use	253	63
Product name only	17	4
Other, unclassifiable	46	12
Audience appeal		
Children	261	65
General audience	134	33
Adults	4	1
Parents	4	1
Place setting		
Home or around home	124	31
Outside (street, field)	139	34
Place of work or profession	1	*
Public place (hotel, movie)	52	13
Other (outer space)	26	7
Uncertain, unclassifiable	61	15
Time setting		
Historical (distant past)	6	2
Contemporary	347	86
Uncertain	50	12
Totals	403	100

*Less than 0.50 percent.

one-third to the general audience.* Almost all identifiable time settings were contemporary, and the home and outdoors were the most frequent place settings. Few CAs seem to be associated with places of work or profession.

Style of Presentation

The structures of CAs were quite different for toys, cereals, candies/sweets, and other products. Whereas almost all toy CAs were filmed live, 80 percent of cereal CAs used animation solely or a mixture of live and animation techniques (Table 1.23).

TABLE 1.23

Use of Animation, by Major Product Type

Product Type	Percent Animated	Percent Non-animated	Percent Mixed	Number of CAs
Toys	–	94	6	73
Cereals	18	20	62	100
Candies/sweets	22	49	29	100
Snack foods	25	69	6	16
Other foods	50	19	31	16
Eating places, meals	–	100	–	42
Household products	–	100	–	5
Personal care products	38	31	31	13
Other misc. products	13	82	5	38
All CAs	16	58	26	
Number of CAs	63	233	107	403

By format, more than 90 percent of toy CAs used an off-stage announcer commenting on the action in the CA. For cereals, candies, snacks, and other foods, a short dramatic skit was most frequently employed. The musical format was most frequent in CAs for eating places (such as the McDonald's jingle). This also was true for 8 of 13 personal care product CAs (see Table 1.24).

―――――

*These same CAs might be seen during evening news programs or other prime time programs.

TABLE 1.24

Form of CA, by Major Product Type
(percent)

Product Type	Off-Stage Voice	On-Stage Voice	Musi-cal	Dra-matic Skit	Other	Num-ber of CAs
Toys	95	1	4	–	–	73
Cereals	3	17	29	51	–	100
Candies/sweets	21	10	32	37	–	100
Snack foods	–	38	–	62	–	16
Other foods	31	12	19	38	–	16
Eating places, meals	10	29	52	9	–	42
Household products	80	–	–	20	–	5
Personal care products	8	31	61	–	–	13
Other misc. products	97	–	–	–	3	38
All CAs	36	13	25	27	*	403

*Less than 0.50 percent.

Depicting characters using the product was the most frequent style of product display. Ninety percent of toy CAs showed children playing with the toy, whereas only 50 percent of cereal announcements showed persons eating cereal. Children and others were more apt to be shown eating candies and other sweets, snacks, and other food products than cereals (Table 1.25).

Who "Speaks for" the Product?

The authoritative voice (announcer or speaking character) for 90 percent of commercials was male—most frequently adult male (Table 1.26). Even representational characters (puppets, animals, monsters) were almost always male. Although females were more often associated with foods, eating places, household products, and candies than with other products, in no product category did female voices or characters represent more than 44 percent of the total for the category.

Children, also were infrequently used as the primary voice representing products (9 percent overall). No toy commercial had children speaking for the product directly; about 20 percent of cereal CAs, 30 percent of personal care products, and 50 percent of "other foods" used children as speakers.

TABLE 1.25

Display Style, by Major Product Type
(percent)

Product Type	Product Picture Display	Product Shown in Use	Product Name Only	Unclassifiable	Number of CAs
Toys	10	90	–	–	73
Cereals	46	50	–	4	100
Candies/sweets	18	76	6	–	100
Snack foods	6	94	–	–	16
Other foods	44	56	–	–	16
Eating places, meals	5	50	24	21	42
Household products	–	100	–	–	5
Personal care products	31	69	–	–	13
Other misc. products	5	5	3	87	38
Totals	21	63	4	12	403

TABLE 1.26

Who "Speaks for" the Product?
(percent)

Sex and Age Group	Toys	Cereals	Candies	Snacks	Other Foods	Eating Places	Household Products	Personal Care	Other Products	Total
Adult male	95	55	62	6	38	67	80	31	94	66
Adult female	5	–	4	–	6	31	20	–	3	6
Total adults	100	55	66	6	44	98	100	31	97	72
Male child	–	16	2	–	12	2	–	31	–	6
Female child	–	3	4	–	38	2	–	–	–	3
Total children	–	19	6	–	50	–	–	31	–	9
Other male	–	26	25	94	6	–	–	38	–	18
Other female	–	–	3	–	–	–	–	–	–	1
Total other	–	26	28	94	6	–	–	38	–	19
Unclassifiable	–	–	–	–	–	–	–	–	3	*
Total males	95	97	89	100	56	69	80	100	94	90
Total females	5	3	11	–	44	31	20	–	3	10
Total CAs	75	100	100	16	16	42	5	13	38	403

*Less than 0.50 percent.

Characters Appearing in the Commercials

In addition to the prime person representing the product, all
characters appearing in CAs were coded by age group, sex, and
race. There was an average of 3.7 characters per CA. Like the
principal speaker, characters in CAs were predominantly males.
Of 1,477 characters studied, 56 percent were male, 24 percent
female, and 20 percent animals or others for whom sex could not
be determined. Of those characters classifiable by sex, therefore,
nearly 70 percent were male (Table 1.27).

Male children were most frequently portrayed, followed by
animal and other characters, male adults, and female children.
Thus, although television advertisers seem to be avoiding the use
of children to sell products directly, they frequently are used as
characters shown enjoying or consuming them. Teens were the
most underrepresented of all groups. Only 37 teens were found
among the 1,477 characters classified, and they were virtually
limited to one product type—candies and sweets.

Males outnumbered females in all categories except household
product CAs (10 of 15 were female), and the sexes were almost
equally divided in CAs for other food products. Male children
dominated toy and snack CAs; female children were not dominant
in any product type. They were outnumbered by animals, monsters,
and such in CAs for cereals, snacks, and miscellaneous products
(primarily movies).

Of characters classifiable as to race, more than 90 percent
were white and 8 percent black. Only 3 out of 1,157 characters
could be identified as Oriental, Indian, or other minority. (See
Table 1.28.)

In all product categories white characters predominated. The
portrayal of blacks was most frequent in snack commercials (27 percent) and candy ads (10 percent). Household and personal care
products were "pure white"; other miscellaneous products were
99 percent so, and other foods 97 percent white.

The population presented in commercial announcements is
hardly representative of that in the "real world." It is predominantly
white and male—about one-half children, with male children outnumbering female children by 2:1 and male adults outnumbering
female adults about 3:1. The teen-ager is forgotten in the world
of television ads—just occasionally seen, eating candy, cakes, and
cookies. And beyond white and black, other ethnic characters are
practically nonexistent.

TABLE 1.27

Age and Sex of Characters Appearing in Commercials, by Major Product Type
(percent)

Age and Sex	Toys	Cereals	Candies	Snacks	Other Foods	Eating Places	House-hold	Pers. Care	Other Misc.	All CAs
Males										
Children	61	36	32	73	19	39	26	46	8	39
Teens	1	–	7	–	–	–	–	–	–	2
Adults	16	16	22	2	16	25	7	22	59	21
Animals	–	15	3	9	16	2	–	–	16	7
Total male	78	67	64	84	51	66	33	68	82	69
Females										
Children	19	28	20	16	26	28	27	7	8	22
Teens	–	–	5	–	–	–	–	–	–	1
Adults	3	5	11	–	23	6	40	25	2	7
Animals	–	–	–	–	–	–	–	–	8	1
Total female	22	33	36	16	49	34	67	32	18	31
Total characters classifiable by sex	(244)	(315)	(265)	(45)	(43)	(125)	(15)	(28)	(102)	(1,182)
Others	(48)	(111)	(84)	(12)	(–)	(10)	(–)	(7)	(23)	(295)
Total children	66	48	39	70	45	62	53	43	12	48
Total teens	1	–	10	–	–	–	–	–	–	2
Total adults	16	15	25	2	39	29	47	37	50	23
Total animals, others	17	37	26	28	16	9	–	20	38	27
Total characters	(292)	(426)	(349)	(57)	(43)	(135)	(15)	(35)	(125)	(1,477)

TABLE 1.28

Race of Characters Appearing in Commercials,
by Major Product Type

Product Type	Percent White	Percent Black	Percent Other	Total Classi- fied	Not Classi- fied
Toys	92	7	1	273	19
Cereals	92	8	–	303	123
Candies/sweets	90	10	–	261	88
Snacks	73	27	–	41	16
Other foods	97	3	–	36	7
Eating places	92	8	–	122	13
Household products	100	–	–	15	–
Personal care products	100	–	–	28	7
Other miscellaneous	99	1	–	78	47
Total all products	92	8	*	1,157	320

*Less than 0.50 percent.

Program Promotion

Another form of CA is the message promoting programs on the station. Although shorter and less frequent, it is intended to increase the audiences for future programs. In addition to investigating the general distributions of promos on the stations, the major question asked in the analysis of program promos was whether any programs were being promoted that might be considered inappropriate for the predominantly child viewing audience, either by reason of general content or by time period in which the program was scheduled.

Of a total of 119 promos recorded, most were for programs at other periods on the stations, rather than for adjacent, upcoming shows or the same program the following week (Table 1.29).

Weekend programs between 7:00 am and 6:00 pm were most frequently promoted (46 percent of all promos), followed by weekday evening programs broadcast between 6:00 and 9:00 pm (18 percent) and weekend evening programs (12 percent). Time period of promoted programs is given in Table 1.30.

There were no promos aired for programs after 9:00 pm on weekdays, and only two for programs on the weekend after 9:00 pm. The latter were two promos for the movie series Great Entertainment.

TABLE 1.29

Type of Promotional Announcement

	Number	Percent
Promo for:		
Next week's show	5	4.2
Upcoming show	8	6.7
Other programs	102	85.7
Other (TV code, station promos)	4	3.4
Totals	119	100.0

There were promos for all types of programs (Table 1.31).
Variety programs, sports events, and situation comedy were the
most frequently promoted (37 percent of all promos), followed by
cartoon comedy and movies (18 percent).

Although many promoted programs were for children and family
audiences, many were not. Some of the latter include quiz programs
such as "What's My Line?," variety shows (Cher, for example, was
the most promoted of all programs, with eight promos), sports
(NBA playoffs), news, and specials. (See Appendix F for a complete
listing of promos by time period and program type.)

There also is little similarity between the distribution of promoted programs and the current weekend broadcast schedule for
children. These are compared in Table 1.32.

TABLE 1.30

Time Period of Promoted Programs

Time Period	Number	Percent
Weekdays		
7:00am–12 noon	11	9.2
12 noon– 6:00pm	11	9.2
6:00pm–9:00pm	21	17.6
after 9:00 pm	–	–
Saturday–Sunday		
7:00am–12 noon	24	20.2
12 noon– 6:00pm	31	26.1
6:00pm– 9:00pm	14	11.8
after 9:00pm	2	1.7
Others, unknown	5	4.2
Totals	119	100.0

TABLE 1.31

Format Categories of Promoted Programs

Format	Number of Promos	Percent
Situation comedy	13	10.9
Family drama	4	3.4
Cartoon comedy	11	9.2
Other comedy	1	0.8
Animal adventure	1	0.8
Action–adventure drama	2	1.7
Movies	10	8.4
Variety	17	14.3
Quiz	4	3.4
Sports events	14	11.8
Other entertainment	1	0.8
Total entertainment programs	78	65.6
Children's news	7	5.9
Documentary	6	5.0
Animal/nature films	4	3.4
Interviews/panel formats	4	3.4
Discussion/debate	1	0.8
Other information	10	8.4
General news, weather, sports	6	5.0
Total information	38	31.9
Other promos (TV Code, station)	3	2.5
Total promos	119	100.0

TABLE 1.32

Time of Programs Broadcast and Promos for Programs, Compared by Format Categories

Format	Percent of Total Program Time	Percent of Promos
Cartoon comedy	42	9
Other comedy	10	15
Action–adventure	23	2
Variety/quiz	4	18
Other entertainment	—	21
Children's information	21	27
Other (news, station, TV Code)	—	8
Totals	(1,223 minutes)	(119 promos)

Cartoon comedy and other drama programs were least promoted in proportion to their broadcast during children's viewing hours. Whereas variety, quiz, and other entertainment (sports and movies) received 39 percent of promos, they constituted only 4 percent of children's program time. On the other hand, there was a slightly higher proportion of promos for children's informational programs (27 percent) than the amount of time they were actually broadcast (21 percent).

COMMERCIAL PRACTICES

Different practices are used in the CAs for different products. For all CAs, a series of general questions was asked (to be answered "yes" or "no"), including whether there was a tie-in with the adjacent program or characters (for instance, program host or characters used to sell the product) or the use of any well-known personalities or characters in the commercial or endorsing the product. In addition, specific questions were directed at CAs for toys, cereals, and other foods. Finally, each CA was classified according to one or more "themes" (claims, appeals) used to promote the sale of the product.

Program and Personality Tie-ins

Although the tie-in or endorsement was not a common practice in the CAs, some CAs did utilize such devices. None of the 403 CAs were directly tied in with adjacent programs. None used program hosts or characters to sell products. Well-known personalities, however, were associated with 7 percent of all CAs. Examples include sports figures Stan Musial, Johnny Bench, and Brooks Robinson, as well as cartoon figures from Walt Disney and Fred Flintstone and Barney in the Fruity Pebbles-Cocoa Pebbles cereal commercials.

Actual endorsement of products occurred in only eight CAs (2 percent). One was an on-camera endorsement by Johnny Bench of Batter-Up, an outdoor baseball batting rig; another was in a Sugar Pops CA, with horseman J. D. Ramsa practicing for a five-mile relay.

About 10 percent of toy and cereal commercials utilized personality tie-ins, and the few endorsements were seen primarily in toy ads (Table 1.33).

TABLE 1.33

Use of Personality Tie-ins and
Endorsements, by Product Category

Product Category	Total Number of CAs	Percent Utilizing Personalities	Percent Utilizing Endorsements
Toys	73	10	7
Cereals	100	12	1
Candies/sweets	100	7	—
Snacks	16	—	—
Other foods	16	—	—
Eating places	42	—	—
Household products	5	—	—
Personal care products	13	—	—
Other miscellaneous products	38	5	—
All products	403	7	2

Disclaimers and Qualifiers

Audio or visual disclaimers include such phrases as "batteries not included," "items sold separately," and "available only at . . . ." Overall, audio qualifiers occurred in 22 percent of the CAs and video qualifiers in 11 percent. These were not always the same, however. In only 8 percent were there simultaneous and similar audio and visual reinforcing messages.

Toys most frequently used audio qualifiers exclusively (55 percent). About 10 percent of cereal and candy CAs used audio and visual qualifiers presented simultaneously (Table 1.34).

Premiums and Contests

Stick-ons, magnets, silly scissors, black-light figures, magic cards, and miniature license plates were offered as free premiums in packages of cereals. Other premium offers required a visit to the store and a purchase—for instance, iron-on decals at Buster Brown stores, Kool Aid Komix at "participating stores," and gifts of toys or games with a visit to a Ground Round restaurant. A few required either purchase or money in addition—such as a dish for 49 cents at Papa Gino's and a "free" milk mug with cookie and milk labels.

TABLE 1.34

Use of Audio and Visual Disclaimers,
by Product Category

Product Category	Total CAs	Percent Using Audio Qualifiers	Percent Using Video Qualifiers	Percent Using Both
Toys	73	55	14	–
Cereals	100	24	15	13
Candies/sweets	100	12	10	10
Snacks	16	–	–	–
Other foods	16	–	–	–
Eating places	42	5	10	5
Household products	5	–	–	–
Personal care products	13	38	31	31
Other miscellaneous prod.	38	16	5	5
All products	403	22	11	8

TABLE 1.35

Use of Premiums or Contests,
by Product Category

Product Category	Total CAs	Percent Using Premiums	Percent Using Contests
Toys	73	–	–
Cereals	100	47	–
Candies/sweets	100	10	6
Snacks	16	–	–
Other foods	16	–	–
Eating places	42	21	5
Household products	5	–	–
Personal care products	13	31	–
Other miscellaneous products	38	–	–
All products	403	17	2

Only four CAs used contests as a selling device. These included
a trip to Disney World in a Razzles candy sweepstakes, a Tootsie
Roll sweepstakes, and the hope of winning a party and radio in a
clown contest for Ground Round restaurant.

Toy commercials used neither contests nor premium offers. Nearly half of all cereal CAs utilized premium offers. Candies, and the restaurant ads mentioned above, also utilized these devices (Table 1.35).

Special Effects

The judgment of visual and other effects that might be misleading to a child is difficult.* Because of the difficulty in making a reliable judgment, we did not attempt to measure the precise number of CAs utilizing such devices. The monitors were asked, however, to make notes on what seemed unusual use of visual techniques that, in their judgment, might tend to mislead or confuse a young child. Some of these are listed below as illustrative of the types of visuals used.

Product	Special Effect
Pop Tarts toasted pastry	animated talking toaster in home of boy who eats Pop Tarts
Apple Jacks	box of Apple Jacks at end of commercial shown much larger than the group of children sitting at the table
Three Musketeers	magic shown in which finger snapping produces the candy bar
Trix	animated rabbit joins real children for breakfast; he is able to change his size at will
Rice Krispies	the "cereal that talks to you"—animated men dance and talk on breakfast table of real children; little men jump out of box
Cheerios	box of Cheerios supered over scene of family activity and never put into perspective
Dusty doll	several tight close-ups of doll, making her look as big as life; not put into perspective in order to judge size
TTP Wild Riders	sounds of engines, and motorcycles leaps and landings

*This is an area that needs considerably more research. Because of the broad perspective of the present study, we could not investigate this aspect in detail.

Levi's	shows a typical boy wearing Levi's and all that can happen to him; film is run backward: waiter's tray goes from ground to his hand, bike rider is on ground, then bike rights itself, boys zip up a pole, and so forth
Superbug (movie)	exaggerated takeoff of a car, film of a car climbing walls, steering wheel that punches, and so on
Escape to Witch Mountain (movie)	trailer flying over countryside, children starting car from back seat by giving verbal commands, animated dogs chasing children
Wizard of Oz dolls	dolls shown walking alone and very large on screen—almost lifelike
Dr. Steele doll	extreme close-up of doll makes it seem too large
Dusty doll	sound of real softball being hit, golf ball being teed, close-up of doll making her seem larger than she is

Product Information

Price, size, quantity, materials, durability, and other information was infrequently an integral part of CAs. Five percent of all CAs mentioned price, and only 8 percent gave objective information about the nature of the product. We did not include vague or unsupportable claims such as "fast action treads" or "sporty stripes" on a toy car. Some examples of CAs that did give price/product information are below.

Product	Price Information
U.S. postal stamp kit	many exciting stamp kits, $2 each
U.S. postal stamp kit	$3.50 per set
Papa Gino's	49 cents for premium of flying pizza dish
Antique, flea, and crafts fair	$1.00 admission for adults
Crimson Travel	Martinique week: $359 + 15 percent tax Montreal weekends: $99 + 15 percent tax Disney World: prices given for adults and children
Arby's Roast Beef	sandwich sale—2 for $1.50
Heavy Metal record	2 records $6.88, 2 tapes $9.88

MGM records and tapes	albums $4.47, eight-track tapes $5.47
Buster Brown shoes	natural leather sandals
Honeycombs	each honeycomb one inch in diameter by tape measure
Koogle spread	12 ounces written visibly on label in close-up
Tang	description of vitamin content
Reese's peanut butter cup	"real milk chocolate and peanut butter"
Philadelphia Imitation cream cheese	one-half the calories of regular cream cheese
Frosted Flakes	fortified with eight essential vitamins
Raisin Bran	two scoops of raisins (size of scoops not indicated)
Sky Ace	made of tough plastic
Rice Krispies	vitamin content described
Topps baseball cards	ten cards and stick of gum, 660 cards in complete set
Pop Tarts	six vitamins and iron, real fruit filling
MGM records	describes the songs in the album

Practices in Toy Commercials

Some additional questions were asked with respect to toy CAs. One technique used was the use of real-life sounds to accompany the selling of the toy. Three examples were found.

Product	Sound Accompanying the CA
Blazin' SSP	with ultrasonic sound-effects
Dusty doll	sound of real softball being hit, golf ball being teed, and so on; doll is shown doing athletic stunts with real sounds in background
TTP Wild Riders	sound of motorcycle engines heard while boys play with small plastic motorcycle toy

Other toy CAs (about 20 percent) showed items in the CA that were not included for sale with the toy. Examples are given below.

Product	Items Sold Separately
Johnny Bench Batter-Up	bat and mounting stand used with toy not included
Match Box cars	racing ramp and runways over which cars glide not included

| G. I. Joe adventure sets | pool where submarine set is used not included; other props not included |
| TTP Wild Riders | ramp the motorcycles leap off is not for sale |

In almost 60 percent of toy CAs, multiple items were offered for sale or were sold separately. In a sense this represents two commercials in one.

Product	Items Sold Separately
Topps baseball cards	cards and gum sold separately
Gold Medal PJ	Olympic gymnast set and balance beam sold separately
Habitrail	sections of the Habitrail hamster house that snap on are sold separately
Gumball bank	three types of banks and gum refills are sold separately
Barbie's World	Malibu Barbie, camper, and townhouse are sold separately
Free Spirit bike	servicing sold separately
Best of the West collection	all of the figurines are sold separately
Wizard of Oz dolls	all dolls and Emerald City are sold separately or in sets
TTP tower and cars	each racer is sold separately
Dr. Steele doll	Dr. Steele and the two other dolls are sold separately
Evel Knievel stunt stadium	doll and stadium sold separately
Dusty doll	doll and athletic sets sold separately
Blazing SSP	separately sold cars are displayed
TTP Wild Riders	riders and motorcycles sold separately

Basic Themes in Children's Advertising

Although little product information was given, all sorts of claims and appeals were used to sell products. Sixteen "themes" were developed for classifying the major appeals of the verbal content of the CAs.*

---

*It is important to mention here that only the manifest verbal appeals included in spoken or printed form as slogans or claims for the product are classified. No attempt was made to judge the total visual impact of the CA, although it is realized that many times this may be more important than the obvious verbal claims and appeals—especially to children.

Altogether, we identified 661 themes or appeals in the 403 commercials. Some appeals were specific to different product types, of course ("taste" for cereals and foods, for example). Therefore, they are analyzed by product type in Table 1.36.

In all food product CAs there was some emphasis on taste or flavor and on texture; cereals and other foods frequently used health and nutrition as an appeal. Lacking this claim, candies more frequently attempted to sell the idea of fun or happiness and the uniqueness of the particular product. Snack foods, while placing most emphasis on taste and texture, also stressed convenience and associations with other foods ("tastes a little like chocolate, a little like peanuts"). Eating places emphasized taste and texture of their foods, but also appealed to peer status (such as "have your party at Brighams—the best one you and your friends will have").

For toys, two major themes predominated—action/speed/power and appearance of the product. Personal care products and toys were the only ones to state anything about the quality of manufacture or materials, and economy or price was rarely mentioned except by other products (airline travel offers).

General superiority claims included such superlatives as "the best," "outstanding," and "fantastic," with little or no support for the claim. These were most frequent in movie ads.

Health, Nutrition, and the Advertising
of Edibles

There are complaints over the legitimacy of advertising of edibles to children. Some medical experts have questioned the effect of advertising sugared cereals, candies, and snack foods on children's nutritional habits. Others question the effects on the dental health of children. It is not the purpose here to review the evidence or expert opinion in any detail. The question, having been raised, however, is relevant to this study of CAs for food products.

From the overall list of CAs, detailed categories of food products were analyzed. Overall, 68 percent of all CAs were for food products (including eating places), and 44 percent were for sugared foods. This tabulation of sugared foods does not include Koogle peanut spread (classified as a snack) or a gumball bank (with gum) and a crushed ice machine (with syrup) classed as toys.

Of all food products, therefore, 64 percent were sugared; the bulk (45 percent) were either sugared cereals or candies. Regular food products—dairy products, fruit, bread, and other prepared foods—together accounted for less than 5 percent of all CAs and 7 percent of all edibles (see Table 1.37).

TABLE 1.36

Basic Themes or Appeals of the CAs, by Product Type
(percent)

Theme/Appeal	Toys	Cereals	Candy	Snacks	Other Foods	Eating Places	House-hold	Pers. Care	Other Prod.	All Prod.
Appearance	19	3	3	–	–	2	–	18	–	5
Quantity/size/amount	5	3	6	–	3	–	–	5	–	3
Convenience/ease of use	9	–	5	17	12	–	–	5	–	4
Taste/flavor/smell	4[a]	36	30	46	37	26	–	–	–	27
Texture	–	12	19	17	18	22	–	–	–	12
"Fun"/happiness	9	2	15	–	–	5	44	32	–	8
Health/nutrition	–	34	4	–	21	–	–	9	–	14
Peer status/popularity	–	2	–	–	–	17	45	–	–	2
Action/power/speed	37	4	–	–	–	–	–	18	–	7
Adventure	7	3	–	–	–	–	–	–	–	2
Comparative/associative	–	1	–	20	9	–	–	–	–	2
Economy/price	1	–	–	–	–	5	–	–	16	1
Uniqueness	–	–	15	–	–	2	–	–	–	4
Quality of manufacture or materials	15	–	–	–	–	–	–	18	–	1
Newness	3	–	–	–	–	–	–	–	–	b
General superiority	1	–	3	–	–	21	11	–	84	7
Totals	100	100	100	100	100	100	100	100	100	100
Total themes (base)	(78)	(224)	(185)	(30)	(33)	(42)	(9)	(22)	(38)	(661)
Total CAs	(73)	(100)	(100)	(16)	(16)	(42)	(5)	(13)	(38)	(403)

[a]Gumball bank classified under toys also mentioned taste of the gum.
[b]Less than 0.50 percent.

TABLE 1.37

CAs for Food Products

Food Product	Number of CAs	Percent of all CAs	Percent of CAs for Food Products
Sugared cereals*	76	18.9	27.8
Candy bars*	47	11.7	17.2
Eating places	40	9.9	14.6
Unsugared cereals	24	5.9	8.8
Cakes and cookies*	22	5.4	8.0
Fruit drinks*	20	5.0	7.3
Peanut spread	11	2.7	4.0
Ice cream, desserts*	9	2.2	3.3
Milk, dairy products	6	1.5	2.2
Fruits	5	1.3	1.8
Chips	5	1.2	1.8
Canned, prepared foods	3	0.8	1.1
Gum (regular)*	2	0.5	0.7
Bread	2	0.5	0.7
Grocery stores	2	0.5	0.7
Total food products	274	68.0	100.0
All other products	129	32.0	—
Total CAs	403	100.0	—

*Sugared foods.

Several additional questions were asked with respect to the advertising of edibles (Table 1.38). Snacks and candies rarely mention nutritional value, whereas more than 40 percent of cereal CAs do.* These references might be in a simple form—"Vitamin charged" (Fruit Brutes), "Freakies has vitamins"—or a more complete one—"Fortified with eight essential vitamins and iron."

One-fourth of cereal commercials used "sweetness" as a selling point, but were not advertised as snack products. "Sweetness" references in cereal CAs included "nature's sweet golden bran" (Raisin Bran), "chocolaty goodies" (Cocoa Pebbles), "fruit flavored

---

*These figures represent "mentions" of these selling points in some form. In the previous analysis of "themes," we classified the major assertions and claims.

TABLE 1.38

Questions on the Advertising of Edibles

	Percent of CAs with "Yes" Answers			
Question	Cereals	Candies	Snacks	Other Foods
Is there any reference to nutritional value of the product?	43	8	—	44
Is "sweetness" mentioned as a selling point?	25	2	—	—
Is food referred to as a snack?	—	24	56	31
Is product shown or represented as part of a balanced meal?	91	2	6	6
Is it represented as a substitute for a balanced meal?	—	—	—	—
Is "taste" or "flavor" other than "sweetness" mentioned?	61	68	88	81
Are ingredients specified as either natural or artificial?	3	19	69	31
Is caloric value stated?	—	—	—	6
Total CAs	(100)	(100)	(16)	(16)

sweeties" (Fruit Brute), and "frosted oat cereal with sweet surprises" (Lucky Charms).

Ninety percent of cereal CAs represented their products as part of a balanced meal, but neither cereals nor other foods were portrayed as a meal substitute. Cereals were most often shown on the breakfast table with other foods. Sometimes only verbal reference was made—"start your day with a complete and balanced breakfast" (Froot Loops), "part of your good breakfast" (Lucky Charms), "part of a balanced breakfast" (Honeycombs), "adds a golden touch to a balanced breakfast" (Crunchy Nuggets).

A majority of all products mentioned taste or flavor as a selling point. Cereals seldom specified any ingredients; and although they frequently presented vitamin and nutritional values, none stated caloric values.

NONCOMMERCIAL ANNOUNCEMENTS

Noncommercial announcements (NCAs) have received little attention, primarily because of the current concern over advertising to children. In this study we logged 92 NCAs that were classified as to style of presentation, use of animation, audience appeal, "cause" or type of organization making the appeal, and who "spoke for" the cause. In addition, characters appearing were classified by age group, sex, and ethnic status.

NCAs generally are presented in a straightforward manner, with about 75 percent nonanimated and 50 percent using an off-stage voice or announcer. There were various other styles represented, however, including all-musical NCAs and short dramatic skits to illustrate a problem or concern (Table 1.39).

Although some NCAs (such as several recently produced nutrition and safety announcements) were designed specifically for the child audience, less than 25 percent were judged to be directed specifically

TABLE 1.39

Number of NCAs, by Style, Use of Animation,
and Audience Appeal

	Number	Percent
Style of presentation		
Off-stage voice	49	54
On-stage announcer	10	11
Musical structure	12	13
Dramatic skit	15	16
Other style	5	6
Total	91*	100
Use of animation		
Animated	25	27
Nonanimated	66	73
Mixed	—	—
Total	91	100
Audience appeal		
Children	20	22
Adults	8	9
General audience	57	62
Parents	6	7
Total	91	100

*Only 91 of 92 NCAs could be classified in detail.

TABLE 1.40

Number of NCAs, by Cause

Cause	Number	Percent
Health and safety		
Athletics (AAU, Olympics, good sports competition)	3	3.2
Health care (anti-smoking, lung cancer, American Dental Association)	10	10.9
Nutrition (nutrition labeling, eat fresh fruits, eat good breakfast, Dairy Council)	9	9.8
Safety (National Safety Council, seat belts, Red Cross, toy safety, bike safety)	10	10.9
Total	32	34.8
Ecology and the environment		
Animal care (MSPCA, Humane Society)	2	2.2
Anti-pollution/anti-litter (keep America beautiful, recycling, USDA, Forestry Service)	13	14.1
Total	15	16.3
Youth organizations		
Girls Clubs, Girl Scouts, Boys Clubs, Cub Scouts, YMCA, Camp Fire Girls	13	14.1
Other voluntary and nonprofit organizations		
Voluntary help programs (Big Sisters, Foster Parents, Voluntary Action Center)	4	4.3
UNICEF	1	1.1
Reading	1	1.1
Museums	5	5.4
Total	11	11.9
Pro-social announcements		
Anti-discrimination (brotherhood, equal rights, Campaign for Human Development)	5	5.4
Religious organization messages (sharing, kindness, growing up, reputation)	5	5.4
Total	10	10.9
Miscellaneous, other causes and organizations		
Boston Bicentennial	6	6.5
Government organizations (Post Office, IRS, Department of Tourism)	3	3.3
Consumerism (Better Business Bureau, Junior Consumer Tip)	2	2.2
Total	11	12.0
Total, all NCAs	92	100.0

at children. Most were classified for the general audience, although about 15 percent made appeals directly to parents or adults in general. Several contained appeals for funds or other adult appeals, such as the Foster Parents program.

NCAs on Behalf of Causes

Sixteen categories of "causes" were developed from the NCAs broadcast. (A complete listing of all NCAs is given in Appendix G.) They were grouped under six major headings for further analysis. The basic distribution of the 92 NCAs by cause is given in Table 1.40.

The largest single category of NCAs was for ecological causes (14 percent), followed by health care (11 percent), safety (11 percent), and nutrition announcements (10 percent). NCAs on behalf of health-safety, ecology, and nutrition causes were more frequently animated (41 percent were animated) than those for youth organizations, other voluntary organizations, and pro-social announcements, of which only 4 percent used animation (Table 1.41).

In terms of audience appeal, health, safety, ecology, pro-social, and other miscellaneous NCAs appealed to children more frequently than did those for youth and voluntary organizations, although in no category was youth the most important audience category (see Table 1.42).

Who "Speaks for" the Cause?

The authoritative voice in NCAs, as in CAs, was male (in 80 percent), and in 52 percent the announcer or character who gave the message was an adult male (Table 1.43). This was true for all

TABLE 1.41

Use of Animation in NCAs, by Cause

Cause	Percent Animated	Percent Nonanimated	Total NCAs
Health	38	62	32
Ecology	53	47	15
Youth organizations	—	100	13
Other voluntary	9	91	11
Pro-social	—	100	9
Miscellaneous	36	64	11
All causes	27	73	91

TABLE 1.42

Audience Appeal of NCAs, by Cause

Cause	Primary Appeal to (percent)				Total NCAs
	Children	Adults	General	Parent	
Health/safety/nutrition	25	3	59	13	32
Ecology/environment	33	–	60	7	15
Youth organizations	–	31	69	–	13
Other voluntary/nonprofit	–	18	73	9	11
Pro-social	44	–	56	–	9
Other miscellaneous	27	9	64	–	11
All causes	22	9	62	7	91

TABLE 1.43

Who "Speaks for" the Cause?
(percent)

Authoritative Voice	Health	Ecology	Youth Orgs.	Other Voluntary	Pro-Social	Misc.	Total
Adult male	53	40	46	64	22	82	52
Adult female	3	13	15	18	11	9	10
Total adults	56	53	61	82	33	91	62
Male child	3	–	8	9	22	–	5
Female child	13	–	31	–	11	–	10
Total children	16	–	39	9	33	–	15
Other male	28	47	–	9	34	9	23
Other female	–	–	–	–	–	–	–
Total other	28	47	–	9	34	9	23
Total males	84	87	54	82	78	91	80
Total females	16	13	46	18	22	9	20
Total speakers	(32)	(15)	(13)	(11)	(9)	(11)	(91)

TABLE 1.44

CAs and NCAs Compared by Who "Speaks for"
the Product or Cause

Who Speaks	Percent in CAs	Percent in NCAs
Adult male	66	52
Adult female	6	10
Total adults	72	62
Male child	6	5
Female child	3	10
Total children	9	15
Other male	18	23
Other female	1	–
Total other	19	23
Total males	90	80
Total females	10	20
Total speakers	(403)	(91)

causes except youth organizations, probably because of the number
of announcements for Girl Scouts, Girls Clubs, and Camp Fire
Girls. Even in this group, however, 7 of 13 used male adults or
male children as the chief speaker for the cause.

With the exception of female children, CAs and NCAs showed
somewhat similar patterns with respect to who delivers the message
of the announcement. Adults and males predominated in both (see
Table 1.44).

Character Distributions in NCAs

In addition to the chief speaker for each NCA, all identifiable
characters were classified by age group, sex, and race. In 91
NCAs studied, 252 characters were classified. Age and sex classifications were made for 222 characters (Table 1.45). Unlike the
distribution of primary speakers, the NCA characters were more
evenly divided by sex (57 percent male). Although outnumbered
overall, females exceeded male teen-agers.

Females outnumbered males only in the youth organization
NCAs (29 to 14), but were outnumbered by 2:1 in ecology announcements and other miscellaneous NCAs, and by 3:1 in pro-social
announcements.

TABLE 1.45

Characters in NCAs, by Sex and Age Group

Sex and Age Group	Number	Percent
Male children	54	24.3
Male teens	14	6.3
Male adults	45	20.3
Male animals, other	13	5.9
Total males	126	56.8
Female children	48	21.6
Female teens	17	7.6
Female adults	29	13.1
Female animals, other	2	0.9
Total females	96	43.2
Total classified	222	100.0
Unclassified	30	
Total characters	252	

Blacks constituted 11 percent of 202 classifiable characters, other minorities 5 percent, and whites 84 percent. Blacks were much more frequently seen in pro-social NCAs (26 percent), other voluntary organizations (25 percent), and youth organizations (16 percent); they constituted less than 10 percent in all other categories (Table 1.46).

In contrast with CAs, NCAs' character distributions were some-what more balanced. Although still male-dominated, they portrayed more female teens and adults and greater proportions of blacks and other minorities (Table 1.47).

TABLE 1.46

Race of Characters in NCAs, by Cause

Cause	Percent White	Percent Black	Percent Other	Total Characters Classified
Health/safety/nutrition	89	5	6	84
Ecology/environment	88	4	8	25
Youth organizations	79	16	5	43
Other voluntary orgs.	75	25	—	16
Pro-social announcements	74	26	—	23
Other miscellaneous	91	9	—	11
All causes	84	11	5	202

TABLE 1.47

CAs and NCAs Compared by
Character Distributions

Age, Sex, and Race	Percent in CAs	Percent in NCAs
Male children	39	24
Male teens	2	6
Male adults	21	20
Male animals, other	7	6
Total males	69	56
Female children	22	22
Female teens	1	8
Female adults	7	13
Female animals, other	1	1
Total females	31	44
Total classified for age and sex	(1,182)	(222)
White	92	84
Black	8	11
Other minority	*	5
Total classified for race	(1,157)	(202)

*Less than 0.50 percent.

A COMPARISON OF CHILDREN'S TELEVISION— 1971 AND 1975

In this section current data are compared with those of the author's 1971 report, Saturday Children's Television (published at Newtonville, Massachusetts, by Action for Children's Television). There are, of course, some differences in the two studies that should be kept in mind. First, the 1971 programs were recorded in June; the 1975 programs, in April. Second, the earlier study included only 19 hours of Saturday broadcasting; the present one included 25.5 hours and Sunday morning programming as well. Third, some procedures and definitions were revised, thereby making certain comparisons invalid. Finally, additional analyses were undertaken in the present study that were not done in 1971.

Nevertheless, it is felt that this overall comparison is useful in pointing out certain changes in the composition of children's television. Both studies represent large samples of children's television. There is also a basic repetitive quality to children's television that gives it a similar look whether recorded in April or

September. The major exception is the increase in toy commercials in the pre-Christmas season. In addition, the proportions of time broadcast by the network affiliates and the independent stations remained constant during the two periods. What were the changes?

Amount of Advertising

There was a decrease in the amount of commercial time on all stations from an average of 11.3 minutes to 9.5 minutes per hour. Stated another way, in 1971, 18.8 percent of broadcast time was devoted to commercial messages; in 1975 it was 15.9 percent. This amounts to a 15 percent decrease (Table 1.48). In one sense, however, this decrease is more apparent than real. Although commercial time decreased, the average number of commercial announcements decreased only slightly—from one every 2.8 minutes to one every 2.9 minutes. In other words, there were about as many commercial product announcements and promos per hour in 1975 as in 1971, although the average length of each was less. These comparisons can be seen in Table 1.49.

The overall pattern with respect to reduction of total commercial time and, at the same time, the reduction of the average length of the announcements is not due to exceptional procedures at any one station. The pattern is consistent for all channels except Channel 38, which showed a slight increase in the average length of its commercials. Station-by-station data is presented in Table 1.50.

Types of Advertising

There were only slight shifts in CAs for various product types. No vitamin or medicine commercials were found in 1975; two were broadcast in 1971. Toys, cereals, and candies were the staples for both periods (Table 1.51). Use of animation and format of the CAs showed little change over the four-year period. Also, in both periods about 60 percent of all CAs showed the product in use.

Commercial Practices

The practice of host-selling and program character lead-ins and tie-ins seems to have been discontinued since 1971. We found no such examples in 1975. There are still a small number of celebrity endorsements, however. Although the data are not strictly comparable, the use of audio or visual disclaimers or qualifiers seems to

TABLE 1.48

Distribution of Program Elements,
1971 and 1975

Percent of Time Devoted to	1971	1975
Program content	77.3	79.9
Commercial product announcements	15.5	13.1
Program promotional announcements	3.3	2.8
All commercial announcements	18.8	15.9
Noncommercial announcements	3.5	3.2
Other miscellaneous material	0.4	1.0
Total time	(1,125)	(1,530)

TABLE 1.49

Number and Average Length of
Announcements, 1971 and 1975

	1971	1975
Number of announcements		
CAs	311	403
Promos	95	119
Total commercial	406	522
NCAs	67	92
All announcements	473	614
Average length (mins.)		
CAs	.56	.50
Promos	.40	.36
Total commercial	.52	.47
NCAs	.58	.53
All announcements	.53	.48
Number of announcements per "x" minutes		
CAs	3.6	3.8
Promos	11.8	12.9
Total commercial	2.8	2.9
NCAs	17.0	17.0
All announcements	2.4	2.5

TABLE 1.50

Amount of Advertising, by Station, 1971 and 1975

	1971	1975
Commercial announcements as percent of total broadcast time		
Channel 4	17.9	14.7
Channel 5*	24.8	13.6
Channel 7*	17.5	17.9
Channel 38	16.7	16.7
Channel 56	–	20.2
All stations	18.8	15.9
Average commercial minutes per hour		
Channel 4	10.8	8.8
Channel 5	14.8	8.2
Channel 7	10.5	10.7
Channel 38	10.0	10.0
Channel 56	–	12.1
All stations	11.3	9.5
Average length of commercial announcements		
Channel 4	.52	.49
Channel 5	.53	.48
Channel 7	.53	.44
Channel 38	.50	.53
Channel 56	–	.46
All stations	.52	.47
Number of commercial announcements per "x" minutes		
Channel 4	2.9	3.3
Channel 5	2.1	3.4
Channel 7	3.1	2.4
Channel 38	3.0	3.1
Channel 56	–	2.3
All stations	2.8	2.9

*In 1971, Channel 5 was affiliated with CBS and Channel 7 with ABC. The affiliations were reversed in the interim.

have increased, as have premium offers. Giving price and other information about the product is still an infrequent practice—as it was in 1971 (Table 1.52).

Program Patterns

In 1975 there was a reduction in the proportion of programming devoted to entertainment and an increase in informational programs. Total comedy drama decreased, and action-adventure increased. This was due primarily to the greater amount of recorded-syndicated programming broadcast during the latter period. There also was a slight decrease in the use of animation.

Basic subject matter of the programs was somewhat more diversified in 1975. Whereas crime, interpersonal rivalry, and the supernatural accounted for 56 percent of subject matter in 1971,

TABLE 1.51

Nature of Advertising, 1971 and 1975
(percent)

	1971	1975
Type of product		
Toys	23	18
Cereals	23	25
Candies/sweets	21	25
Other foods	23	18
Vitamins/medicine	1	—
Other products	9	14
Use of animation		
Animated	22	16
Nonanimated	58	58
Mixed	20	26
Format		
Off-stage announcer	40	36
Musical structure	21	24
Dramatic skit	27	27
Other	12	13
Product display style		
Product picture display	28	21
Product in use	62	63
Product name only	2	4
Other	8	12
Total commercials	(311)	(403)

TABLE 1.52

Commercial Practices, 1971 and 1975
(percent)

Type of Practice	1971[a]	1975
Price information	8	5
Premium offers	13	17
Contests	b	2
Program/host tie-ins	5	—
Product endorsements	4	2
Personality tie-ins	b	7
Audio disclaimers	16	22
Visual disclaimers	7	11
Both audio and visual disclaimers	3	8

[a]1971 percentages are based on number of individual CAs (132), not counting repeated exposures. 1975 data are based on total CAs broadcast, including repeats (403).
[b]Not classified separately in 1971.

they amounted to only 34 percent in 1975. The major change noted was a shift away from crime and a greater frequency of domestic subjects (Table 1.53). Also, although the proportions were not large, there were increases in history, religion, race/nationality, education, business, and public affairs. These were due largely to the greater amount of information programming broadcast in 1975.

Nature and Extent of Violence

Although nearly the same proportion of dramatic program segments were classified as "saturated" with violence (30 percent in 1971; 29 percent in 1975), program time in which the violence occurred decreased from 31 percent to 16 percent (see Table 1.54). The explanation for this lies in the number of shorter segments represented by cartoon comedy that contain violence compared with the longer network and situation comedy segments that contain less violence.

The modest decrease in the amount of violence in children's television is reflected in the categories of violence. The percent of program segments containing one or more acts of human violence—with and without weapons, natural violence, deaths, and violence directed at humans—all showed some decrease (Table 1.55).

TABLE 1.53

Nature of Programming, 1971 and 1975
(percent)

	1971	1975
Entertainment program time	89	79
Informational program time	11	21
Format of programs		
Comedy drama	61	52
Action–adventure (including crime)	16	23
Variety	5	4
Other entertainment	6	–
Informational	12	21
Origin of programs		
Local	13	13
Recorded–syndicated	19	35
Network	68	52
Use of animation		
Animated	66	57
Nonanimated	33	36
Mixed	1	7
Subject matter		
Domestic (marriage, home)	–	10
Crime (police, robberies)	28	10
Historical (events)	1	6
Religion (church, clergy)	–	2
Love and romance	3	2
Supernatural (ghosts, magic)	14	10
Nature and animals	6	6
Race/nationality	2	4
Education/schools	–	1
Business/industry	1	3
Government/public affairs	2	4
Science/scientists	8	3
Entertainment world (sports, show business)	8	13
Armed forces/war	3	1
Literature/fine arts	2	1
Interpersonal rivalry	14	14
Crafts/hobbies	*	2
Other	8	8
Total program time (minutes)	(732)	(1,223)

*Less than 0.50 percent.

TABLE 1.54

Extent of Violence in Drama Segments, 1971 and 1975

	1971	1975
Percent of drama segments		
Saturated with violence	30	29
With violence subordinate	23	29
With violence incidental	29	24
With no violence	18	18
Number of segments	(79)	(70)
Percent of time in dramatic segments		
Saturated with violence	31	16
With violence subordinate	21	25
With violence incidental	38	34
With no violence	10	25
Total time (mins.) in dramatic segments	(651)	(918)

TABLE 1.55

Nature of Violence in Dramatic Segments, 1971 and 1975

	1971	1975
Percent of Segments with		
"Chase" scenes	53	50
Deaths	6	1
Injuries	8	27[a]
Violence with weapons	57	50
Violence without weapons	37	31
Natural/accidental violence	25	16
Violence directed at humans	52	30
Death or injury as a direct result of violence	4	23[a]
Suspenseful/frightening situations	19	24[b]
Number of segments	(79)	(70)

[a]Study definitions were changed. In 1971 only "permanent" injuries were counted; in 1975 any immediate injury to another was classified.

[b]This small increase could well be due to differing interpretations in the two study periods.

Although this comparison of the extent and nature of violence does not adequately fulfill the requirements of a "violence index" recommended by the surgeon general, it does demonstrate the feasibility of such an index if conducted periodically on similar samples of children's television.

Unfortunately, the 1971 analysis was not as detailed with respect to program promotion, NCAs, program popularity, and the distributions of characters as the 1975 study. With regard to the last consideration, it is doubtful that the sexual and racial distributions have improved since 1971. There is some evidence presented by John Doolittle and Robert Pepper in "Children's TV Ad Content: 1974" (Journal of Broadcasting 19, 2 [Spring 1975]: 131-42), to indicate that the opposite is true.

2

CHILDREN'S COMMERCIAL
TELEVISION AFTER SCHOOL

AN OVERVIEW OF INDEPENDENT
STATION PROGRAMMING

Of the 73 independent stations in the universe, programming
and audience data were available for 68. The following analysis is
based on a composite of those 68 stations, representing some 350
programs and 202 hours of broadcast time.

Types of Programs

Programs were classified into 19 type categories. The largest
single type was situation comedy (syndicated reruns of Andy Griffith,
Gomer Pyle, I Love Lucy, Green Acres, and so on), followed by
animated cartoons, children's variety programs, and action-
adventure drama. The time devoted to each program type on all
stations is given in Table 2.1.

Defining "children's programs" is, at best, a difficult task.
Looking over the list of after-school programs broadcast, one can
see that a large majority were not originally produced for the child
audience. At most, about 43 percent of all programs could be
classified as designed for children. This is a generous estimate,
however, since many are adapted from material originally produced
for theater presentation (such as Popeye and Little Rascals).
Approximately 18 percent of the time was given to adult-audience
programs, including crime shows, adult westerns, quiz programs,
news, religion, and movies. About 26 percent of programs were
reruns of prime-time situation and family comedies. The remaining
13 percent were Spanish-language programs or other local programs

TABLE 2.1

Types of Programs Broadcast on
Independent Stations

Type of Program	Number of Programs	Total Minutes	Percent of Total Minutes
Situation comedy (Addams Family, Andy Griffith, Beverly Hillbillies, Bewitched, Dick Van Dyke)	90	2,730	22
Family comedy (Leave It to Beaver, Dennis the Menace, Family Affair, Ozzie and Harriet, Partridge Family)	17	510	4
Cartoon comedy (Bugs Bunny, Bullwinkle, Cartoons and Kids, Casper, Flintstones, Tennessee Tuxedo)	54	1,800	15
Other comedy (Little Rascals, Three Stooges)	21	690	6
Animal adventure (Flipper, Jeff's Collie, Timmy and Lassie)	3	90	1
Crime/mystery/detective (Alfred Hitchcock, Avengers, Mission Impossible, Mod Squad)	8	420	3
Action/adventure (Batman, Johnny Sokko, Marine Boy, Robin Hood, Speed Racer, Spiderman, Superman)	36	1,170	10
Western (Big Valley, Bonanza, Rifleman, Cisco Kid)	9	360	3
Fantasy/science fiction (Lost in Space, One Step Beyond, Star Trek)	8	360	3
Other drama (Room 222)	2	60	1
Movies (2 o'Clock Movie, 3 o'Clock Movie, others)	9	600	5
Variety (Banana Splits, Bozo, Frightenstein, Mickey Mouse Club, Presto Clown)	40	1,230	10
Quiz/games/contests (Dealer's Choice, It's Your Bet, What's My Line?)	4	120	1
Sports events	—	—	—
Other entertainment	—	—	—
Total entertainment programs	301	10,140	84
Children's news	—	—	—
Other news (Today's Headlines, 5:30 News, others)	8	210	2
Other children's information (New Zoo Revue)	3	90	1
Spanish-language programs (Ana del Aire, Ayudan a Dios, Mis Tres Amores, Sube Pelayo, Villa Alegre)	19	885	7
Other informational (Praise the Lord, religious films)	4	180	1
Total information programs	34	1,365	11
Type unknown (Adam Murphy, Cap't. Andy, Debbie's Place, For or Against, Penthouse Barnyard)	15	645	5
Total all programs	350	12,150	100

that could not be classified by type or intended audience. In effect, there has been a relabeling of programs produced for prime-time television as "children's television."

The distribution of programming in different market sizes and on UHF and VHF stations varied considerably (see Table 2.2). Whereas VHF stations carried larger proportions of situation comedies, adult crime and western drama, and movies, UHF stations were more diversified in programming. There were greater proportions of family drama, other comedy drama, action-adventure and fantasy drama, as well as of news, children's information, Spanish-language, and religious programs on UHF stations than on VHF stations.

Small-market stations specialized more in westerns, children's information, news, and Spanish-language programs; medium-sized markets in situation comedy, family comedy, crime, fantasy, and children's variety programs. Large-market stations, in contrast, focused more heavily on other children's comedy programs, action-adventure drama, and movies.

The Child Audience for After-School Programs

Two measures were used to describe the child audience for the programs: the 2-11-year-old child audience rating (percent of all children 2-11 years old in the market who are watching) and the child audience percentage (percent of total persons watching who are 2-11 years old).

By market size, independent stations in large markets showed a lower average child audience rating than did those in smaller markets (Table 2.3). VHF station programs were rated higher, on the average (15.0), than UHF station programs (10.4). The highest average 2-11 child ratings were for programs on small-market VHF stations (17.6); the lowest were on large-market UHF stations (8.1).

Although child audience ratings for UHF stations were lower than for VHF stations, the percent of total audience who are children was somewhat higher on UHF stations (50.2 percent and 57.4 percent, respectively). Thus, we have an interesting anomaly—stations with the highest 2-11 child audience ratings (small-market VHF stations) have the lowest child percent of total audience (47.6 percent), and stations with the lowest average child rating (large-market UHF stations) have the largest percentage of children of the total audience (58.2 percent). The types of programs that drew the highest child audience ratings and child percent of total audience are given in Table 2.4. Highest-rated programs were children's variety, cartoon comedy, situation comedy, action-adventure drama, and other comedy drama, all with a child rating of ten or better.

TABLE 2.2

Types of Programs Broadcast, by Type of Station and Market Size

(percent)

Program Type	Market Size			Type of Station		All
	Small	Medium	Large	VHF	UHF	Stations
Cartoon comedy	13	16	15	16	15	15
Other comedy drama	33	40	33	43	29	34
Situation comedy	24	31	21	39	16	24
Family comedy	6	7	3	2	5	4
Other comedy	3	2	9	2	8	6
Action/adventure drama	19	22	23	19	23	22
Animal adventure	–	2	1	–	1	1
Action-adventure	9	5	13	7	12	10
Crime/mystery-detective	3	7	3	7	2	4
Western	6	1	3	5	2	3
Fantasy/science fiction	1	6	3	–	5	3
Other drama	–	1	1	–	1	1
Variety/quiz	10	15	11	12	12	12
Other entertainment	4	1	7	10	3	5
Information	21	6	11	–	18	12
Children's information	3	1	–	–	–	1
News	5	1	1	–	3	2
Spanish-language programs	12	3	8	–	12	8
Religious programs	1	1	2	–	2	1
Total time classified (minutes)	(2,340)	(2,625)	(6,540)	(3,870)	(7,635)	(11,505)
Type unknown (minutes)	(240)	(315)	(90)	(90)	(555)	(645)
Total time studied (minutes)	(2,580)	(2,940)	(6,630)	(3,960)	(8,190)	(12,150)

TABLE 2.3

Average Ratings and Percent of Child Audience,
by Market Size and Type of Station

Type of Station and Market Size	Average Rating	Child Audience Percentage*	Number of Programs for Which Data Available
VHF stations			
Small market	17.6	47.6	20
Medium market	16.1	43.0	28
Large market	13.7	49.7	66
Total VHF stations	15.0	50.2	114
UHF stations			
Small market	11.2	56.1	38
Medium market	14.2	56.7	50
Large market	8.1	58.2	93
Total UHF stations	10.4	57.4	181
All stations			
Small market	13.4	53.2	58
Medium market	14.8	55.4	78
Large market	10.4	54.7	159
Total all stations	12.2	54.6	295

*Percent of total viewers who are children 2-11 years old.

The highest proportions of child audience to total audience were
for action-adventure drama, children's variety, cartoon comedy,
other comedy drama, and animal adventure programs—all with more
than 60 percent child audience.

Individual program titles, ratings, and percent child audience
figures are given in Table 2.5. Generally speaking, higher-rated
programs were those syndicated to several independent stations.
The most popular program was the revival of Mickey Mouse Club,
carried on 29 of the 73 independent stations studied during the sample
period; it had an average child rating of 22.8 and a 68 percent child
audience.

This section has attempted to outline the patterns of independent
station after-school programming and the extent of the child audience
for that programming. Approximately 70 percent of these stations
are independent UHF stations, and more than half are in large
markets with 850,000 or more television households. Although
program patterns vary by type of station and market size, the staple

commodities of independent station programming are situation and family comedy, cartoon and other comedy, children's variety, and action-adventure drama. These categories account for two-thirds of total broadcast time between 3:00 and 6:00 pm on weekdays.

Many of the programs draw more than 10 percent of all children in the community, and many have child audiences of 60 percent or more. For example, at 4:30 pm on a weekday afternoon in New York City, 35 percent of children 2-11 may be watching Bugs Bunny cartoons. This represents some 1,158,000 children. Another 211,000 children may be watching syndicated reruns of Gilligan's Island on another independent station at the same time. It is not necessary to consider the largest market to get a perspective on the number of child viewers, however. In Atlanta, at 4:30 pm on the same weekday, 83,000 children may be watching Leave It to Beaver, and

TABLE 2.4

Average Child Rating and Average Percent
Child Audience, by Type of Program

Program Type	Average Rating	Percentage Child Audience	Number of Programs for Which Data Available
Variety/quiz	19.8	70.3	37
Cartoon comedy	15.1	70.1	52
Situation comedy	12.4	45.6	89
Action-adventure	12.0	73.5	32
Other comedy drama	10.8	61.3	21
Family comedy	9.9	45.6	17
Animal adventure	9.0	61.0	2
Fantasy/science fiction	6.5	33.0	8
Crime/mystery/detective	6.0	22.0	8
Western drama	4.8	26.2	6
News	1.5	41.0	2
Other drama	1.0	31.0	2
Other entertainment (movies)	0.5	10.0	8
Spanish-language programs	0.2	28.8	6
Children's information	*	*	*
Religious programs	*	*	*
Type unknown	10.0	66.4	5
Total all programs	12.2	54.6	295

*Data not available.

TABLE 2.5

List of Programs, with Number of Stations
on Which Each Appeared, Average Child
Rating, and Average Percent Child Audience

Program	Number Stations Carrying	Stations for Which Data Available	Average Rating	Average Percent Child Audience
Mickey Mouse Club	29	28	22.8	68
Flintstones	23	23	17.2	64
Gilligan's Island	23	23	9.5	54
Popeye	11	11	15.0	78
Three Stooges	11	11	11.7	56
Batman	10	10	13.1	74
Leave It to Beaver	10	10	12.6	46
Movies	10	8	0.5	10
Bewitched	9	9	13.9	46
I Love Lucy	9	9	14.3	42
Little Rascals	9	9	9.3	66
Speed Racer	9	9	14.7	80
News	8	2	1.5	41
I Dream of Jeannie	7	7	11.3	45
Munsters	6	6	9.7	54
Programs appearing on five stations				
Banana Splits		4	7.2	82
Bugs Bunny		5	17.6	69
Mod Squad		5	7.8	26
Star Trek		5	5.6	28
Sube Pelayo		3	0.3	25
Programs appearing on four stations				
Andy Griffith		4	10.5	37
Gomer Pyle		4	12.2	41
Hogan's Heros		4	8.5	29
Superman		4	11.5	66
Villa Alegre		1	*	73
Film (varied)		*	*	*
Programs appearing on three stations				
Black Buffalo		*	*	*
Bozo		1	5.0	91
Bullwinkle		3	3.3	67
Casper		3	15.7	79
Dick Van Dyke Show		3	15.7	36
Father Knows Best		3	2.7	32

Program	Stations for Which Data Available	Average Rating	Average Percent Child Audience
Spiderman	2	6.0	79.5
Tennessee Tuxedo	2	7.5	79.0
New Zoo Revue	*	*	*
Programs appearing on two stations			
Addams Family	2	9.0	52
Beverly Hillbillies	2	11.0	38
Big Valley	2	3.0	18
Cisco Kid	*	*	*
Get Smart	2	3.0	38
Green Acres	2	3.5	40
Hilarious World of Frightenstein	2	20.5	79
Huckleberry Hound and Friends	2	20.5	79
Lone Ranger	1	3.0	45
Lost in Space	2	12.0	58
Mis Tres Amores	1	0.0	6
Nanny and the Professor	2	9.0	45
Real McCoys	1	1.0	21
Rifleman	2	8.0	28
Robin Hood	1	1.0	40
Room 222	2	1.0	31
Super Heros	2	4.0	74
Programs appearing on one station only			
Alfred Hitchcock	1	0.0	4
Avengers	1	0.0	14
Ayudan a Dios	1	0.0	19
Bill Cosby	1	2.0	40
Bonanza	1	4.0	21
Captain Cheasepeake	1	2.0	57
Cool Ghoul Show	1	7.0	75
Dealer's Choice	1	3.0	31
Debbie's Place	1	20.0	73
Dennis the Menace	1	2.0	80
Family Affair	1	15.0	70
Flipper	1	16.0	53
Flying Nun	1	7.0	62
Hazel	1	3.0	38
Honeymooners	1	3.0	30
Jeff's Collie	1	2.0	69
Johnny Sokko	1	12.0	80
Kid Komix	1	11.0	79

(continued)

(Table 2.5 continued)

Program	Stations for Which Data Available	Average Rating	Average Percent Child Audience
Magilla Gorilla	1	4.0	71
Marine Boy	1	10.0	84
Mission Impossible	1	8.0	30
Mister Ed	1	3.0	33
My Favorite Martian	1	4.0	55
One Step Beyond	1	0.0	5
Ozzie and Harriet	1	2.0	30
Partridge Family	1	15.0	44
Penthouse Barnyard	1	5.0	63
Petticoat Junction	1	7.0	47
Please Don't Eat the Daisies	1	2.0	37
Porky and Friends	1	9.0	59
Presto the Clown	1	17.0	90
Puff 'n Stuff/Lidsville	1	13.0	83
Rambling Rod	1	16.0	64
Tarzan	1	21.0	44
That Girl	1	1.0	50
Thrillers	1	0.0	7
Data not available			
Adam Murphy			
Ana del Aire			
Captain Ahab			
Captain Andy			
Captain Hook's Private Adventures			
Cartoons and Kids			
Entre Brumas			
En San Antonio			
For or Against			
Hechizada			
It's Your Bet			
Kaleidoscope			
The King Is Coming			
Nuestro Mexico			
Praise the Lord			
Revista Femenina			
Sin Palabras			
Timmy and Lassie			
What's My Line?			

*Data not available.

2,000 more The Real McCoys on another channel. Meanwhile, in South Bend-Elkhart, Indiana, another 24,000 are viewing Batman on the local independent station.

These figures demonstrate a consistent pattern in which the independent stations are reaching the after-school child audience in large numbers. One reason, of course, is that there is no children's television provided by the network stations at this time (except for an occasional after-school special). What is available for the child, then, are the few Public Broadcasting Service children's programs, adult soap operas and talk shows on the networks, or situation comedy, cartoons, and action-adventure on the independent stations. Children are choosing to watch the last in large numbers.

To gain a more detailed picture of what they are watching, the rest of this chapter is devoted to an analysis of programming, commercial practices, and other aspects of broadcasting in the after-school hours on a sample of ten of these independent stations.

CHILDREN'S PROGRAMMING ON TEN INDEPENDENT STATIONS

Of 30 hours of broadcast material analyzed on the ten independent stations, 78 percent was devoted to actual program material, 20 percent to commercial announcement time, and the remainder to noncommercial and other announcements. There was a fairly consistent pattern for all ten stations studied, with program matter ranging from 76 to 82 percent of total time, and CAs from 16 to 22 percent (see Table 2.6).

This section is designed to analyze the actual program fare with respect to type of program, subject matter, settings of the stories, the extent and nature of violence, and the composition of characters.

Program Fare

There was a pattern of sameness on all ten stations studied. More than 96 percent of all programming was recorded-syndicated. Less than one hour in 30 was local, and only three of the stations carried any locally originated programming. Buffalo's WUTV carried two minutes of News Capsule for the Deaf, Atlanta's WTCG broadcast seven minutes of baseball, and Louisville's WDRB presented Presto Clown, which, although containing portions of cartoon comedy, was the only local program intended for children found on any of the ten stations. About 30 percent was animated programming, 10 percent mixed animation and live on film, and the remainder nonanimated.

TABLE 2.6

Total Time Studied, by Station and Type of Material

Station	Channel	Type of Material						
		Program Matter	Comm'l. Product Ancmts.	Program Promotion	Total Comm'l. Time	NCAs	Other[a]	Total
		Minutes						
New York	5	137	25	9	34	8	1	180
Washington	20	136	25	13	38	5	1	180
Buffalo	29	147	28	2	30	2	1	180
Detroit	50	137	36	5	41	1	1	180
Milwaukee	18	141	28	7	35	4	b	180
Louisville	41	146	20	9	29	4	1	180
Norfolk	27	145	30	3	33	2	b	180
Atlanta	17	141	33	5	38	1	b	180
Seattle	11	137	30	9	39	1	3	180
Sacramento	40	141	36	1	37	1	1	180
Total all stations		1,408	291	63	354	29	9	1,800
		Percent						
New York		76	14	5	19	5	c	100
Washington		76	14	7	21	3	c	100
Buffalo		82	16	1	17	c	c	100
Detroit		76	20	3	23	c	c	100
Milwaukee		78	15	4	19	2	c	100
Louisville		81	11	5	16	2	c	100
Norfolk		81	16	2	18	c	c	100
Atlanta		78	18	3	21	c	c	100
Seattle		76	17	5	22	c	2	100
Sacramento		78	20	1	21	c	c	100
Total all stations		78	16	4	20	2	c	100

a Station identification and other miscellaneous transitional material.
b Less than 30 seconds.
c Less than 0.50 percent.

Four categories of programming accounted for two-thirds of all time. Cartoon comedy was the largest single category for all stations combined (26 percent), followed by situation comedy (20 percent), children's variety (11 percent), and crime/mystery/detective programs (10 percent). (The last category includes Batman, Mod Squad, and the end of an afternoon movie.) There was no informational programming. Detailed categories are given in Table 2.7 for all ten stations combined. (A list of program titles of all programs monitored is presented in Appendix C.)

There were differences in program types on the various stations. New York, Buffalo, Milwaukee, and Seattle exceeded the average for cartoon comedy; Milwaukee, Norfolk, Atlanta, and Seattle carried more than 50 percent other comedy; and Washington, Buffalo, Detroit, and Sacramento were highest in action-adventure programming (Table 2.8).

Subject Matter of the Programs

Different program types tended to focus on different subject areas. For all programs combined, four subjects accounted for more than 60 percent of all subjects treated: domestic (21 percent), interpersonal rivalry (16 percent), crime (15 percent), and the supernatural (11 percent). None of the programs dealt with war, race-nationality, language, or religion; and a minimum of time was devoted to historical topics, education, business or industry, government, literature or the fine arts, or crafts and hobbies (Table 2.9).

Cartoon comedy dealt primarily with interpersonal rivalries between characters, crime, romance, and domestic topics. Other comedy dealt mostly with domestic subjects, and action-adventure with crime, science, and interpersonal rivalry. Variety and other entertainment programs generally dealt with various topics, led by the entertainment world, the supernatural, crafts, and nature/ animals.

Time and Place Settings

The images reflected in the basic time and place settings of after-school programming for children presented a rather ethnocentric picture of the world. They most often took place in the United States (79 percent) and in the city (57 percent) (Table 2.10). City settings were not often found in foreign locales, however. Of more than 20 hours of dramatic format programming, about 100

TABLE 2.7

Time Devoted to Various Program Types,
All Stations Combined

Program Type	Minutes	Percent
Situation comedy (I Love Lucy, Gilligan's Island, Addams Family, Munsters)	280	19.9
Family comedy (Leave It to Beaver, Partridge Family)	112	8.0
Cartoon comedy (Casper and Friends, Bugs Bunny and Friends, Kid Komix, Popeye, Flintstones)	364	25.9
Other comedy drama (Three Stooges, Banana Splits, Little Rascals)	76	5.4
Animal adventure (Timmy and Lassie)	26	1.8
Crime/mystery/detective (Batman, Mod Squad)	145	10.3
Action-adventure (Marine Boy, Speed Racer)	83	5.9
Western drama	–	–
Fantasy/science fiction (Star Trek, Lost in Space)	115	8.2
Other drama (Room 222)	24	1.7
Movies	20	1.4
Variety (Mickey Mouse Club, Presto Clown)	154	10.9
Quiz	–	–
Sports events (baseball)	7	0.5
Other entertainment	–	–
Total entertainment programs	1,406	99.9
Children's news	–	–
Documentary/travel	–	–
Animal/nature films	–	–
Interviews/panels	–	–
Discussion/debate	–	–
Music and fine arts	–	–
Foreign-language programs	–	–
Other informational (news for the deaf)	2	0.1
Total information	2	0.1
Total all program types	1,408	100.0

TABLE 2.8

Type of Program, by Station
(percent)

Station	Cartoon Comedy	Other Comedy	Action- Adventure	Variety/ Quiz	Other	Infor- mation	Total Minutes
New York	67	—	9	24	—	—	137
Washington	26	28	46	—	—	—	136
Buffalo	40	—	43	16	—	1	148
Detroit	—	33	52	—	15	—	137
Milwaukee	40	50	10	—	—	—	141
Louisville	10	26	33	31	—	—	145
Norfolk	16	66	18	—	—	—	145
Atlanta	13	66	—	16	5	—	141
Seattle	35	52	—	13	—	—	137
Sacramento	13	28	51	8	—	—	141
All stations	26	35	26	11	2	*	1,408

*Less than 0.50 percent.

minutes took place in foreign locales—but only 19 minutes in foreign cities. Time settings were most often contemporary; and when historic settings were presented, they were most often in the humorous context of cartoon comedy.

Extent of Violence

If the overall level of violence has been reduced in all of children's television, as is claimed by the newer network productions, it is far from true for independent station programming. Overall, more than 60 percent of stories viewed contained some observable act of violence, and about 30 percent were "saturated" with violent acts. These latter programs had little more than the violent action (albeit often in humorous contexts) to sustain the story. Cartoon comedy and the older action-adventure programs accounted for most of the violent episodes (Table 2.11).

Although each individual act of violence was not tallied and classified, monitors were asked to record and classify program segments with chase scenes, deaths, injuries, and so on, in order to obtain an index of the nature of the violence in the programs.

For all programs, human violence with weapons was the most common type, followed by human violence without weapons. The violence was most frequently directed at other humans (see Table 2.12).

TABLE 2.9

Subject Matter of the Programs,
by Type of Program
(percent)

Subject Matter Category[a]	Cartoon Comedy	Other Comedy	Action-Adventure	Variety	Information	All Types
Domestic (marriage, home, family)	10	41	13	8	—	21
Crime (robberies, police, crime detection)	13	10	27	7	—	15
Historical (association with historical events)	6	—	2	—	—	2
Religion (church, clergy, religious customs)	—	—	—	—	—	—
Love and romance (relations between sexes)	12	9	—	—	—	6
Supernatural (magic, the occult)	9	12	5	23	—	11
Nature and animals (hunting, exploring)	7	5	4	13	—	7
Race/nationality (minorities, foreign)	—	—	—	—	—	—
Education (schools, teachers, training)	2	6	—	4	—	3
Business and industry (labor, private business)	4	2	—	—	—	2
Government/public affairs (law, politics, government)	—	3	—	—	—	1
Science and scientists (medicine, technology)	—	3	23	—	—	7
Entertainment world (sports, show business)	7	2	3	23	—	7
War/armed forces	—	—	—	—	—	—
Literature/fine arts	1	—	—	7	—	1
Interpersonal rivalry (jealousy, conflict)	27	7	23	—	—	16
Crafts/hobbies	1	—	—	15	—	2
Language (words, spelling)	—	—	—	—	—	—
Other, not classifiable above	1	—	—	—	100	b
Total minutes	(634)	(794)	(590)	(301)	(2)	(2,321)

[a]Each program segment was classified into one or two subject categories.
[b]Less than 0.50 percent.

TABLE 2.10

Time and Place Settings of Dramatic
Format Programs
(percent)

	Cartoon Comedy	Other Comedy	Action-Adventure	All Drama
Time settings				
Distant past	35	—	12	14
Recent past	9	12	4	9
Contemporary	36	88	31	55
Future	—	—	44	13
Time uncertain	20	—	9	9
Total time (mins.)	(364)	(492)	(370)	(1,226)
Place settings				
U.S., city	38	82	39	56
U.S., rural	42	13	16	23
Foreign, city	5	—	—	1
Foreign, rural	4	5	12	7
Outer space	—	—	27	8
Place uncertain	11	—	6	5
Total time (mins.)	(364)	(492)	(370)	(1,226)

TABLE 2.11

The Extent of Violence

Extent of Violence	Cartoon Comedy	Other Comedy	Action-Adventure	All Drama
Percent of segments				
With no violence	14	69	12	30
With incidental violence	5	9	6	6
With violence subordinate	41	9	44	32
Saturated with violence	40	13	38	32
Total segments (no.)	(42)	(23)	(16)	(81)
Percent of time				
With no violence	11	75	7	36
With incidental violence	3	8	6	6
With violence subordinate	46	7	48	31
Saturated with violence	40	10	39	27
Total time (mins.)	(364)	(492)	(370)	(1,226)

TABLE 2.12

The Nature of Violence

	Percent of Segments			
	Cartoon Comedy	Other Comedy	Action- Adventure	All Seg- ments
Segments with				
Chase scenes	55	22	31	41
Deaths	5	–	13	5
Injuries	31	9	44	27
Human violence with weapons	69	22	56	53
Human violence without weapons	50	22	50	42
Natural and accidental violence	10	4	38	14
Death/injury through violence	24	4	19	17
Violence directed at humans	48	22	50	41
Frightening situations	7	4	44	14
Total segments	(42)	(23)	(16)	(82)

Although deaths did not occur frequently, there were injuries in about one-fourth of the stories, most often in action-adventure programs.

Action-adventure stories also contained more natural or accidental violence as well as dangerous, frightening, or highly suspenseful situations offering the threat of violence or injury. Cartoon comedy, equally violent in most respects, often employed the "chase" scene and, it is interesting to note, more frequently employed human violence with weapons than other types of stories. A sample of typical scenes is presented below.

Examples of Violence

"Oil's Well that Ends Well" (Popeye)
> During chase in which Popeye follows a car driven by Brutus, he smashes the car and Brutus with his fist, after having been run over twice by the car.

"Innertube Antics" (Kid Komix)
> Donkey character, during course of cartoon, steps on shovel several times, getting hit in the nose; hits innertube, which hits

back; tries to pull innertube and gets thrown back, narrowly
avoiding being impaled on a pick-axe; instead sits down on a
fork. Then he is caught in a ladder, is hit, and is shot into
the air like a helicopter, landing on electrical wires. He is
electrocuted again when he cuts down a power-line pole.

"Girl Daredevil" (Speed Racer)

Twinkie and Speed Racer drive over Niagara Falls on two ropes,
then fall into a secret cave of Mr. Brosh. They are attacked
by leopards, shot at by Mr. Brosh, and fought hand-to-hand by
bodyguards.

Marine Boy

Marine Boy and the Ocean Patrol tangle with Dr. Diablo, who
is creating "gillmen." Gillmen chase Marine Boy; they fight
with fists as well as ray guns and Ocean Patrol missiles.
Marine Boy uses karate on gillmen.

"Hold That Lion" (Three Stooges)

Episode revolves around an inheritance. All three are beaten
by man demanding money, chase man on train, injure each
other with hammer and gun, and run into lion's cage, after
which the lion escapes.

"Toby Tortoise Returns" (Mickey Mouse Club)

Scene is a fight ring—Hare vs. Tortoise. Max (hare) pummels
slower Toby. After being knocked out of the ring, Toby hides
in his shell. Max, going in after him, gets his hand caught in
a mouse trap. He then pours a bucket of water into Toby's
shell. Toby, after having been filled with fireworks, becomes
a fighting machine and wins the bout.

Batman

Robin is tied to a clock; they both are trapped in steam that
will kill them if they do not escape; they blow up a wall, then
go to beat their captors.

Overall, 57 of 81 dramatic stories contained such types of
activity in more or less concentrated form. About half of them
contained all three types of violence: with weapons, without weapons,
and natural-accidental.

Deaths occurred in various ways. A witch died after being
struck by lightning (Kid Komix); Superman smashed several Brainiacs
to pieces (Kid Komix); a man was killed by "the Mob" in a movie
segment; the boss of a restaurant was murdered (Flintstones); and
a girl was shot (Mod Squad). Injuries also occurred in ingenious
ways. A dog was blown up by dynamite; people fell off cliffs, were
shot into the air, and crashed through roofs; other characters were
scalded in boiling water, were attacked by death forces, run over
by cars, electrocuted, and—occasionally—shot by other people.

When not being killed or maimed, the characters often found themselves in such dire circumstances that miracles were required to escape death or injury. They were chased by others wielding hatchets or by animals acting as we might assume they would act when provoked. They were trapped in animal cages, steam rooms, and inside vehicles, and exposed to death rays and hostile humanoids.

Child Audiences

Nielsen rating data for February-March 1975 were used to provide estimates of the extent of the child audience for the programs on the various stations. Although these were not for the exact period studied on the ten stations, they should provide reasonable estimates of the child viewing audiences. Few of the programming schedules changed radically during the interim period.

Of the total audiences viewing the 30 hours of programming studied, almost two-thirds, on the average, were children 2-11. This average varied from about 44 percent in Norfolk-Portsmouth to 85 percent in New York City. In eight of the ten markets, 50 percent or more of the audience were children aged 2-11. Table 2.13 presents the overall 2-11 rating and child audience percentage, by station, averaging all program types.

By program type, three-fourths of the audience for variety and cartoon comedy were children, two-thirds for action-adventure programs, and over one-half for other comedy programs—situation comedy, family comedy, and the older movie theater comedies (Three Stooges, Little Rascals). Other program types (such as information and other entertainment programs) were presented too infrequently to obtain any stable averages for the child audience (Table 2.14).

Characters in the Programs

Up to five major characters in the programs were classified by sex, age group, and minority status. This provided a picture of the "population" of after-school children's television and the resulting sexual and social images that are reinforced daily by these programs. A total of 405 major characters were classified in 92 program segments studied. A "character" was defined to include all persons, animals, or other anthropomorphic beings who played a major role in the story—or, in the case of variety or information programs, who acted as hosts, panelists, or guests.

TABLE 2.13

Average Rating and Percent Child Audience,
by Station

City	Number of Segments Rated	Average Rating	Average Percent Child Audience
New York	13	32.0	84.7
Washington	10	11.2	71.7
Buffalo	14	11.4	72.9
Detroit	5	8.2	49.8
Milwaukee	10	18.4	68.2
Louisville	8	23.9	77.6
Norfolk	7	7.1	44.0
Atlanta	9	9.7	45.0
Seattle	9	16.4	61.2
Sacramento	7	15.7	56.6
All stations	92	16.3	65.8

TABLE 2.14

Average Rating and Percent Child Audience,
by Program Type

Program Format	Average Rating	Average Percent Child Audience	Number of Program Segments
Cartoon comedy	17.9	75.1	42
Other comedy drama	13.4	51.8	23
Action-adventure	15.4	65.9	16
Variety/quiz	23.1	75.1	8
Other entertainment	0.0	4.5	2
Information	8.0	40.0	1
All programs	16.3	65.8	92

After-school programming hardly gives a representative picture of society. Of 405 characters, 289 were male and 101 female. The remainder were animal or other characters for which sex could not be determined (Table 2.15). By age distribution, 14 percent were children, 8 percent teens, and 71 percent adult characters, with the

TABLE 2.15

Sex, Age Group, and Ethnic Status of the Characters

	Number	Percent
Male children		
White	29	7.2
Black	1	0.2
Other minorities	2	0.5
Unknown (animals and others portraying male children)	8	2.0
Total male children	40	9.9
Male teens		
White	17	4.2
Black	—	—
Other minorities	—	—
Unknown (animals and others portraying male teens)	3	0.7
Total male teens	20	4.9
Male adults		
White	149	36.8
Black	3	0.7
Other minorities	2	0.5
Unknown (animals and others portraying male adults)	53	13.1
Total male adults	207	51.1
Male, age and race unknown	22	5.4
Total males	289	71.4
Female children		
White	11	2.7
Black	—	—
Other minorities	1	0.2
Unknown (animals and others portraying female children)	2	0.5
Total female children	14	3.4
Female teens		
White	9	2.2
Black	—	—
Other minorities	—	—
Unknown (animals and others portraying female teens)	3	0.8
Total female teens	12	3.0
Female adults		
White	59	14.6
Black	2	0.5
Other minorities	1	0.2
Unknown (animals and others portraying female adults)	7	1.7
Total female adults	69	17.0
Female, age and race unknown	6	1.5
Total females	101	24.9
Other characters, age, sex, and race unknown	15	3.7
Total all characters	405	100.0

remainder animals and others with age indeterminable. Thus, for every female there were 2.9 males. For children, the ratio was 1:2.9; for teens, it was 1:1.7; and for adults, 1:3.0. When others were portrayed, the ratio was 1:3.9.

If not precisely the same, the predominant pattern remained for all categories of programs. In cartoon comedy, the ratio of females to males was 1:4.0; in other comedy 1:2.1; in action-adventure drama, 1:3.5; and in variety, 1:2.1. (See Table 2.16.)

Ethnic or racial status was coded for 70 percent (282) of 405 major characters. Of these, 96 percent were white, 3 percent black, and 1 percent other minorities. The pattern was consistent for all types of programs (Table 2.17).

Analysis of character distributions is only one of several indexes that might be used to describe the world portrayed by any segment of the mass media. These distributions become the repetitive, reinforcing images to which the audience is exposed on a regular basis. Although we may be concerned with the imitative behavior of children with respect to acts of violence portrayed, or with the lack of diversity in the subject matter of the programs, the distribu-

TABLE 2.16

Age and Sex of Characters, by Program Type
(percent)

Sex and Age Group	Cartoon Comedy	Other Comedy	Action-Adventure	Variety and Other	Total
Male children	7	17	9	7	10
Male teens	3	5	9	4	5
Male adults	57	46	57	57	53
Male animals, other	13	–	3	–	6
Total males	80	68	78	68	74
Female children	2	2	3	14	4
Female teens	3	2	4	7	3
Female adults	14	28	14	9	18
Female animals, other	2	–	1	2	1
Total females	20	32	22	32	26
Total children	9	19	12	21	14
Total teens	6	7	13	11	8
Total adults	70	74	71	66	71
Total animals, other	15	–	4	2	7
Total classified	(155)	(114)	(77)	(44)	(390)

TABLE 2.17

Race of Characters, by Program Type

Characters in	Percent White	Percent Black	Percent Other Minorities	Number of Characters Classified
Cartoon comedy	98	—	2	62
Other comedy	96	3	1	109
Action–adventure	97	3	—	72
Variety, other	92	5	3	39
All types	96	3	1	282

tion of characters may have a more lasting and subtle long–term influence than we might at first believe. The connection between viewing the world of the mass media and effects on those who are continually exposed to it has not been adequately demonstrated. However, we do know that the world of after–school children's television bears little relationship to the world in which we live.

ADVERTISING ON THE INDEPENDENT STATIONS

The 12–Minute Rule

According to the 1974 FCC Report and Policy Statement on Children's Television Programs, the Association of Independent Television Stations agreed to the same limits on the amount of time devoted to advertising to children as was adopted by the National Association of Broadcasters. By 1976 there was to be a reduction in commercial time to 9.5 minutes per hour on Saturday and Sunday, and to 12 minutes per hour on weekdays.

Five of the 10 independent stations studied exceeded this amount during the 3:00–6:00 pm period in May 1975. The stations ranged from a high on two stations of more than 15 minutes to a low on another station of just over 6 minutes. The average for all stations was 11.92 minutes per hour; and in 16 of the 30 hours studied, commercial time exceeded 12 minutes (Table 2.18).

Number and Length of Commercials

A total of 487 CAs was studied. This figure represents 487 exposures of 262 different versions of CAs for 218 products. More than 80 percent of all CAs were 30 seconds long, 10 percent were 60 seconds long, and the remainder either 10- or 15-second spots or 120-second commercials for records, specialized schools, and so on. In addition, 139 promos were broadcast. The average length of commercials was thus somewhat greater than that usually found on weekend children's television. The ten stations varied somewhat in the amount of commercial material during the three-hour period studied on each. There was a low of 48 commercial announcements on one station and a high of 72 on another. The average announcement was .56 minutes in length for all stations combined—or one commercial announcement every 2.9 minutes. (See Table 2.19.)

Types of Products Advertised

The types of products most frequently advertised in the after-school hours were miscellaneous products and services, such as record offers, schools, movies, and amusements. In order, these were followed by toys, cereals, candies, and eating places. Table 2.20 presents a detailed list of products advertised. (All commercials are listed in Appendix E.)

Toy CAs were primarily for dolls and outdoor toys. Sugared cereal CAs outnumbered those for unsugared cereals by 3:1; and

TABLE 2.18

Number of Commercial Minutes per Hour,
by Station

Station	Channel	Minutes per Hour			Average Minutes per Hour
		3:00–4:00pm	4:00–5:00pm	5:00–6:00pm	
New York	5	10.41	11.24	12.83	11.49
Washington	20	14.42	12.42	10.84	12.56
Buffalo	29	9.00	9.50	12.09	10.20
Detroit	50	15.16	14.39	12.58	13.71
Milwaukee	18	11.59	8.59	14.76	11.65
Louisville	41	6.25	11.33	11.41	9.66
Norfolk	27	8.17	12.58	12.09	10.95
Atlanta	17	14.43	12.50	10.34	12.42
Seattle	11	10.25	14.16	14.98	13.13
Sacramento	40	10.67	15.50	13.09	13.09
Total all stations		110.35	122.21	125.01	357.57
Average all stations		11.04	12.22	12.50	11.92

TABLE 2.19

Number and Length of Commercial
Announcements, by Station

Station	Number of CAs	Time (mins.)	Aver-age Length	Percent of Total Time (180 min. = 100%)	One CA per "x" Minutes
New York	70	34	.49	18.9	2.9
Washington	66	38	.58	21.1	2.7
Buffalo	54	31	.57	17.2	3.3
Detroit	69	41	.59	22.8	2.6
Milwaukee	67	35	.52	19.4	2.7
Louisville	50	29	.58	16.1	3.6
Norfolk	48	33	.69	18.3	3.8
Atlanta	62	37	.60	20.6	2.9
Seattle	68	39	.57	21.7	2.6
Sacramento	72	37	.51	20.6	2.5
All stations	626	354	.56	19.7	2.9

CAs for candy bars, cakes and cookies, and carbonated beverages
constituted the bulk of CAs for sweets. Only a few CAs were broadcast for other foods individually (milk, bread, fruits) or for snack
foods, although many were aired for quick meals and eating places.
Household and personal care products accounted for approximately
7 percent of all CAs. Of all miscellaneous products, recreations
(amusement parks, race tracks) and record offers were the most
frequently advertised.

Basic Structure of the CAs

Overall, about 10 percent of CAs used animation solely, and
about 20 percent used some form of animation. The form of the
commercials was mixed, with the off-stage announcer most frequent,
dramatic skits second, and musical forms third. (See Table 2.21.)

More than 50 percent of CAs showed the product being used,
and about 30 percent showed only pictures or drawings of the product.
Only one-half were classified as appealing directly to children, and
about one-third to the adult audience. Almost all identifiable time
settings were contemporary, and outdoor settings around home were
the most frequent. Few CAs seemed to be associated with places
of work or profession.

TABLE 2.20

Number and Percent of CAs, by Specific
Product Type

Product Type	Number	Percent
Toys		
Cars, planes, trains	1	0.2
Dolls and doll play sets	59	12.1
Indoor games, puzzles	3	0.6
Outdoor games and toys	21	4.3
Toy stores	—	—
Other toys, hobbies, crafts	6	1.2
Total toys	90	18.5
Cereals		
Sugared cereals	65	13.3
Unsugared cereals	20	4.1
Total cereals	85	17.4
Candies/sweets		
Candy bars, packaged candies	23	5.1
Chewing gum (sugarless)	1	0.2
Chewing gum (regular)	7	1.4
Cakes and cookies	16	3.3
Ice cream, puddings, desserts	2	0.4
Soft drinks (carbonated)	12	2.5
Fruit drinks and ices	9	1.8
Juice drinks (orange, grape)	—	—
Other candies, sweets	1	0.2
Total candies/sweets	73	14.9
Snacks		
Chips—potato, corn, other	1	0.2
Peanut butter and spreads	—	—
Other snacks	1	0.2
Total snacks	2	0.4
Other foods		
Canned, prepared packaged foods	4	0.8
Fruits and fruit juices	1	0.2
Vegetables	—	—
Meats	1	0.2
Bread	—	—

(continued)

(Table 2.20 continued)

Product Type	Number	Percent
Milk, dairy products	2	0.4
Other foods	1	0.2
Total other foods	9	1.8
Eating places		
Restaurants, meals	50	10.3
Grocery stores, supermarkets	4	0.8
Other	1	0.2
Total eating places	55	11.3
Vitamins/medicines		
Vitamins	–	–
Medicines, analgesics	–	–
Other	–	–
Total vitamins/medicines	–	–
Household products		
Cleansers, detergents	2	0.4
Appliances	6	1.2
Tools, hardware	8	1.6
Other household products (Dixie Cups)	2	0.4
Total household products	18	3.6
Personal care products		
Shampoos, deodorants, soaps	6	1.2
Health (sauna suit, exerciser)	7	1.4
Clothing (shoes, other)	4	0.8
Other	2	0.4
Total personal care	19	3.8
Other miscellaneous products		
Motion pictures	14	2.9
Recreation/amusements	36	7.4
Books/magazines	9	1.8
Record offers	26	5.3
Automobiles (repair, parts)	16	3.3
Airlines (travel offers)	1	0.2
Schools	13	2.7
Hi-fi and stereo stores	7	1.4
Other miscellaneous products	14	2.9
Total miscellaneous	136	27.9
Total all products	487	100.0

TABLE 2.21

Commercial Announcements, by Style
of Presentation

	Number of CAs	Percent
Type of CA		
Animated	50	10.3
Nonanimated	381	78.2
Mixed	56	11.5
Form		
Off-stage voice	226	46.4
On-stage announcer	67	13.8
Musical structure	88	18.1
Dramatic skit	99	20.3
Other	7	1.4
Display style		
Product display only	155	31.8
Product shown in use	256	52.6
Product name only	42	8.6
Other, unclassifiable	34	7.0
Audience appeal		
Children	238	48.9
General audience	69	14.2
Adults	177	36.3
Parents	3	0.6
Place setting		
Home or around home	140	28.7
Outside (street, field)	117	24.0
Place of work or profession	36	7.4
Public place (hotel, movie)	86	17.7
Other (outer space)	17	3.5
Uncertain, unclassifiable	91	18.7
Time setting		
Historical (distant past)	7	1.4
Recent past	1	0.2
Contemporary	460	94.5
Uncertain	19	3.9
Totals	487	100.0

Who "Speaks for" the Product?

The authoritative voice (announcer or speaking character) for 90 percent of commercials was male—most frequently adult male (Table 2.22). Even representational characters (such as animals or monsters) were almost always male. Although females were more often associated with personal care, household products, cereals, and eating places, in no product category did female voices or characters account for more than 21 percent.

Children also were infrequently used as the primary voice representing products (5 percent overall). Only cereals, candies, and snack and other foods used children to speak for them.

Characters Appearing in the Commercials

In addition to the prime person representing the product, all characters appearing in the CAs were coded by age group, sex, and race. There was an average of 3.2 characters per CA. Like the principal speaker, characters in CAs were most frequently male. Of 1,538 characters classified, 55 percent were male, 32 percent female, and 13 percent animals or others for which sex could not be determined. Of those characters classifiable by sex, therefore, more than 60 percent were male (Table 2.23).

Male children were most frequently portrayed as characters, followed by male adults and female children. Thus, although television advertisers seem to avoid using children to sell products directly, they are frequently used as characters shown enjoying or consuming them. Teen-agers were the most underrepresented group. Only 126 teen characters were found among the 1,538 classified. They were most frequently found in CAs for candies and sweets.

Males outnumbered females in all product categories. The sexes were more equally balanced in CAs for personal care and for other food products. Male children dominated toy CAs; female children were not dominant in any one product type and most often appeared in cereal commercials.

Of characters classifiable by race, 95 percent were white and 5 percent black. Only 1 out of 1,287 characters could be identified as a member of another minority (Table 2.24).

All product categories contained predominantly white characters. The portrayal of blacks was most frequent in snack and other food commercials (29 percent combined, 6 out of 21 characters). Household and personal care products were almost "pure white."

The population shown in CAs is hardly representative of the "real world." It is predominantly white and male. The teen-ager

TABLE 2.22

Who "Speaks for" the Product?
(percent)

Sex and Age Group	Toys	Cereals	Candies	Snacks and Other Foods	Eating Places	House- hold Prod.	Pers. Care	Other Prod.	Total
Adult male	92	32	58	82	82	83	79	95	75
Adult female	8	5	8	9	13	17	21	4	8
Total adults	100	37	66	91	95	100	100	99	83
Male child	–	2	12	9	–	–	–	–	3
Female child	–	12	2	–	–	–	–	–	2
Total children	–	14	14	9	–	–	–	–	5
Other male	–	49	20	–	3	–	–	1	12
Other female	–	–	–	–	2	–	–	–	*
Total other	–	49	20	–	5	–	–	1	13
Total males	92	83	90	91	85	83	79	96	90
Total females	9	17	10	9	15	17	21	4	10
Total CAs	(90)	(85)	(73)	(11)	(55)	(18)	(19)	(136)	(487)

*Less than 0.50 percent.

TABLE 2.23

Age and Sex of Characters Appearing in Commercials, by Major Product Type
(percent)

Age and Sex	Toys	Cereals	Candies	Snacks	Other Foods	Eating Places	House- hold	Pers. Care	Other Misc.	All CAs
Males										
Children	60	37	21	–	34	35	6	21	13	31
Teens	–	–	15	–	–	–	8	9	5	4
Adults	11	10	24	67	22	29	46	23	48	26
Animals	–	11	*	–	–	2	–	–	1	3
Total males	71	58	60	67	56	66	60	53	67	64
Females										
Children	28	34	8	–	22	19	–	–	10	18
Teens	*	1	16	–	–	2	9	6	6	5
Adults	1	7	16	33	22	12	31	41	17	13
Animals	–	–	–	–	–	1	–	–	–	*
Total females	29	42	40	33	44	34	40	47	33	36
Total characters classifiable by sex	(234)	(256)	(223)	(3)	(18)	(192)	(35)	(47)	(331)	(1,339)
Others	–	(72)	(53)	(2)	–	(18)	–	–	(54)	(199)
Total children	–	55	24	–	56	50	6	21	20	43
Total teens	*	1	25	–	–	2	17	15	10	8
Total adults	12	13	32	60	44	38	77	64	55	34
Total animals, others	–	31	19	40	–	10	–	–	15	15
Total characters	(234)	(328)	(276)	(5)	(18)	(210)	(35)	(47)	(385)	(1,538)

*Less than 0.50 percent.

92

TABLE 2.24

Race of Characters Appearing in Commercials,
by Major Product Type

Major Product Type	Percent White	Percent Black	Percent Other	Total Class-ified	Not Class-ified
Toys	94	6	*	233	1
Cereals	95	5	—	249	79
Candies/sweets	95	5	—	222	54
Snacks	67	33	—	3	2
Other foods	72	28	—	18	—
Eating places	96	4	—	170	40
Household products	100	—	—	35	—
Personal care products	98	2	—	47	—
Other miscellaneous	95	5	—	310	75
Total all products	95	5	*	1,287	251

*Less than 0.50 percent.

is least often seen in the world of television ads. Beyond white and black, characters of other racial or ethnic groups are practically nonexistent.

Advertising of "Adult" Products to Children

It has been argued that all advertising to children is inappropriate. Given that such advertising does exist on children's television, however, most people would agree that some types of product advertisements are more appropriate for children than others. Traditionally, toys, cereals, candies, and snack foods have constituted the bulk of children's advertising. Questions have been raised as to the appropriateness not only of some of these products, but even more so of certain motion picture ads and of CAs for hazardous household products, over-the-counter drugs and medicines, and other products considered potentially harmful to a child.

To obtain a measure of the appropriateness of advertising in the after-school hours, all CAs were coded according to the percent of total persons viewing who were children (percent child audience).*

*Figures used should be considered as the best available estimates of the child audience. Programs were recorded in May and

TABLE 2.25

Commercials Appearing on Programs, by
Percent Child Audience

Product Type	Percent of CAs on Programs with Child Audiences of				Total CAs
	0–29%	30–49%	50–69%	70% or more	
Toys	3	4	37	56	90
Cereals	5	14	38	43	85
Candies	9	26	40	25	73
Snacks/other foods	18	46	9	27	11
Eating places	11	14	29	46	55
Household products	33	39	11	17	18
Personal care prods.	26	42	21	11	19
Other misc. prods.	15	35	26	24	136
All products	11	23	31	35	487

Generally speaking, those products traditionally advertised to children appeared most often on programs with higher child audiences. There were, however, significant numbers of commercials for household, personal care, and other "adult" products advertised on programs with large child audiences. A general picture of this advertising can be seen by examining the product types and the number of commercials for each that appeared on programs with 50 percent or greater child audiences (Table 2.25).

Although the cutoff point must be somewhat arbitrary, programs for which 50 percent or more of the audience is children could well be defined as "children's programs"–regardless of the intent or the content of the program. Two-thirds of 487 CAs were broadcast on programs for which 50 percent or more of the audience was children. More than three-fourths of CAs for toys, cereals, and eating places were broadcast on such programs, as were more than one-half of those for candies and miscellaneous products. Three product types had one-third or less of their CAs on large child audience programs–snacks and other foods, personal care products, and household products.

––––––––

June 1975. Rating data were obtained from the Nielsen Station Index reports for February–March 1975. Most of the program schedules remained the same.

To obtain a more detailed perspective on the appropriateness of advertising matter for children, a list was prepared of specific CAs broadcast on programs with child audiences of 25 percent or greater. The list (see Table 2.26) included ads for restaurants, foods, supermarkets, magazines, or record offers—although many of these items probably are not in the purchasing perspective of the child.

Program Promotion

Another form of commercial announcement is the message promoting programs on the station. Although shorter and less frequent, they are intended to increase the audiences for future programs. In addition to investigating the general distribution of promos on the stations, the major question asked in the analysis of program promos was "whether any programs were being promoted that might be considered inappropriate for the predominantly child viewing audience, either by reason of general content or by time period in which the program was scheduled."

Of a total of 129 promos recorded, two-thirds were for programs at other periods on the stations—rather than for adjacent, upcoming shows or for the same program the following week (Table 2.27).

Weekday programs between noon and 6:00 pm were most frequently promoted (41 percent of all promos), followed by weekday evening programs (6:00-9:00 pm, 29 percent), and weekend evenings (7 percent). Time period of promoted programs is given in Table 2.28.

Eight promos were aired for programs after 9:00 pm on weekdays, and one for a program on the weekend after 9:00. These included three promos for Bonanza, and one each for Police Surgeon, Dinah, and Nashville. The remainder were for evening movies. (See Appendix F for a complete listing of promos by time period and program type.) Promos most frequently were for situation comedy and action-adventure drama. Ninety percent of promos were for entertainment programs on the stations. Informational programs were not given such attention (see Table 2.29).

Altogether, about 10 percent of promos shown between 3:00 and 6:00 pm could be called promos for adult programming (ignoring, for the moment, the scheduled time of the promoted program). These were Mod Squad, The Untouchables, Dragnet, The FBI, Bonanza, Police Surgeon, Dinah, Hee Haw, and movies shown after 9:00 pm.

TABLE 2.26

Selected Commercial Announcements Appearing on Programs
with 25 Percent or Greater Child Audience

Product Name	Program on Which CA Appeared	Percent Child Audience
Hoover spin drier	Banana Splits	89
RCA XL 100 television sets	Speed Racer	80
N.Y. Cosmos soccer team	Flintstones	79
Harrow's swimming pools (2)	Flintstones	79
Bracelets and pendants	Flintstones	79
Sawyer Secretarial School	Batman	74
Lafayette Technical Academy	Batman	71
Motocross Champions	Batman	71
Musk Dust deodorant	Batman	71
Sweet Kleen laundry and dry cleaning	Mickey Mouse Club	71
Joey Chitwood Daredevil Show	Three Stooges	71
Supertrack drag racing	Three Stooges	71
George's TV and Radio	Heckle and Jeckle Show	68
Total Trim power mower	Gilligan's Island	63
Dodge car service and tune-up	Flintstones	60
Dodge dealer	Flintstones	60
Weider Total Body Shaper	Munsters	59
Sauna Slim suit	I Love Lucy	49
Wrestling	I Love Lucy	49
Panasonic tape and recorders	I Love Lucy	49
Bell Air Chevrolet trucks	Leave It to Beaver	47
J & G Motors (used cars)	Leave It to Beaver	47
Music and Sound, Inc.	Leave It to Beaver	47
World Book insurance	Leave It to Beaver	47
Culligan water softener	Partridge Family	44
Sears department store	Partridge Family	44
Protein 21 shampoo	Lucy Show	43
Delta Airlines	Lucy Show	43
EZ Dun vinyl repair kit	Star Trek	40
K-Tel Fishin' Magician	Star Trek	40
Irish Spring soap	Star Trek	40
Aloha Bobby and Rose (movie)	Star Trek	40
Harness racing	Star Trek	40
Rabbit (Volkswagon)	Star Trek	40
Ferry auto supplies	Star Trek	40
Tech hi-fi	Star Trek	40
Rain Jet rotary massage	Hazel	38
Datsun Little Hustler pickup truck	Hazel	38
American Motors	Bewitched	38
Dick Bolch Chevrolet	Bewitched	38
Standard Technical Institute	Bewitched	38
Federal Way furniture store	Bewitched	38
Ever Clear glass cleaner	Dick Van Dyke	38
20-Mule Power bathroom cleaner	Dick Van Dyke	38
MBTI Data Processing School	Dick Van Dyke	38
Computer Date Match	Dick Van Dyke	38
Gimbel's jade sale	Dick Van Dyke	38
Sun's chlorine feeder	Dick Van Dyke	38
Marsh's carpets	Mod Squad	27
Port-a-Dolly	Mod Squad	27
Head and Shoulders shampoo	Mod Squad	27
Noxzema	Mod Squad	27
Costello Chevrolet	Mod Squad	27
Harrold Ford	Mod Squad	27

96

TABLE 2.27

Type of Promotional Announcement

	Number	Percent
Promo for:		
Next week's show	1	0.7
Upcoming show	35	25.2
Other programs	91	65.5
Other (TV Code, station promos)	12	8.6
Totals	139	100.0

TABLE 2.28

Time Period of Promoted Programs

Time Period	Number	Percent
Weekdays		
7:00am–12 noon	6	4.3
12 noon– 6:00pm	57	41.0
6:00pm– 9:00pm	40	28.8
After 9:00pm	8	5.8
Saturday-Sunday		
7:00am–12 noon	4	2.9
12 noon– 6:00pm	7	5.0
6:00pm– 9:00pm	10	7.2
After 9:00pm	1	0.7
Others and unknown	6	4.3
Totals	139	100.0

COMMERCIAL PRACTICES

Various commercial practices are used in the CAs. For all commercials studied, a series of general questions was asked (to be answered "yes" or "no"), including whether there were program tie-ins in which the host or program characters participated in the selling of products, personality tie-ins and endorsement of products, and audio and visual disclaimers. In addition, specific questions were asked that were relevant to toys and food products. Each commercial was then classified by one or more "themes" (product claims and appeals) used to promote the sale of the product.

TABLE 2.29

Types of Programs Promoted on the
Independent Stations

Program Type	Number of Promos	Percent
Situation comedy	30	21.6
Family comedy	9	6.5
Cartoon comedy	11	7.9
Other comedy	1	0.7
Animal adventure	—	—
Crime/mystery/detective	6	4.3
Action–adventure drama	18	13.0
Western drama	3	2.2
Fantasy/science fiction	5	3.6
Movies	12	8.6
Variety	11	7.9
Quiz/games/contests	5	3.6
Sports	1	0.7
Other (lineup of entertainment programs on the stations)	9	6.5
Total entertainment	121	87.1
Children's news	—	—
Documentary/travel	—	—
Animal/nature films	9	6.5
Interviews/panels	1	0.7
Discussion/debate	—	—
Music/fine arts	1	0.7
Other information	1	0.7
General news/weather/sports	—	—
Total information	12	8.6
TV Code, station promos	6	4.3
Total all promos	139	100.0

Program and Personality Tie-ins

Although the practice was not extensive, we found some examples
of program tie-ins, the use of well-known personalities in the CAs,
and celebrity endorsements. Six (1.2 percent) were tied in with a
program character, 5 (1.0 percent) used endorsements, and 24
(4.9 percent) utilized famous personalities or cartoon figures in
the CAs.

Tie-ins with program personalities occurred on two stations. In Sacramento, Capt. Mitch, a station personality who "fills" between cartoons and other program segments, gave CAs for a Mickey Mouse bicycle safety flag available for $3.00 to television viewers only, advertised Pachinko Palace games, and drew the winner of free tickets to the California Expo Playground. In Detroit, at the end of the Bill Kennedy movie, Mr. Kennedy gave an ad for The Golden Coach, featuring a show directly from Las Vegas.

There were endorsements by Jane Powell for an exercise machine, Dina-Gym, and by J. D. Ramsa for Kellogg's Sugar Pops. In addition, recording personalities promoted television record offer CAs—Frankie Laine, Chubby Checker, and Johnny Mathis are examples.

Other uses of personalities not directly selling or endorsing products were more frequent than program host tie-ins and direct endorsements. These included Flintstone characters in the Pebbles cereal CAs, Redd Foxx eating hot dogs, Popeye drinking a soft drink in a Red Barn restaurant CA, Cesar Romero for Famous Upholstering, Jim Lucus for the Joey Chitwood Daredevil Show, and many recording personalities—Al Jolson, the Beatles, and the Who, among others. Jimmy Walker from the Good Times program also sells Panasonic equipment. A summary of these practices is presented in Table 2.30.

TABLE 2.30

Use of Personalities and Endorsements,
by Product Category

Product Category	Total CAs	Percent Using Program Tie-ins	Percent Using Person- alities	Percent Using Endorse- ments
Toys	90	3	—	—
Cereals	85	—	4	1
Candies/sweets	73	—	—	—
Snacks, other foods	11	—	27	—
Eating places	55	—	4	—
Household products	18	—	6	—
Personal care products	19	—	5	5
Other misc. products	136	2	10	2
All CAs	487	1	5	1

Disclaimers and Qualifiers

Traditionally, audio and visual disclaimers have included such phrases as "sold separately" and "batteries not included," in toy commercials. These phrases were noted in the present study covering a broader range of product types. Presented either verbally only or visually only, or both, such disclaimers included "supplies are limited," "while quantities last," "limited offer," "available only at . . .," "check your newspaper," "available by mail," "not sold in stores," "Monday and Wednesday only," "good only when adult purchases ticket," and "in specially marked boxes."

About 20 percent of CAs utilized some form of audio qualifier, 10 percent used visual disclaimers, and 5 percent utilized both simultaneously. Such disclaimers were most frequent in toy commercials (audio only). Other products used visual qualifiers more often (Table 2.31).

Premiums and Contests

Use of contests in conjunction with product sales was infrequent. One was a drawing for a free ticket to a playground, another a Duncan yo-yo contest. Premiums, however, were used extensively by some product categories—especially cereals and eating places. Cereal premiums consisted of the familiar iron-on patches, "bike

TABLE 2.31

Use of Audio and Visual Disclaimers,
by Product Type

Product Type	Total Number of Commercials	Percent Using Audio Disclaimers	Percent Using Video Disclaimers	Percent Using Both
Toys	90	51	1	1
Cereals	85	20	16	16
Candies/sweets	73	1	—	—
Snacks, other foods	11	—	—	—
Eating places	55	22	11	6
Household products	18	17	33	17
Personal care products	19	—	16	—
Other misc. products	136	15	12	5
All CAs	487	21	9	6

TABLE 2.32

Use of Premiums or Contests,
by Product Category

Product Category	Total CAs	Percent Using Premiums	Percent Using Contests
Toys	90	–	1
Cereals	85	33	–
Candies/sweets	73	1	–
Snacks, other foods	11	9	–
Eating places	55	31	–
Household products	18	17	–
Personal care products	19	5	–
Other miscellaneous products	136	12	–
All product CAs	487	14	*

*Less than 0.50 percent.

clickers," and plastic figures included in the boxes and those requiring proof of purchase and a sum of money to be mailed in. Other product categories were more varied in the offers made. Following is a sample list of some from various eating places:

"Fun cup and fun coin" worth 5¢ on the next purchase (Burger Chef)
"Prizes for everyone" with a visit (Burger Queen)
"Free admission to Atlanta Braves game" with purchase (Burger King)
"Free Tweetie Bird glass" with an order of 49¢ (Hardee's)
"Swim rings" only 99¢ with visit (Holly Farms)
Free ice cream (Spoon and Straw restaurant, second anniversary)
Free "Great American Birthday Game" with any purchase (Winchell's
    Donut House)

For other products there were free introductory offers, free demonstrations, free three-piece wallets, sheriff's badges, books, and records. Probably the most valuable prize was offered by a Chevrolet dealer who was "giving away" a free ten-speed bike with any car purchase—presumably by the parent. The statistical picture on the use of premiums and contests can be seen in Table 2.32.

Product Information

If television advertising were more information-oriented, sub-stantial amounts of product information could be given in the CAs—

including price, weight, size, materials, durability, ingredients, and warnings of dangers. Another method is the comparative claim. We found no product CA that included a warning about its use, over-use, or potential hazard to the young child. Also, none used any comparative claim.

Price information was given by nearly 20 percent of commercials, and other informative product descriptions by about 10 percent. Most of these, however, were in CAs for household, personal care, and other miscellaneous products (see Table 2.33).

What is probably most interesting about the above figures is the lack of information given about products traditionally advertised to children—toys, cereals, candies—whereas other products give at least minimal information. For example, Port-a-Dolly is lightweight steel and loads up to 200 pounds; Total Trim power mowers have the throttle on the handle and an instant height adjuster. Even Atlanta Braves belts and T-shirts let the viewer know the colors and materials they are made of. And there is no doubt about the number of all-time greatest hits on the many records offered for sale. It obviously is not necessary to know the number of flakes in a box of corn flakes, but it might prove helpful to know the nutritive and caloric values of such cereals or whether toys are made of plastic, paper, or metal.

Other Commercial Practices

Direct appeal to children to ask parents to purchase products is no longer a common feature of product advertising. We found

TABLE 2.33

CAs Giving Price and Other Product
Information, by Product Category

Product Category	Total CAs	Percent Giving Price Information	Percent Giving Other Product Descriptions
Toys	90	2.2	5.6
Cereals	85	—	3.5
Candies	73	—	6.8
Snacks, other foods	11	—	9.1
Eating places	55	18.2	1.8
Household products	18	61.1	27.8
Personal care products	19	57.9	10.5
Other products	136	37.5	19.1
All CAs	487	17.5	9.9

only two examples. One suggested that the viewer "tell anyone going to the store to buy Golden Flakes" (potato chips), and another more directly said, "Have your parents bring you to the [Edgewater] Park." We did not attempt to classify more indirect attempts to urge children to pressure parents into buying certain items, although the bicycle premium given by an auto dealer represents one outstanding example.

Toy Commercials

A few additional questions were asked with respect to toy CAs. One concerned the showing of items that were not for sale. Examples include an Evel Knievel trail bike being demonstrated going over a ramp that is not sold and a bicycle safety flag attached to a bicycle not for sale. Selling of multiple items in the same commercial is a much more frequent practice. Of 90 toy commercials, 44 (49 percent) portrayed two or more items "sold separately."

Advertising of Edibles

Table 2.34 lists eight separate questions that were asked about each cereal, candy, or other food CA.

Although many food products used nutritional value as a selling point, some references were more complete and prominent than others. In cereals, Sugar Smacks, Sugar Frosted Flakes, and Raisin Bran all asserted that they are "fortified with eight essential vitamins and iron." Trix cereal, however, simply said it is "vitamin enriched," and Boo Berry cereal only indirectly alluded to nutrition when one character said, "Someone's come for a nutritious breakfast." An ice cream commercial referred to the nutrition of dairy foods. The nutrition appeal was somewhat secondary in the chocolate peppermint Pop Tarts commercial, which spoke of chocolate-flavored crust, a layer of tasty white frosting, plenty of pink minty filling, and six vitamins and iron.

Twenty percent of cereal commercials used "sweetness" as a selling point, but none advertised them as snack products. Ninety percent of cereals represented their products as part of a balanced meal, but none suggested that they were substitutes for a balanced meal.

Many food products mentioned taste or flavor other than sweetness as a selling point. Few food products specified any ingredients aside from vitamins and minerals added, and none stated caloric values.

TABLE 2.34

Questions on the Advertising of Edibles

Question	Percent of CAs with "Yes" Answers		
	Cereals	Candies	Snacks and Other Foods
Is there any reference to nutritional value of the product?	41	11	18
Is "sweetness" mentioned as a selling point?	22	—	—
Is food referred to as a snack?	—	14	9
Is product shown or represented as part of a balanced meal?	94	8	9
Is it represented as a substitute for a balanced meal?	—	—	—
Is "taste" or "flavor" other than "sweetness" mentioned?	74	49	36
Are ingredients specified as either natural or artificial?	4	3	9
Is caloric value stated?	—	—	—
Total CAs	(85)	(73)	(11)

Overall, 46 percent of all CAs in the after-school hours were for food products (including eating places), and 28 percent were for foods high in sugar content. Sixty-one percent of all edibles were sugared—the bulk (40 percent) being either sugared cereals or candies. Regular food products—dairy products, fruit, bread, and other prepared foods—together accounted for less than 3 percent of all CAs and 6 percent of all edibles (see Table 2.35).

Basic Themes in After-School Advertising
to Children

Although only about 10 percent of CAs gave useful information about the nature of their products, many unsubstantiated claims and appeals were used to sell. Sixteen "themes" were developed for classifying the major appeals of the verbal content of the CAs.*

———

*Only manifest verbal appeals in spoken or printed form, such as slogans or claims for the product, were classified. No attempt was made to judge the total visual impact of the CA, although it is

TABLE 2.35

CAs for Food Products

Food Product	Number of CAs	Percent of All CAs	Percent of CAs for Food Products
Sugared cereals*	65	13.3	29.0
Eating places	51	10.5	22.8
Candy bars*	25	5.2	11.2
Unsugared cereals	20	4.1	8.9
Cakes and cookies*	16	3.3	7.2
Carbonated beverages*	12	2.5	5.4
Fruit drinks*	9	1.9	4.0
Regular gum*	7	1.4	3.1
Canned, prepared foods	4	0.8	1.8
Grocery stores	4	0.8	1.8
Ice cream, desserts*	2	0.4	0.9
Milk, dairy products	2	0.4	0.9
Chips	2	0.4	0.9
Sugarless gum	1	0.2	0.4
Fruits	1	0.2	0.4
Other sweets*	1	0.2	0.4
Meats	1	0.2	0.4
Other foods	1	0.2	0.4
Total food CAs	224	46.0	100.0
All other products	263	54.0	
Total CAs	487	100.0	

*Sugared foods.

By classifying each CA for from one to three themes (appeals to buy, slogans, and product claims), we identified 735 themes in the 487 commercials studied. Themes varied, of course, for different product types. They are analyzed in Table 2.36.

In all food product CAs there was some emphasis on taste or flavor. Cereals and other foods frequently used health and nutrition as an appeal. Lacking this claim, candies more frequently attempted to sell other ideas—quantity, texture, or "fun." Eating places placed less emphasis on taste and texture of their foods than on price and convenience.

realized that many times this may well be more important than the obvious verbal claims and appeals—especially to the child.

TABLE 2.36

Basic Themes or Appeals of the CAs, by Product Type
(percent)

Theme/Appeal	Toys	Cereals	Candy	Snacks	Other Foods	Eating Places	House-hold	Pers. Care	Other Prod.	All Prod.
Appearance	17	7	7	–	8	–	–	7	5	7
Quantity/size/amount	13	3	16	–	–	11	–	–	7	8
Convenience/ease of use	6	–	2	50	8	20	32	16	7	7
Taste/flavor/smell	2	36	35	50	25	14	–	5	1	19
Texture	2	10	11	–	–	9	–	5	–	6
"Fun"/happiness	16	1	10	–	8	3	–	–	12	7
Health/nutrition	–	34	7	–	17	–	–	32	–	13
Peer status/popularity	2	1	2	–	–	–	–	9	1	2
Action/power/speed	22	7	–	–	–	–	4	4	3	6
Adventure	1	1	–	–	–	–	–	–	–	*
Comparative/associative	–	–	1	–	–	–	7	–	–	*
Economy/price	–	–	1	–	8	30	32	11	18	8
Uniqueness	2	–	6	–	–	4	11	–	10	4
Quality of manufacture or materials	1	–	1	–	17	–	7	7	11	3
Newness	3	–	–	–	8	–	–	4	4	2
General superiority	13	–	1	–	–	9	7	–	21	7
Totals	100	100	100	100	100	100	100	100	100	100
Total themes (base)	(117)	(211)	(120)	(2)	(12)	(56)	(28)	(44)	(145)	(735)
Total CAs	(90)	(85)	(73)	(2)	(9)	(55)	(18)	(19)	(136)	(487)

*Less than 0.50 percent.

For toys, three major themes predominated: action/speed/power, appearance of the toy, and "fun." Personal care products often were concerned with health and convenience, while household products more frequently emphasized convenience or ease of use as a selling point. Economy or price was the most frequent appeal of eating places, household products, and other products.

General superiority claims consisted of those familiar superlatives stated by schools that "will change your life completely" or offer you a "fantastic future," and by record albums that are "electrifying," "incredible," and the "most exciting new record package ever offered!" They also were used by ads for movies that are "brilliant," "full of excitement," and "the most entertaining picture of our time," and for other products offering "the best deal in town."

NONCOMMERCIAL ANNOUNCEMENTS

One measure of station performance is the frequency and nature of the unpaid noncommercial or public-service announcements broadcast. These messages often are designed as pro-social material and presented as part of the stations's public interest responsibilities. We therefore examined these announcements for the "cause" or type of organization making the appeal, the intended audience, style of presentation, and character compositions.

NCAs appear much less frequently in the after-school hours than on weekend children's television. Only 52 NCAs were logged in the 30 hours studied on 10 stations. They accounted for only 29 minutes, or 1.6 percent of total time. On weekend television there were 48 minutes of NCAs in 25.5 hours studied—3.2 percent of total time. Stated another way, in the after-school hours, there was an average of one NCA every 35 minutes; on weekend children's television there was one every 17 minutes.

The ten stations studied varied considerably in the number of NCAs broadcast. New York's WNEW led the list with 14 such announcements, whereas Seattle's KSTW provided only one in the three hours studied. Station comparisons are given in Table 2.37.

Style of Presentation

Overall, NCAs are presented in a rather straightforward manner. About 90 percent did not use animation, and about half used an off-stage voice or announcer giving the message. There were various other styles represented, however, including on-stage announcers or speakers, all-musical formats, and short dramatic skits illustrating the problem or cause (Table 2.38).

TABLE 2.37

Number and Time of NCAs, by Station

Station	Number of NCAs Broadcast	Minutes	Percent of Total Time	One NCA per "x" Minutes
New York	14	8.00	4.4	12.9
Washington	8	5.00	2.8	22.5
Buffalo	5	2.17	1.2	36.0
Detroit	3	1.42	0.8	60.0
Milwaukee	6	3.67	2.0	30.0
Louisville	6	4.42	2.5	30.0
Norfolk	4	1.66	0.9	45.0
Atlanta	3	1.17	0.7	60.0
Seattle	1	.50	0.3	180.0
Sacramento	2	.67	0.4	90.0
All stations	52	28.85	1.6	34.6

TABLE 2.38

Number of NCAs, by Style, Use of
Animation, and Audience Appeal

	Number	Percent
Style of presentation		
Off-stage voice	28	54
On-stage announcer	12	23
Musical structure	3	6
Dramatic skit	7	14
Other style	2	4
Total	52	100
Use of animation		
Animated	2	4
Nonanimated	49	94
Mixed	1	2
Total	52	100
Audience appeal		
Children	4	8
Adults	6	11
General audience	38	73
Parents	4	8
Total	52	100

Although some NCAs were designed specifically for children, many seemed appropriate for the general audience, and about 20 percent made appeals directly to parents or adults. Examples include local health department announcements warning parents not to "gamble with your child's health," a U.S. Savings Bond NCA showing a man at a retirement party, and Social Security announcements for adult working people. (A list of all NCAs recorded is in Appendix G.)

NCAs on Behalf of Various Causes

Six major categories composed of 16 subcategories of "causes" were developed by examining the NCAs broadcast. The basic distribution is given in Table 2.39.

The largest single category of NCAs was for health care causes (17 percent), followed by anti-pollution (14 percent) and safety and youth organizations (12 percent each).

Who "Speaks for" the Cause?

The authoritative voice in NCAs, as in CAs, was male (82 percent), and in 74 percent the announcer or character who gave the message was an adult male (Table 2.40). This was generally true for all types of causes.

With the exception of a slightly greater proportion of adult females in NCAs, CAs and NCAs showed quite similar patterns with respect to who delivers the message. Adults and males dominate in each (see Table 2.41).

Character Distributions in NCAs

In addition to the chief speaker for each NCA, all identifiable characters were classified by age group, sex, and race. In 52 NCAs studied, 138 characters were so classified, of which 121 could be classed by age and sex. Quite unlike the distribution of primary speakers, the NCA characters were almost evenly divided by sex (49 percent male). (See Table 2.42.)

Blacks constituted 23 percent of 117 classifiable characters, other minorities 5 percent and whites 72 percent. Blacks were much more frequently seen in NCAs for voluntary organizations (48 percent) and youth organizations (32 percent). (See Table 2.43.)

TABLE 2.39

Number of NCAs, by Cause

	Number	Percent
Health and safety announcements		
Athletics (keep physically fit)	1	1.9
Health care (center for nonsmoking, Society to Prevent Blindness)	9	17.3
Nutrition (Ad Council, Cookie Monster)	1	1.9
Safety (safety on subway, how to report a fire, Red Cross, lawn mower safety)	6	11.6
Total	17	32.7
Ecology and the environment		
Animal care (wild baby animals, Dept. of Fish and Wildlife)	2	3.8
Anti-pollution/anti-litter (Keep America Beautiful, clean up, protect wilderness)	7	13.5
Total	9	17.3
Youth organizations		
Boy Scouts, Girl Scouts, Boys Clubs	6	11.6
Other voluntary and nonprofit organizations		
Voluntary help programs (Upward Bound, Goodwill, United Negro College Fund)	5	9.6
UNICEF/CARE	1	1.9
Reading/education (RIF)	2	3.8
Museums (Metropolitan Museum of Art, Afro-American Cultural Center)	5	9.6
Total	13	24.9
Pro-social announcements		
Religious/anti-discrimination messages (God's love, be yourself, gossip)	4	7.7
Miscellaneous other causes		
Government organizations (Social Security, savings bonds)	3	5.8
Totals	52	100.0

TABLE 2.40

Who "Speaks for" the Cause?[a]

Authoritative Voice	Health	Ecol- ogy	Youth Orgs.	Other Volun- tary	Pro- Social	Misc.	Total
Adult male	12	8	4	11	–	2	37
Adult female	3	–	2	2	1	–	8
Total adults	15	8	6	13	1	2	45
Male child	1	–	–	–	–	–	1
Female child	–	1	–	–	–	–	1
Total children	1	1	–	–	–	–	2
Other male	1	–	–	–	1	1	3
Other female	–	–	–	–	–	–	–
Total other	1	–	–	–	1	1	3
Total males	14	8	4	11	1	3	41
Total females	3	1	2	2	1	–	9
Total speakers	17	9	6	13	2	3	50[b]

[a]Because of the small numbers in each category, table is in frequencies rather than percentages.
[b]Two NCAs could not be classified.

TABLE 2.41

CAs and NCAs Compared by Who "Speaks for" the Product or Cause

Who Speaks	Percent in CAs	Percent in NCAs
Adult male	75	74
Adult female	8	16
Total adults	83	90
Male child	3	2
Female child	2	2
Total children	5	4
Other male	12	6
Other female	a	–
Total other	13	6
Total males	90	82
Total females	10	18
Total speakers	(487)	(50)[b]

[a]Less than 0.50 percent.
[b]2 NCAs were not classified.

TABLE 2.42

Characters in NCAs, by Sex and Age Group

Sex and Age Group	Number	Percent
Male children	21	17.3
Male teens	7	5.8
Male adults	29	23.9
Male animals, other	2	1.7
Total males	59	48.7
Female children	29	24.0
Female teens	12	9.9
Female adults	19	15.7
Female animals, other	2	1.7
Total females	62	51.3
Total classified	121	100.0
Unclassified	17	
Total characters	138	

TABLE 2.43

Race of Characters in NCAs, by Cause

Cause	Percent White	Percent Black	Percent Other	Total Characters Classified
Health/safety/nutrition	86	8	6	36
Ecology/environment	81	13	6	16
Youth organizations	68	32	—	19
Other voluntary orgs.	52	48	—	23
Pro-social announcements	60	20	20	15
Other miscellaneous	75	25	—	8
All causes	72	23	5	117

In contrast with CAs, NCA character distributions were much more representative with respect to sexual and racial distributions. They portrayed more female children, adults, teens, and animals. Blacks and other minorities also were given more prominence (Table 2.44).

TABLE 2.44

CAs and NCAs Compared by
Character Distributions

Age, Sex, and Race	Percent in CAs	Percent in NCAs
Male children	31	17
Male teens	4	6
Male adults	26	24
Male animals, other	3	2
Total males	64	49
Female children	18	24
Female teens	5	10
Female adults	13	15
Female animals, other	*	2
Total females	36	51
Total classified by age and sex	(1,339)	(121)
White	95	72
Black	5	23
Other minority	*	5
Total classified by race	(1,287)	(117)

*Less than 0.50 percent.

SUMMARY OF CHAPTERS 1 AND 2

These two chapters represent detailed content analyses of 25.5 hours of weekend commercial children's television and 30 hours of after-school programming on independent television stations. There were some surprising similarities as well as differences in these two samples. The major differences resulted from the difference in program sources. On the weekend, more than half of all programming is network-originated, whereas independent stations rely almost solely on syndicated reruns of former network fare. There are similar patterns in the extent and nature of advertising and in the basic character distributions in both program and advertising matter.

Preliminary classification of more than 200 hours of programs between 3:00 and 6:00 pm on 68 independent stations revealed a process of relabeling programs originally produced for prime time adult television as "children's television." Approximately 60 percent of all such programs were not originally designed for children. They include situation and family comedy, adult crime and western drama, and other adult and family entertainment.

In both samples, large child audiences watched these programs.
In the after-school hours, nearly two-thirds of the audience were
children 2-11 years old. In some markets the figure was much
higher. Child audiences also were larger for the independent UHF
stations and in large market areas than for VHF and small market
areas. In both samples, nearly three-fourths of the audience for
cartoon comedy and action-adventure drama were children. Other
types of programs—such as situation comedy, family drama, and
space-fantasy stories—drew at least one-third of their viewers from
the 2-11-year-old audience.

Distribution of Broadcast Time

On five Boston stations, 80 percent of total time was devoted to
program material and 16 percent to CAs, with the remainder of
time taken up by noncommercial and station identification material.
Independents showed a similar pattern, with 78 percent program
matter, 20 percent CAs, and about 2 percent NCAs. Time devoted
to commercial messages ranged from a low of 14 percent to a high
of 20 percent of the total time on each Boston station; for the
independents, the range was 16-23 percent. The major difference
in commercial messages was their length, with weekend announcements shorter, on the average, than those in the after-school hours.

The Programs

In Boston, about 80 percent of each hour was devoted to entertainment programs, and more than half of this was cartoon comedy.
On the ten independent stations, nearly all programming was entertainment (99.9 percent), also dominated by cartoon comedy.
Weekend programming contained more informational material
(13 percent of total time) than did that of the after-school hours.
Only two of the five Boston stations originated any local children's
programs, and there was less than one hour in 30 on the independents.
Current fare on the weekends also had a higher degree of animation
than on weekdays. Nearly two-thirds of weekend programs used
some form of animation, whereas only 40 percent of independent
after-school programs did so. Both samples of programming
presented an ethnocentric picture of the world. Time and place
settings showed major emphasis (about 80 percent) on contemporary
U.S. settings.
Subject matter treated in the programs also showed a consistency
between the two samples. Five subject areas accounted for nearly

60 percent of weekend and 70 percent of after-school programming: domestic (home, family), interpersonal rivalry, the entertainment world, crime, and the supernatural. Little emphasis was placed on historical topics, religion, race/nationality, education, business, government, war, literature and the fine arts, crafts, or language.

Violence in the programs appeared most frequently in the most popular programs—cartoon comedy and action-adventure dramas. Eight out of ten weekend and two-thirds of after-school dramatic segments contained some incidental or more serious violence, and about one in four weekend and one in three weekday segments were judged as "saturated" with violence. That is, there was little in the story to maintain interest beyond repeated acts of violence—usually in the context of interpersonal rivalries in cartoon comedies. Although few deaths resulted from the violence, there were substantial numbers of injuries. The most popular form of violence involved weapons.

Advertising

Overall, there were 403 product commercials and 119 program promotional announcements on the weekend and 487 product commercials and 139 promos in the after-school sample. Thus, about one minute in six on weekends and one minute in five on weekdays was devoted to commercial messages. On a per-hour basis, Boston stations averaged 9.5 minutes, and independent stations 11.9 minutes, of advertising per hour. Stations varied considerably from this average, however. Applying the current NAB Code Authority guidelines for maximum permissible nonprogram material, several stations exceeded the recommended maximum in various one-hour periods.

The types of products advertised on weekends and on weekdays showed some differences. On weekends, cereals and candies accounted for almost half of all ads, with toy commercials, other foods, and other products accounting for the rest. In the after-school hours, about one-third of all advertising was for products not normally found in or around children's programs. These included ads for recreation and amusement centers, record offers, and household and personal care products.

For the most part, the commercials were presented in a straightforward manner. Toy commercials were not animated, whereas cereals were frequently animated. Overall, 40 percent of weekend and 20 percent of weekday commercials used some form of animation. The off-stage announcer was the format most frequently used to present commercial messages.

Advertising of Edibles

In Boston, 68 percent of commercials and 46 percent of those on independent stations were for edible products. Nearly two-thirds were for highly sugared products (64 percent and 61 percent, respectively). About 20-25 percent of all cereal commercials used "sweetness" as an appeal to sell their products. In both samples, about 90 percent of cereal ads represented their product as part of a balanced meal. They also frequently referred to vitamin and other nutritional components of the cereals. However, no food products stated caloric values, and only a few noted whether ingredients were either artificial or natural.

Nutritional foods such as bread, milk, fruits, or vegetables were infrequently advertised, accounting for only 4 percent of weekend commercials and less than 2 percent of those in the after-school hours.

Commercial Practices

Several commercial practices were investigated. On weekend television no examples of host selling or program tie-ins were found. In the after-school hours, a few examples were found on two of the independent stations. There were, however, endorsements of products—primarily toys and cereals—by celebrities, sports figures, or well-known cartoon characters.

Disclaimers or qualifiers also were used—often in toy commercials. Many items were verbally or visually qualified with such phrases as "items sold separately," "limited offer," and "specially marked boxes." Although it has been recommended that such disclaimers be presented both verbally and visually, they are most often presented only verbally. Overall, about one product commercial in four used disclaimers of any kind. Related to the use of disclaimers is the practice of selling several products in one commercial message. This practice was most frequent in toy commercials, in which more than one item was offered for sale or "sold separately."

Premium offers (either enclosed in the package or through coupons or visits to stores) were used in nearly half of all cereal ads and in 17 percent of all commercials in Boston (14 percent on the independent stations).

Although no attempt was made to classify special or misleading visual or other effects in detail, some common examples included exaggerated sound effects, extreme close-ups, and animated objects talking with real children.

Advertisers infrequently appealed directly to the child to ask or otherwise influence his or her parents to buy products. None were found that used comparative claims; neither were any warnings or cautions about the use of products given.

Basic themes or appeals of the commercials varied by product type. For toys, action/power/speed and appearance were important. For cereals, taste/flavor or health/nutrition appeals were most frequent. Other appeals included convenience or ease of use, fun/happiness, improved peer status, and the uniqueness of the product.

Little or no product or price information was given. Less than 10 percent of CAs in either sample gave even minimal product information (ingredients, size, weight, materials). On weekend television, about 5 percent gave price information; on weekdays, nearly 18 percent did. This was due to the greater number of adult-oriented products: travel offers, record offers, and household items.

Program Promotion

As one might expect, weekend and weekday program promotional announcements showed quite different patterns. About 60 percent of weekend promos were for Saturday-Sunday programs, whereas week-day promos were most frequently for weekday programming (80 percent). Also, whereas only 2 of 119 weekend promos were for programs broadcast after 9:00 pm, nine of 139 independent station promos were found for late programming.

Weekend television also more frequently promoted informational programs (32 percent). Almost 90 percent of weekday promos were for entertainment programs, led by situation comedies and action-adventure dramas.

NCAs

Although much less time was devoted to noncommercial, public-service announcements than to commercial material on all stations, weekend television contained about twice as many NCAs as the weekday sample did. On the weekends, 92 NCAs were aired, representing 3.2 percent of total time, or an average of one announcement every 17 minutes. In the after-school sample, 52 were broadcast, representing 1.6 percent of the time, or about one every 35 minutes.

By type, similar distributions were found in both samples except that independent stations broadcast a much greater proportion of NCAs for miscellaneous voluntary and nonprofit organizations (such as UNICEF, CARE, Goodwill). Most frequent in both samples were NCAs for health and safety causes, and there were substantial proportions for ecology and the environment.

Also, in both samples, a large number of NCAs were not addressed specifically to children. Some were addressed specifically to parents or to adults, appealing for funds or voluntary aid.

Character Distributions

Characters in programs, CAs, and NCAs were classified by sex and race. Such frequency counts provide a basic index of the extent of sexual and racial bias in continuing portrayals. Of 400 major characters on weekend children's programs, 301 were male and 88 female—about 3.4 males to every female. Of 405 characters in after-school programs, 289 were male and 101 female—2.9 males to each female. Sixty percent of characters were adults on weekend television; the figure was 70 percent on after-school television. In both samples, teen-agers were the most underrepresented group, with about 12 percent on weekend television and 8 percent on weekdays. Program characters were predominantly white (89 percent on weekends; 96 percent in the after-school hours); blacks numbered 7 percent and 3 percent, respectively. Other minorities were portrayed even less frequently.

The patterns found in program character distributions held for characters in the commercials. Of 1,477 characters in Boston television commercials, males outnumbered females by a ratio of 2.2 to 1. On independent television, the ratio was 1.8 to 1. This was especially true for adult characters, for whom the respective ratios were 3:1 and 2:1 male. On Boston television 92 percent of commercial characters were white; in the after-school sample, 95 percent were white. Black characters appeared most frequently in snack food commercials (27 percent and 33 percent, respectively) but represented only 8 percent of weekend and 5 percent of weekday commercial characters overall.

The important, authoritative voice who "speaks for" the product also was classified by sex and demonstrated an even more extreme sex bias. In both samples 90 percent of the speakers giving the prime commercial message were male (or male voices). Although female speakers were more frequent for some product types (household products, foods, eating places), they never represented a majority in any product category.

In NCAs character distributions were somewhat more representative and balanced, although still reflecting the same patterns as programming and commercial advertising. On weekend television,

57 percent were male, 84 percent white, 11 percent black, and
5 percent other minorities. NCAs broadcast on weekdays also
showed more balanced distributions: 49 percent male, 51 percent
female, 72 percent white, 23 percent black and 5 percent other
minorities.

3

SEASONAL VARIATIONS IN TELEVISION ADVERTISING TO CHILDREN

THE NATURE AND EXTENT OF CHILDREN'S ADVERTISING

Increase in Advertising Time

On Boston network television, there was a 17 percent increase in the proportion of time devoted to product commercials—from 12.8 percent of total time in April to 15 percent in November (Table 3.1). At the same time there were drastic overall reductions in time devoted to program promotion and, especially, to noncommercial, public-service announcements. In effect, there was a substitution of Christmas advertising for all other types of announcements.

There was an overall pre-Christmas increase in the frequency of product commercials from an average of one every 3.9 minutes in April to one every 3.4 minutes in November (see Table 3.2). This tendency was the most pronounced on WCVB, Channel 5 (ABC), and WBZ, Channel 4 (NBC); Channel 7, WNAC (CBS), had almost maximum levels of product advertising in both periods.

There was a great reduction in the frequency of noncommercial messages. In April, one could expect a noncommercial, public-service message on an average of every 16 minutes. In November, there was one every 50 minutes. The extreme in this case was Channel 7 (CBS), which televised only three such messages in each period (one every 130 minutes, on the average).

Exceeding of Ten-Minute Limit for Nonprogram Time

Section XIV of the current NAB Code Authority Guidelines sets standards for nonprogram material on children's television. Child-

TABLE 3.1

Distribution of Total Time, April and November

Type of Material	Minutes		Percent	
	April	November	April	November
Program time	966.63	788.77	80.6	82.2
Product commercial time	154.25	144.25	12.8	15.0
Program promotion time	29.89	15.48	2.5	1.6
Total CA time	184.14	159.73	15.3	16.6
NCAs	36.77	8.72	3.1	0.9
Other miscellaneous time	12.46	2.78	1.0	0.3
Total time monitored	1,200.00	960.00	100.0	100.0

ren's programming time is defined as ". . . those hours other than prime time in which programs initially designed primarily for children under 12 years of age are scheduled." Time limitations are detailed as follows:

> Within this time period on Saturday and Sunday, non-program material shall not exceed 10 minutes in any 60-minute period after December 31, 1974 and nine minutes 30 seconds in any 60-minute period after December 31, 1975.

Nonprogram material includes "billboards, commercials, promotional announcements and all credits in excess of 30 seconds per program, except in feature films. . . . Public Service announcements and promotional announcements for the same program are excluded from this definition."

The definition of nonprogram time used in this book was less inclusive than that specified by the NAB. Since only commercial announcements and program promotional announcements were tabulated, study definitions can be considered more "conservative" than those quoted above. They are referred to here as "commercial minutes." Billboards and credits were not timed separately, and program promotional announcements for the same program (such as previews of next week's program) were not tabulated in the analysis.

In the April study of weekend commercial children's television, several instances were found in which Boston network-affiliated stations exceeded the limits of ten minutes of commercials per hour. The pattern was similar in the November sample, in which 8 of the 15 full one-hour periods studied exceeded 10 minutes of

TABLE 3.2

Number and Type of Announcements, by Station,
April and November

Station and Type of Announcement	Number of Announcements		Number per "x" Minutes*	
	April	November	April	November
Channel 4 (NBC)				
Product commercials	102	94	3.8	3.5
Program promotion	15	18	26.0	18.3
Total CAs	117	112	3.3	2.9
NCAs	41	11	9.5	30.0
Total Channel 4	158	123	2.5	2.7
Channel 5 (ABC)				
Product commercials	81	67	5.2	3.6
Program promotion	44	14	9.5	17.1
Total CAs	125	81	3.4	3.0
NCAs	30	5	14.0	48.0
Total Channel 5	155	86	2.7	2.8
Channel 7 (CBS)				
Product commercials	124	123	3.1	3.2
Program promotion	36	31	10.8	12.6
Total CAs	160	154	2.4	2.5
NCAs	3	3	130.0	130.0
Total Channel 7	163	157	2.4	2.5
All stations				
Product commercials	307	284	3.9	3.4
Program promotions	95	63	12.6	15.2
Total CAs	402	347	2.9	2.8
NCAs	74	19	16.2	50.5
Total all stations	476	366	2.5	2.6*

*For all stations in November, one announcement, on the
average, every 2.6 minutes (minutes broadcast/number of announcements).

nonprogram material as defined above. The figures are given in
Table 3.3.

Increase in Toy Advertising

There was not only an increase in the frequency of commercial
messages but also a shift in types of products advertised. This is

seen in an almost threefold increase in toy advertising between April and November, and a relative decrease in all other product types (Table 3.4).

Channel 7 (CBS) had the greatest shift in toy advertising and the largest November proportion of toy commercials of the three

TABLE 3.3

Number of Commercial Minutes per Hour,
November Sample[a]

Time Period	Ch. 4 NBC	Ch. 5 ABC	Ch. 7 CBS
7:00- 8:00am	6.08	6.00	9.84
8:00- 9:00am	10.67	9.42	9.59
9:00-10:00am	7.91	12.00	10.68
10:00-11:00am	10.75	10.34	10.00
11:00am-12 noon	5.08[b]	—	10.42
12 noon- 1:00pm	10.75	—	10.25
1:00- 2:00pm	—	—	5.33[c]

[a]Figures for November 22 on Channels 5 and 7, for November 29 on Channel 4.

[b]11:00-11:30 am.

[c]1:00-1:30 pm.

TABLE 3.4

Commercial Announcements, by Major Product
Type, All Stations, April and November

Major Product Type	Number of Announcements		Percent of Total	
	April	November	April	November
Toys	53	135	17.3	47.5
Cereals	72	56	23.5	19.7
Candies/sweets	83	56	27.2	19.7
Snacks	16	1	5.2	0.3
Other foods	11	5	3.6	1.8
Eating places	19	15	6.2	5.3
Vitamins, medicines	—	1	—	0.3
Household products	5	3	1.6	1.1
Personal care products	11	3	3.6	1.1
Other products	36	9	11.8	3.2
Total all products	306	284	100.0	100.0

stations. Whereas in April less than 20 percent of commercials were for toys, by November nearly 50 percent were toy commercials (Table 3.5). (A complete listing of all commercial announcements is in Appendix H.)

A more specific listing of products advertised is given in Table 3.6. Only sugared cereals and candy bar commercials continued to represent a significant proportion of the November ads. Almost every other specific type of product advertising was reduced to accommodate the large increase in toy advertising.

Advertising of Edibles

Besides toys, edible food products were the only other sizable category of children's television advertising in November and April.

TABLE 3.5

Type of Product Advertised, by Station,
April and November

Major Product	Number		Percent	
Type and Station	April	November	April	November
Toys				
Channel 4 (NBC)	20	41	19.8	43.6
Channel 5 (ABC)	12	28	14.8	41.8
Channel 7 (CBS)	21	66	16.9	53.7
All stations	53	135	17.3	47.6
Cereals				
Channel 4	24	22	23.7	23.4
Channel 5	11	11	13.6	16.4
Channel 7	37	23	29.8	18.7
All stations	72	56	23.5	19.7
Candies/sweets				
Channel 4	24	15	23.8	16.0
Channel 5	26	15	32.1	22.4
Channel 7	33	26	26.6	21.1
All stations	83	56	27.2	19.7
All other products				
Channel 4	33	16	32.7	17.0
Channel 5	32	13	39.5	19.4
Channel 7	33	8	26.6	6.5
All stations	98	37	32.0	13.0
Total product				
commercials	306	284	100.0	100.0

TABLE 3.6

Specific Products Advertised, All Stations, April and November

Specific Product Types	Number		Percent	
	April	November	April	November
Toys				
Cars, planes, trains	20	27	6.5	9.5
Dolls and doll play sets	22	44	7.2	15.5
Indoor games and toys	2	39	0.7	13.7
Outdoor games and toys	—	13	—	4.6
Toy stores	—	1	—	0.4
Other toys, hobbies, crafts	9	11	2.9	3.9
Total toys	53	135	17.3	47.5
Cereals				
General (cereal company)	1	—	0.3	—
Sugared cereals	59	44	19.3	15.5
Unsugared cereals	12	12	3.9	4.2
Total cereals	72	56	23.5	19.7
Candies/sweets				
Candy bars, packaged candies	45	30	14.7	10.6
Chewing gum (sugarless)	—	—	—	—
Chewing gum (regular)	2	—	0.7	—
Cakes and cookies	16	16	5.2	5.6
Ice cream, puddings, desserts	6	5	2.0	1.8
Soft drinks (carbonated)	—	—	—	—
Fruit drinks and ices	14	2	4.6	0.7
Juice drinks	—	—	—	—
Other sweets (such as Fluff)	—	3	—	1.1
Total candies/sweets	83	56	27.2	19.7
Snacks				
Chips	5	1	1.6	0.3
Peanut butter spread	11	—	3.6	—
Other snacks	—	—	—	—
Total snacks	16	1	5.2	0.3
Other foods				
Canned, prepared packaged foods	3	3	1.0	1.1
Fruits	5	—	1.6	—
Vegetables	—	—	—	—
Meats	—	—	—	—
Bread	2	—	0.7	—
Milk, dairy products	1	2	0.3	0.7
Other foods	—	—	—	—
Total other foods	11	5	3.6	1.8
Eating places				
Restaurants, meals	17	15	5.5	5.3
Grocery stores, supermarkets	2	—	0.7	—
Other	—	—	—	—
Total eating places	19	15	6.2	5.3
Vitamins/medicines				
Vitamins	—	—	—	—
Medicines	—	1	—	0.3
Total vitamins/medicines	—	1	—	0.3
Household products				
Cleansers, detergents	1	—	0.2	—
Appliances	—	—	—	—
Tools, hardware	—	—	—	—
Other household products	4	3	1.3	1.1
Total household products	5	3	1.6	1.1
Personal care products				
Shampoos, deodorants, soaps	7	1	2.3	0.4
Health care (sauna suit)	—	—	—	—
Other personal care (clothing)	4	2	1.3	0.7
Total personal care	11	3	3.6	1.1
Other miscellaneous products				
Motion pictures	30	7	9.8	2.5
Recreation/amusements	1	1	0.3	0.4
Books and magazines	—	—	—	—
Record offers	1	—	0.3	—
Automobiles (repair, parts)	—	—	—	—
Airlines and travel offers	4	1	1.3	0.4
Schools	—	—	—	—
Hi-fi and stereo stores	—	—	—	—
Other miscellaneous products	—	—	—	—
Total miscellaneous	36	9	11.8	3.2
Total all products	306	284	100.0	100.0

Although reduced from 65 percent of all advertising in April to 47 percent in November, food advertising was still a major part of children's television advertising.

There was not equal emphasis on all food products, however; highly sugared foods dominated the food commercials. A list of all specific food products is given in Table 3.7. As a percentage of all food commercials, highly sugared products accounted for 71 percent in April (142 of 200 ads) and 75 percent in November (100 of 133). In both periods, foods such as bread, fruits, vegetables, meats, and dairy products were seldom seen.

TABLE 3.7

Commercial Announcements for Edibles,
All Stations, April and November

Food Product[a]	Percent of All Commercials		Percent of Food Commercials	
	April	November	April	November
Sugared cereals[b]	19.3	15.5	29.5	33.1
Candy bars[b]	14.7	10.5	22.5	22.6
Eating places	5.5	5.3	8.5	11.3
Cakes and cookies[b]	5.2	5.6	8.0	12.0
Fruit drinks[b]	4.6	0.7	7.0	1.5
Unsugared cereals	3.9	4.2	6.0	9.0
Peanut spread	3.6	–	5.5	–
Ice cream, puddings, desserts[b]	2.0	1.8	3.0	3.8
Chips	1.6	0.3	2.5	0.8
Fruits	1.6	–	2.5	–
Canned, prepared foods	1.0	1.1	1.5	2.2
Chewing gum (regular)[b]	0.7	–	1.0	–
Bread	0.7	–	1.0	–
Grocery stores	0.7	–	1.0	–
Milk and dairy products	0.3	0.7	0.5	1.5
Other sweets[b]	–	1.1	–	2.2
Total percent	65.4	46.8	100.0	100.0
All other commercials	34.6	53.2		
(Number)	(306)	(284)	(200)	(133)

[a]Ranked by April percentage.
[b]Sugared products.

Toy Advertising and Style of Commercials

Many aspects of commercials were heavily influenced by the dominance of toy advertising in the November sample. For example, toy ads are seldom animated. Thus, three-fourths of all commercials in November were nonanimated, as compared with slightly more than one-half in April (Table 3.8). In terms of style of presentation, the off-stage announcer and musical formats were much more frequent in toy commercials and dominated the overall format for all commercials.

TABLE 3.8

Style and Structure of Commercials,
April and November
(percent)

	April	November
Use of animation		
Animated	18.9	4.6
Nonanimated	55.9	75.3
Mixed	25.2	20.1
Totals	100.0	100.0
Format		
Off-stage voice	35.0	39.0
On-stage announcer	13.4	6.0
Musical structure	22.5	37.0
Dramatic skit	38.8	18.0
Other	0.3	–
Totals	100.0	100.0
Total commercials	(306)	(284)

Increase in Sexism

The effect of the larger number of toy commercials is seen more vividly in the analysis of the "authoritative" voice in all advertising in April and November. Asking the question "Who speaks for the product?," we found that adult male voices were the authoritative ones in 118 out of 135 toy commercials. Although the male voice was most frequent in all categories of product commercials, the November emphasis on toy advertising accentuated this bias. Thus, even more male voices were represented in November than in April (Table 3.9).

TABLE 3.9

Who "Speaks for" the Product?
(percent)

	April	November
Adult male	63.8	80.3
Adult female	4.9	6.3
Total adults	68.7	86.6
Male child	6.8	3.9
Female child	3.9	—
Total children	10.7	3.9
Other male (animal, other)	18.9	9.5
Other female	1.0	—
Total other	19.9	9.5
Unclassifiable	0.3	—
Total males	89.5	93.7
Total females	10.5	6.3
Total commercials	(306)	(284)

Dominance of Male Children in Children's Advertising

More than 1,100 characters were counted in both April and November advertising. Child characters increased from less than one-half of all characters in April commercials to almost two-thirds in November. There was a slight increase in the number of female characters, as a result of the increase in female children appearing in the toy commercials. Overall, however, male characters still outnumbered female characters by more than 2:1 (see Table 3.10).

Increase in Black and Minority Characters

Although slightly more black and other minority characters appeared in November than in April advertising, whites generally dominated all children's advertising (Table 3.11).

COMMERCIAL PRACTICES

In neither the April nor the November sample were there any commercials directly tied in with the program on which they appeared (through host selling or characters). Nor did any use

TABLE 3.10

Age and Sex of Characters Appearing in
Commercials, April and November
(percent)

Age and Sex	April	November
Males		
Children	38.9	46.8
Teens	2.5	1.2
Adults	23.4	14.6
Animals, others	8.3	5.6
Total males	73.1	68.2
Females		
Children	17.5	23.3
Teens	1.5	2.3
Adults	7.0	5.5
Animals, others	0.9	0.7
Total females	26.9	31.8
Total characters class-ified by sex	(930)	(1,097)
Totals, by age group		
Children	45.6	64.6
Teens	3.2	3.2
Adults	24.6	18.5
Animals, others	26.6	13.7
Total characters	(1,152)	(1,191)

TABLE 3.11

Race of Characters Appearing in Commercials,
April and November
(percent)

Race	April	November
White	91.0	87.3
Black	8.7	10.7
Other minority	0.3	2.0
Total classified by race	(888)	(1,025)

comparative claims. Other commercial practices were used to various degrees, however. Some of these may reveal the level of compliance with the NAB Code Guidelines for advertising to children; other practices not specifically covered by the NAB Code are interesting for the manner in which appeals to children were being made.

The percent of commercials for various products that employ the commercial practices investigated is presented in Table 3.12. A majority of all products are shown being used by the characters in the commercials. This is especially true of toy products—nearly all of which are being used by children.

In April about 10 percent, and in November only slightly more than 10 percent, gave any indication of objective product information or description. The small increase overall was due primarily to inclusion of cereal information on vitamin and mineral content in November that was computed separately in the April study. The definition of product information used was a liberal one. If any description (giving size, materials, quantity, ingredients), no matter how slight, was provided, the commercial was classified as having provided some product description. Some examples from the November sample will illustrate this.

Product	Description
Push and Play/Schroeder's piano	"batteries included," "can play real tunes"
Putt-Putt Railroad	"hardwood railroad"
Planet of the Apes fortress and catapult	"27 inches high"
TTP tower and car	"with Ultra-Chrome"
Kellogg's Raisin Bran	"two scoops of raisins," "plump, juicy raisins," "eight vitamins and iron"
Pillsbury chocolate chip cookies	"bake in only 12 minutes"
Chef Boyardee mini ravioli	"lots of meat inside, lots of tomato outside"
Edaville Railroad	"open daily through January 5"

As one can see, the product descriptions seldom give more than very minimal information. Although products are visually represented, it often is difficult for the child (or adult) to determine the materials, physical dimensions, operational procedures, or other necessary consumer information.

Additional information about the products is provided by the disclosures or disclaimers about what is not included. These disclosures, disclaimers, and qualifiers frequently are given in toy and cereal commercials—most often in the audio portion of the

TABLE 3.12

Use of Various Commercial Practices, by
Product Category, April and November

Percent of Commercials That:	April	November
Showed the product in use		
Toys	93	97
Cereals	57	64
Candies/sweets	81	89
All other	54	62
All products	68	85
Gave any objective product description		
Toys	6	10
Cereals	11	43[a]
Candies/sweets	11	9
All other	11	14
All products	10	17
Gave price information		
Toys	8	1
Cereals	—	—
Candies/sweets	—	—
All other	6	3
All products	3	1
Used audio disclaimers, disclosures, or qualifiers		
Toys	49	53
Cereals	26	50
Candies/sweets	—	—
All other	10	11
All products	18	36
Used visual disclaimers, disclosures, or qualifiers		
Toys	—	18
Cereals	18	45
Candies/sweets	—	—
All other	5	22
All products	6	20
Used simultaneous audio and visual disclaimers		
Toys	—	13
Cereals	18	34
Candies/sweets	—	—
All other	5	8
All products	6	14

(continued)

(Table 3.12 continued)

Percent of Commercials That:	April	November
Gave warnings or cautions about the product		
Toys	—	2
Cereals	—	—
Candies/sweets	—	—
All other	—	3
All products	—	1
Used "celebrity" endorsements		
Toys	—	—
Cereals	1	—
Candies/sweets	—	—
All other	—	—
All products	b	—
Used "personalities"		
Toys	4	15
Cereals	17	2
Candies/sweets	5	2
All other	2	19
All products	7	12
Had "contest" offer		
Toys	—	—
Cereals	—	—
Candies/sweets	5	—
All other	—	—
All products	1	—
Used "premium offer"		
Toys	—	—
Cereals	56	41
Candies/sweets	—	—
All other	4	—
All products	14	8
Told children to ask parents to buy product		
Toys	—	—
Cereals	—	—
Candies/sweets	—	—
All other	4	3
All products	1	b

aFigures were not directly comparable because vitamin and mineral content statements were not included in April coding.

bLess than 0.50 percent.

commercial only, sometimes visually, and less frequently simultaneously in both modes.

More than one-half of toy ads, for example, used audio disclaimers; 20 percent used visual disclaimers; but only about 10 percent gave such information simultaneously. The most frequent such disclaimers are items "sold separately," "batteries not included," or "assembly required." For cereals, such statements often refer to premiums—for instance, "in specially marked boxes." There also are occasional disclosures on photographic technique ("filmed in black light") or information such as "non-flying airplane." When such disclosures are given only visually, or only in brief verbal messages, there is some question as to the ability of the viewer to perceive them as an integral part of the commercial.

Warnings or cautions about the use of products are seldom given, even though the product itself may sometimes include such information. The only examples found in the November sample were for the medicine Appedrine ("use only as directed") and for one toy. The toy was an airplane that "should be flown with adult supervision."

If one inspects the products themselves, he or she may find clear indications of caution. An example is the Lite-Brite toy. Although no caution was given in the commercial, the packaging and instructions carefully state that there might be a "shock hazard"; and printed on the container are the warnings "CAUTION: ELECTRIC TOY" and "not recommended for children under 4 years of age." Unfortunately, time did not permit inspection of all products advertised—the above example, however, is illustrative of the problem.

Endorsements of products by celebrities or well-known personalities or characters is a rare practice. However, associations often are made through the use of such characters in the commercials. Cartoon characters, well-known personalities, comic strip characters, and television program characters were used in about 10 percent of commercials. In November, 15 percent of all toy commercials used personality tie-ins. They included Peanuts characters, such as Snoopy; Mr. Spock and others from Startrek; the Flintstone characters; the Waltons; Evel Knievel; Batman; Superman; and Planet of the Apes figures. Also, Boston personality Rex Trailer made commercials for Crimson Travel trips to California.

Contests and premium offers were other techniques used to sell. No contests were used in the November sample of commercials, although premium advertising was still a dominant practice by cereal companies. Sugar Pops, Lucky Charms, Super Sugar Crisp, Trix, Captain Crunch Punch Crunch, and Freakies cereals all employed some form of premium offer—including stickers, figures, and toys—to induce product purchase.

Advertisers seldom directly urged children to pressure their parents to buy the product or service offered. We found only one such case in November, in which the child was told, "Ask your mom or dad to take you to Edaville Railroad." Such practice violates the NAB Code Authority Guidelines for advertising to children.

Special Questions—Toy Commercials

Some advertising practices peculiar to certain products also were investigated. For toys, four questions were asked that relate to NAB Code Guidelines (see Table 3.13).

Some examples of the above cases will illustrate the techniques used. In commercials for toy cars (SSP Smash-up Derby, Thunder-shift 500, SSP Tournament of Thrills), sounds of racing cars, an actual race scene, and derby car smash-up sounds are used. Human-like groans and screams accompany Kar-a-a-ate Men in action, and a very human sneeze is seemingly emitted by Baby Tender Love.

Often there is more than one item offered for sale in the same commercial. This is especially true of toys, such as the doll play adventure sets consisting of several animal and human figures—usually sold separately. Examples include Marx's safari adventure set and safari action set, which include a lion, tiger, gorilla, elephant, a hunter, and so on. Although one can buy the figures separately, the toy may seem to the child to be incomplete if all the items shown are not purchased. Such toys tend to become very expensive indeed.

TABLE 3.13

Special Questions—Toy Commercials

| | Percent "Yes" Answers | |
Question	April	November
Is toy shown in other than normal child environment?	—	1.5
Is sound of real-life objects attributed to the toy?	18.9	8.9
Are items shown that are not included with the toy?	17.0	8.9
Is more than one item in the CA offered for sale?	66.6	42.2
	(N = 53)	(N = 135)

TABLE 3.14

Special Questions—Cereals and Candies

| | Percent with "Yes" Answers | | | |
| | Cereals | | Candies/Sweets | |
Question	April	November	April	November
Is there reference to nutritional value?	49	64	10	2
Is "sweetness" mentioned as a selling point?	31	23	0	12
Is the product referred to as a "snack"?	0	0	19	4
Is it shown as part of a balanced meal?	88	100	2	2
Is it shown as a substitute for a balanced meal?	0	0	0	2
Is "taste" or "flavor" used as a selling point?	56	79	74	93
Are ingredients identified as either "natural" or "artificial"?	3	14	19	0
Is caloric value stated?	0	0	0	0
(N)	(72)	(56)	(83)	(56)

Some commercials offer two major products in the same commercial. Examples include Kenner's Six Million Dollar Man and bionic transport repair station and Meco's Planet of the Apes fortress and Planet of the Apes catapult.

Appeals in Cereal and Candy/Sweets Commercials

Special questions also were asked concerning edible products. These questions investigated nutritional value, sweetness, taste, and ingredient information as selling devices. The questions are presented in Table 3.14.

Nutritional claims included versions of "eight essential vitamins and iron" in many of the Kellogg's cereal ads, and sometimes such statements as "good nutrition" without further specification. In more than 20 percent of cereal ads mention was made of "richness," "secret frostings," "coated with golden sugar," "taste of honey"— all of which are designed to appeal to the "sweetness" of the cereal.

One sweet (Kellogg's chocolate-peppermint frosted Pop Tarts) was
called a "super snack"; Snack Pak dessert and a yogurt "snack and
dessert" represented the snack appeal in the product advertising.
All 56 cereal commercials showed their products as part of a
balanced breakfast (with milk, fruit, and other foods on the table).

Appeals to taste, flavor, and texture were common in all
advertising for edibles. Some examples are "tastes dandy,"
"crunchy taste," "thick and chocolaty," "rich caramel," "powerful
good," "fruity," "fresh and delicious," and "flavors that never grow
old."

Whether ingredients were natural or artificial was not frequently
specified in the commercials. Kellogg's Raisin Bran referred to
"nature's golden bran"; and Kellogg's Apple Jacks were said to have
"bits of real apple"; and Captain Crunch Punch Crunch cereal visually
reminded the viewer (no audio) that there was an "artificial fruit
punch flavor." None of the food advertising stated caloric values.

Major "Themes" in the Commercials

Certain patterns were noted in the verbal and printed statements,
product slogans, and other appeals used in the commercials. These
were called "themes." Sixteen such "theme" categories were found,
and showed various tendencies for different product types (Table 3.15).

Toys were advertised as "new," "fun," with plenty of "action."
"Appearance" was a less-used theme. The major appeal of cereals
was to "health and nutrition," followed by "taste" and "texture."
These account for more than 80 percent of cereal themes. Candies/
sweets did not use nutritional claims; "taste" and "texture," followed
by "quantity or size," were most frequent appeals. Other edibles
more often stressed "appearance," "fun," and "convenience," along
with the "taste" and "texture" appeals of cereals and candies. Other
products also appealed to "fun" along with "action," "adventure,"
and general claims of "superiority."

Overall, and primarily due to the dominance of toy advertising
in November, the greatest increase was shown in the "newness"
and "fun" themes (Table 3.16).

Use of Special Effects in the Commercials

Partly because of the difficulties of definition, no quantitative
data were collected on the use of special effects (unusual camera
angles, extreme close-up photography, speeded-up action, and

TABLE 3.15

Basic Themes in the Commercials,
November Sample*
(percent)

Theme/Appeal	Toys	Cereals	Candies	Other Edibles	Other Products
Appearance	11	2	1	17	–
Quantity/size/amount	1	1	11	9	–
Convenience/ease of use	6	–	8	12	–
Taste/flavor/smell	–	29	31	21	–
Texture	1	20	29	12	–
Fun/happiness	24	3	8	17	30
Health/nutrition	–	35	1	9	9
Peer status/popularity	–	–	–	–	9
Action	23	3	–	–	13
Adventure	4	1	–	–	13
Comparative/associative	–	2	–	3	–
Economy/price	–	–	–	–	–
Uniqueness	1	–	4	–	–
Quality of manufacture	–	–	–	–	–
"Newness"	28	4	1	–	9
General superiority	1	–	6	–	17
Totals	100	100	100	100	100
Total themes (base)	(164)	(155)	(132)	(34)	(23)
Total commercials	(135)	(56)	(56)	(21)	(15)

*Themes were classified according to manifest verbal appeals
in spoken or printed form as slogans or product claims. No attempt
was made to judge the appeals of the visual presentation.

other visual devices). A number of cases were noted that might
be misleading to the child, however. They are listed here as
examples, with the suggestion that more research be conducted to
determine whether, or to what extent, the use of such devices may
lead to misperceptions or exaggerated expectations on the part of
children.

Product	Special Effect
G. I. Joe secret mountain outpost	animated twinkle in Atomic Man's eye
Six Million Dollar Man and bionic transport and repair station	doll appears to be walking independently

Big Wheel	appears to be going much faster than possible
Star Trek U.S.S. Enterprise gift set	rocky environment, lunar surface, and size distortion with close-ups
Child World	animated rabbit walking with children
Kar-a-a-ate Men	appear to be moving without help; human screams are heard
Live-in Train	size distortion by extreme close-ups
Nerf gliders	glider makes exaggerated squeaking noises when it collides with table
Putt-Putt Railroad	size distortion by close-ups
Waltons' farmhouse gift set	figures appear to walk without human help; rocking chair rocks by itself
Evel Knievel stunt cycle	extreme close-ups make speed distorted; difficult tricks are performed
Lite-Brite	extreme close-ups distort size
Evel Knievel stunt and crash car	car seems to be going much too fast
Super Sugar Crisps	filmed under black light (noted visually)
Pillsbury chocolate chip cookies	fast-motion photography
Trix	animated rabbit joins real children; his eyeglasses become models of the cereal
Kellogg's Frosted Flakes (1)	animated tiger comes out of box, sits down, and eats
Kellogg's Frosted Flakes (2)	tiger sits down to eat and spoon-feeds real child
Kellogg's Frosted Flakes (3)	animated tiger feeds child
Chocolite	candy grows larger when unwrapped
3 Musketeers	finger snap magically produces candy bar
Kellogg's Sugar Smacks	animated frog enters kitchen where children are eating
Cheerios	box of Cheerios supered over scene of family activity is never put into perspective

Freakies   animated drawing of Freakies
                                           sparkling
Kellogg's chocolate-peppermint   a talking toaster
  frosted Pop Tarts
Chef Boyardee mini ravioli   animated sparkle in raviolis
Pringles potato chips   never show actual size of a bag
                                           they compare

TABLE 3.16

Basic Themes in the Commercials,
All Products, April and November
(percent)

Theme/Appeal	April	November
Appearance	4	6
Quantity/size/amount	3	4
Convenience/ease of use	3	5
Taste/flavor/smell	25	18
Texture	13	15
Fun–happiness	7	13
Health/nutrition	13	12
Peer status/popularity	2	*
Action	7	9
Adventure	3	2
Comparative/associative	2	1
Economy/price	1	–
Uniqueness	6	1
Quality of manufacture	2	–
"Newness"	*	11
General superiority	9	3
Total	100	100
Total themes (base)	(502)	(508)

*Less than 0.50 percent.

THE COST OF ADVERTISED TOYS

A special analysis of prices was conducted for 67 toys represented
by the 135 toy commercials shown in November. To get an idea of
the costs to the consumer, all items shown or mentioned in the toy
commercials were recorded separately on the coding form. Then

TABLE 3.17

Range of Basic and Total Prices for Toys,
by Type of Toy
(dollars)

Type of Toy	Basic Price Range*	Total Price Range*
18 cars, planes, other	6.76 – 26.16	6.76 – 121.32
20 dolls, doll play sets	4.84 – 22.94	10.46 – 57.79
21 indoor games, toys	2.49 – 29.88	3.97 – 30.77
4 outdoor toys	11.97 – 129.95	13.88 – 129.95
4 crafts, hobbies	2.00 – 12.99	9.87 – 17.86
67 toys, total	2.00 – 129.95	3.97 – 129.95

*See text for definition.

visits were made to local toy stores or department stores.* The
intent was to obtain the total cost of advertised toys at lowest
("discount") prices available. Many of the prices would be somewhat
higher than listed here, were one to buy them in other retail outlets.
Thus, on the whole, this analysis probably is conservative. Naturally,
local sales taxes were not included. Price information as of March
1976 was obtained for each toy advertised and each component
mentioned, shown, or advertised as sold separately. (See Appendix I
for a list of all toy prices.)

Three price figures were computed for each toy product: the
basic item(s) price, additional price of components mentioned with
the basic item as sold separately, and total price—the basic item(s)
plus other components. In some cases, where equal emphasis was
given to two or three items, they are included as basic items advertised.

———

*Special thanks are due Robert Krock, who spent many hours
visiting the following stores to obtain the price information:

Child World (Swampscott, Saugus, Medford, and Dedham, Mass.)
K-Mart (Danvers, Mass.)
Ann and Hope (Danvers, Mass.)
Bradlees (Swampscott, Mass.)
Sears, Roebuck & Co. (Saugus, Mass.)
Woolworth (Lynn, Mass.)
Babyland (Lynn, Mass.)
Honda of Boston (Boston, Mass.)

The range in price figures are summarized in Table 3.17. For 67 toys analyzed, the basic price ranged from $2.00 for one U.S. stamp kit to $129.95 for a ten-speed bicycle.

Two averages were computed for all toys and by type of toy: the arithmetic mean and the median price. For all 67 toys, the average (mean) price for the basic item(s) advertised was $14.25; the average for additional components was $3.55; and the average total price was $17.77. These averages are slightly inflated because of two or three expensive toys. The median basic item price for all toys was $10.99 and for complete items it was $12.00.

Summaries of average price information is given in Table 3.18 by type of toy. Outdoor toys were most expensive (median price $22.46), followed by dolls and doll play sets, crafts and hobbies, and cars and planes. Least expensive (median price $9.99) were indoor games and toys (other than cars and dolls).

Arguing that toy advertising on television benefits the consumer, a statement by the Toy Manufacturers of America, Inc., before the Federal Trade Commission in 1971 stated:

One benefit stems from the fact that strong competition in the toy industry dictates that a toy must be relatively low in price if it is to sell in any quantity. Because we produce toys on a mass basis, because we advertise them on a mass basis, more toys are available to Americans at lower prices relative to disposable family incomes than in any other country of the world. To the consumer, the results of this system are highly beneficial.

TABLE 3.18

Mean and Median Prices for Toys,
by Type of Toy
(dollars)

	Mean Prices			Median Prices		
	Basic	Add'l.	Total	Basic	Add'l.	Total
Type of Toy	Price	Price	Price	Price	Price	Price
18 cars, planes, other	11.82	6.84	18.56	10.90	*	11.92
20 dolls, doll play sets	13.80	3.83	17.61	12.92	*	14.84
21 indoor games, toys	11.92	.55	12.48	8.88	*	9.99
4 outdoor toys	46.44	.75	47.18	21.92	*	22.46
4 crafts, hobbies	7.46	5.94	13.40	7.43	*	12.94
67 toys, total	14.25	3.55	17.77	10.99	*	12.00

*Less than one-half of items in category had components sold separately.

For example, in the United States, the average or
mean income per household is about $13,000. The
average toy purchase is approximately $2.98 . . . .[1]

The disparity between the average of $2.98 and the current
prices of television-advertised toys in this study is considerable.
Since the statement was made in 1971, part of the disparity could
be accounted for by inflation, of course. It is more probable, however, that television-advertised toys are considerably more expensive,
on the average, than the average toy purchase price quoted. According to the Toy Manufacturers statement, this is most likely true:

It is true, of course, that many toys advertised on
television cost more than $2.98. (Because they cost
more to design and produce.) But even many of these
reach the consumer at a price close to, or sometimes
below, that paid by the retailer, because a highly advertised "loss leader" item serves as a traffic builder.[2]

In any case it is the parent who will be asked to pay the $11.00
or $12.00 average price for a television-advertised toy, since
children, especially younger ones, seldom have that amount of
money to spend.

SEASONAL VARIATIONS IN THE ADVERTISING
CONTENT OF ONE NEW YORK INDEPENDENT
TELEVISION STATION

One New York independent television station was monitored in
November to provide some index of change in the advertising content
during the after-school hours. Although the sample was inadequate
to generalize to all independent stations, comparison of the advertising on WNEW in New York City between 3:00 and 6:00 pm in June
and November showed greater differences than that of the network-
affiliated Boston stations.
        Overall, there was a 67 percent increase in the total number
of product commercials presented (48 in June, 80 in November).
There also was a corresponding increase in the number of commercial minutes per hour. Although time standards for independent
stations are much more liberal than for weekend children's programming on network affiliates, this independent station seemed to
maximize the amount of children's advertising in the after-school
period. Commercial minutes on WNEW-TV increased from an
average of 11.49 in June to 14.22 in November (Table 3.19).

TABLE 3.19

Number of Commercial Minutes per Hour,
New York, June and November

Time Period	Minutes per Hour	
	June	November
3:00–4:00 pm	10.41	13.50
4:00–5:00 pm	11.24	14.50
5:00–6:00 pm	12.83	14.67
Average mins. per hr.	11.49	14.22

More than the network-affiliated Boston television stations,
WNEW showed a very large increase in toy advertising. Representing
46 percent of all ads in June, toys constituted 85 percent in November
(67 of 80 commercials). The data are given in Table 3.20.

As on Boston television, the emphasis on toy commercials led
to increased numbers of males as speakers (from 77 percent in
June to 85 percent in November), more child characters in the
population of commercials (from 61 percent to 82 percent), and a
slight increase in the proportion of other minorities represented
(although a slight reduction in the percentage of blacks—unlike
Boston television). (See Tables 3.21, 3.22, and 3.23.)

TABLE 3.20

Commercial Announcements, by Major Product
Type, New York, June and November

Major Product Type	June		November	
	Number	Percent	Number	Percent
Toys	22	45.8	67	83.7
Cereals	5	10.4	2	2.5
Candies/sweets	7	14.6	3	3.8
Snacks	–	–	–	–
Other foods	1	2.1	3	3.8
Eating places	5	10.4	2	2.5
Vitamins, medicines	–	–	–	–
Household products	–	–	2	2.5
Personal care products	–	–	1	1.2
Other products	8	16.7	–	–
Totals	48	100.0	80	100.0

TABLE 3.21

Who "Speaks for" the Product?
New York, June and November
(percent)

	June	November
Adult male	69	81
Adult female	21	15
Total adults	90	96
Male child	4	3
Female child	2	—
Total children	6	3
Other male	4	1
Other female	—	—
Total other	4	1
Total commercials	(48)	(80)

TABLE 3.22

Age and Sex of Characters in the Commercials,
New York, June and November
(percent)

Age and Sex Group	June	November
Males		
Children	43	50
Teens	3	1
Adults	17	9
Animals, others	—	1
Total males	63	61
Females		
Children	24	32
Teens	6	1
Adults	6	5
Animals, others	1	1
Total females	37	39
Total classified by sex	(133)	(229)
Total children	61	81
Total teens	8	2
Total adults	20	14
Total animals, others	11	3
Total characters	(147)	(231)

TABLE 3.23

Race of Characters in Commercials,
New York, June and November
(percent)

Race	June	November
White	94	90
Black	6	4
Other minorities	–	6
Total classified by race	(135)	(217)

Overall, the figures for the New York independent station
suggest that whatever commercial tendencies one might find in
network-affiliated stations probably are more extreme on the
independent stations. A much larger sample would be necessary
to verify this assumption, however.

SUMMARY OF CHAPTER 3

The primary purpose of this study was to analyze the differences
in advertising content in the spring (April 1975) and the pre-Christmas
season (November 1975). In addition, a special analysis was made
of the cost of television-advertised toys. Following is a brief
summary of the findings.

Amount of Advertising

There was a 17 percent increase in advertising, from 12.8 percent
of total time in April to 15.0 percent in November. Noncommercial, public-service announcements and program promotion
were cut back to accommodate this increase in pre-Christmas
advertising.
As was found in April, stations continued to exceed the NAB Code
Authority Guidelines of ten-minutes of nonprogram material
per hour on Saturday children's television.
The greatest increase was in toy advertising—from 17.3 percent
of all ads in April to 47.5 percent in November. All other
product categories decreased both in frequency and as a proportion of all advertising.

Nature of Advertising

In both April and November a pattern of sexism was noted. Males
dominated as the authoritative voice in all commercials (93.7

percent in November). Also, in an analysis of over 1,000 characters in the ads, males constituted approximately 70 percent; and male children outnumbered female children 2:1.

There was a slight increase in the proportion of black and minority characters in the November ads, primarily through the increase in the number of children portrayed in toy commercials.

Advertising of Edibles

Ads for edibles constituted 65 percent of all commercials in April and 47 percent in November. Highly sugared products accounted for 71 percent of ads for edibles in April and 75 percent in November.

Commercial Practices

Although many commercial practices in children's television that have received criticism occurred very infrequently or not at all (such as host selling, program tie-ins, comparative claims), other practices continued.

Although they did not directly endorse the product, well-known personalities, celebrities, cartoon, comic, or program characters were sometimes employed as integral parts of the commercials.

Few children's ads gave any objective product information: how the product operates, its size, quantity, ingredients, materials, or price information. Rather, selling appeals tended to have such themes as "fun," "action," or the "newness" of toys; the "taste," "texture," or "nutritional value" of cereals.

Nearly two-thirds of cereal referred to the nutritional value, about one-fourth used "sweetness" as an appeal, and more than three-fourths used other "taste" or "flavor" appeals. None stated caloric values in the ads, and few identified ingredients—whether natural or artificial.

A frequent practice of cereal commercials continued to be the use of premium offers (41 percent of cereal ads did so in November).

Real-life sounds of racing cars, human voices, and other sound effects were sometimes associated with toys.

About one-half of all toy ads used disclosures or qualifiers such as "sold separately," "batteries not included," or "assembly required." About 20 percent used only visual disclosures, and only 10 percent used simultaneous audio and visual disclosures.

Other commercial practices involved the use of special effects–
   animation, extreme close-up photography, camera angles.
   Several examples were noted.
A more and more frequent practice seemed to be the offering of
   more than one item for sale in a single commercial.

Cost of Television-Advertised Toys

Analysis of the prices of 67 television-advertised toys revealed an
   overall price range from $3.97 to $129.95.
The average (mean) price for basic toys advertised was $14.25;
   with additional "sold separately" items added, the average was
   $17.77.
Median basic item cost for 67 toys was $10.99; the median price
   including all components shown was $12.00.
On the average, the most expensive toys were outdoor toys (median
   $22.46); dolls and doll play sets, which included many components
   ($14.84); and crafts and hobbies ($12.94). The least expensive
   were indoor games and other indoor toys ($9.99).

New York Independent Television in the After-School Hours

Comparison of one New York independent television station between
   3:00 and 6:00 pm in June and November showed more extreme
   changes than weekend children's television. For example,
   commercial time averaged more than 14 minutes per hour,
   or nearly 24 percent of total time in November, compared with
   11.5 minutes, or about 19 percent in June. Toy commercials
   accounted for 84 percent of all advertising in November (67 of
   80 commercials).

   This chapter details research conducted as a follow-up to the
April 1975 investigation of weekend and after-school commercial
children's television.[3] The procedures used were the same as in
those studies, and are not included here in detail. The focus of
this chapter, however, is principally on advertising matter. Thus
a comparison is possible between the amount and nature of advertising to children during the spring and that in the pre-Christmas
period.
   Saturday morning children's programs on the three network-
affiliated commercial television stations in Boston were videotaped
on November 22 and 29, 1975. This represents a total of 16 hours
of children's programming. Data for the same three stations during
the April study were retabulated so as to represent comparable
samples for the two periods.

Funds did not permit full analysis of independent station advertising during the after-school hours in November. Ten such stations were studied in April. However, one station (WNEW, Channel 5, in New York City) was studied to provide some indication of changes on such stations.

NOTES

1. Statement by the Toy Manufacturers of America, Inc., presented at the Hearings on Modern Advertising Practices, Federal Trade Commission, November 10-11, 1971, p. 16.

2. Ibid., p. 17.

3. F. Earle Barcus, Weekend Commercial Children's Television and Television in the After-School Hours (Newtonville, Mass.: Action for Children's Television, 1975).

CONCLUSION
Rachel Wolkin

"If they can get you asking the wrong questions, they don't have to worry about answers." This "proverb" was cited by George Comstock of the Rand Corporation in writing about the direction of children's television research. Its philosophy is particularly appropriate for the policy implications of this study. If critics of current advertising and programming practices are confined by industry's determination to discourage possible change, critics will be asking the wrong questions and the industry will not be required to provide meaningful answers.

The right question to ask must be "How can children's television reflect stimulating diversity in programming and at the same time avoid commercial practices that are detrimental to a child's mental and physical growth?" This question must be posed not only to broadcasters, but repeatedly to those agencies congressionally mandated to protect the public interest.

The first condition for change is that the television industry must accept some economic flexibility. Positive change cannot take place unless there is a slackening of the rigid adherence to present commercial practices, which place the highest premium on programs that are the most profitable. This condition for change is derived from the proposition that programming in the public interest can be achieved only when television serves the interests of children as well as the financial interests of the broadcasters and advertisers.

Balancing economic interests against the public interest, the American legal system has determined in numerous cases that regardless of economic hardship, the public must be protected. When children are the public in need of protection, the courts have been particularly careful to guarantee adequate safeguards. Laws restricting child labor, for example, reflect the stronger societal commitment to the well-being of children as against economic interests. More recently, the television industry, following Banzhaf v. FCC, absorbed the economic impact of the ban on cigarette commercials because of the "greater public interest" argument. Children's television itself has responded to the 40 percent reduction of commercial time on weekends without suffering undue economic hardship. These examples point to the conclusion that the threat of economic change need not be viewed by critics as an insurmountable obstacle to improved children's television.

Advertising, as the revenue basis for programming, is most susceptible to economic change. William Melody, an economist at the University of Pennsylvania, wrote in Children's Television:

> The question of protection from harm is not that children
> should be shielded from exposure to any and all adver-
> tising on television. Clearly, children always have and
> always will be exposed to advertising. The issue is whether
> children should be protected from being isolated as a
> specialized audience for the specific purpose of applying
> pinpoint and tailor-made advertising directed toward
> their particular vulnerabilities as children. The point
> to be considered is not whether children should be per-
> mitted to observe and grow up in the television-advertising
> game as played by adults. Rather, the question is, should
> children be protected from being singled out as the most
> vulnerable and malleable target for direct attack by tele-
> vision advertisers?[1]

Future regulation of commercial practices on children's televi-sion could vary from the complete elimination of all advertising to the prohibition of products that are harmful to a child's health. An additional issue of commercial practice is the types of advertising techniques that should be allowed or prohibited on children's televi-sion.

Lewis A. Engman, former chairman of the Federal Trade Commission (FTC), raised eight points for consideration in his address to the Young Lawyers Section of the American Bar Associa-tion. He noted that "spokesmen representing all views" have recognized these issues as problems needing solutions. The list is included here as an initial guideline reflecting rational, if somewhat conservative, thought. Reevaluation was recommended for the following:

1. The distortion of product performance in regard
   to speed, time, motion or size, through the use of
   visual techniques;
2. Confusion over sales prices and what accessories,
   props, and other items are included in a given sales
   price;
3. Advertisements which encourage the purchase of food
   items—especially those involving soft drinks, candy,
   snacks, etc.—without at the same time explaining
   how the product fits into a well-balanced nutritious
   program;

4. The use of premiums and contests to create an
   artificial demand for a specific product;

5. The practice of encouraging children to act as surrogate
   salesmen for the manufacturer by directly or indirectly
   suggesting that they ask their parents to purchase a
   given product;

6. The exposure of children to advertisements for
   products which promise to affect the user's mood
   or well-being;

7. The use of program characters—either live or
   animated—to sell products to children; and

8. The use of material which can reasonably be expected
   to frighten children or promote anxiety or which
   portrays appeals to violent or dangerous behavior or
   which portrays children in unsafe acts.[2]

Added to this list can be the recommendation that each point be
very critically evaluated in light of the child's vulnerability to
commercial messages. Strictly interpreted, the application of this
additional recommendation creates a strong argument for prohibiting
the advertising of certain products.

Current self-regulatory practices affecting ads for highly
sugared cereals provide a particularly apt example of the need for
federal regulation. The voluntary code of the NAB states, regarding
the advertising of these edibles, "Each commercial for breakfast-
type products shall include at least one audio reference to and one
video depiction of the role of the product within the framework of
a balanced regimen." This guideline has resulted in commercials
for cereals with over 50 percent sugar that assert the cereal forms
part of a balanced breakfast. Even with industry guidelines the
child is being sold, with the aid of sophisticated marketing techniques,
a product saturated with an ingredient detrimental to dental health,
in a manner that might easily lead the child to believe that a food's
sweetness is a primary concern in making nutritional choices.
Since highly sugared cereals constitute almost 19 percent of the
products advertised on weekend commercial children's television,
the health implications of these "nutritional" messages are significant. Despite the warnings of dentists and nutritionists, such
commercials are permitted. It is clear that, in this instance, the
best efforts of industry are not sufficient. When 98 percent of the
population suffers from tooth decay, it does not seem unreasonable
for the FTC to regulate nutritional messages directed to young
viewers. The issue of sugared-cereal advertising is just one example
of the need for new direction in formulating commercial policies.
Advertising of any food or beverage highly saturated with sugar
raises equally important policy questions.

Toys are second only to food products in the amount of advertising on children's television. Toy advertising practices can be seen as deceptive on several counts. Special effects, inadequate price information, and highly manipulative ad themes operate to mislead the child. Misleading special effects include visual distortion of the toy's size and audio distortion of the toy's noise-making ability. Furthermore, toys frequently are depicted with items that are not part of the unit being sold. These practices confuse and frustrate the child. The disparity between what is allegedly promised and what the child receives creates anger and confusion. Daniel Yankelovich, Inc., in its study Mothers' Attitudes Towards Children's Television Programs and Commercials noted: "This type of misrepresentation leads to frustration, anger, disappointment, tears, etc. Often this anger is expressed against the mother, not the sponsor."[3] Dr. Richard Feinbloom of Harvard pointed out that one reason for this confusion and disappointment is that "the child responds as much to the setting as to the object advertised."[4]

Themes used in child-oriented commercials take advantage of the child's propensity to confuse the toy and the setting in which it is placed. As the Barcus study demonstrates, many ads imply that product purchase will guarantee fun, popularity, happiness, power, and speed. Toy advertising practices illustrate the willingness of advertisers and broadcasters to manipulate the child's susceptible nature. Furthermore, they demonstrate that self-regulatory guidelines have not adequately restricted such techniques. Federal protection of the young consumer is necessary to ensure that she or he receives fair treatment from the advertiser and is protected from "unfair and deceptive acts or practices."

The use of premiums as a selling device combines the worst aspects of food and toy advertising practices. Of the cereal commercials monitored for the study, 47 percent used this mechanism to entice the child. This advertising technique is unfair because it encourages the child to choose his breakfast food on the basis of a toy's attractiveness, which is totally unrelated to the properties of the cereal. It is difficult enough for a child to make reasoned consumer choices, without this added confusion. It is not reasonable to expect that a child will disregard the promise of an attractive "free" toy and choose another cereal, without a toy, because it is more nutritious.

In each of these areas—food, toys, and premiums—two changes could be suggested: the elimination of all advertising of these products or the enactment of enforceable regulations promulgated by the FTC to guarantee that only fair advertising practices are used on children's television. The FTC has ample authority to regulate "unfair or deceptive acts or practices in commerce."[5]

This has been interpreted in part to mean that a practice is unlawful if it has an unfair impact on a particular consumer group. The audience's level of competence is to be taken into account.[6] The FTC thus has the authority to impose more stringent regulation of advertising directed to children than that directed to adults. The results of this study most strongly indicate that the FTC should exercise its authority to prohibit confusing and manipulative selling practices for all products, and the advertising of products potentially detrimental to children's health, such as heavily sugared foods, vitamins, and fireworks. Lewis Engman concluded his address with the following caveat: "If television advertising deceives our children, if it frustrates them through false and misleading promises, if it promotes the sale of dangerous toys or other products, if it fosters dietary habits which endanger their health—if it does these things, I think television will soon find itself circumscribed by legal restrictions and requirements."[7] That address was delivered in 1973. The industry has not reformed itself; and it is time that the FTC act, or else be deemed to have abdicated its responsibility to children.

The Federal Communications Commission (FCC) likewise has a responsibility to children as part of its congressional mandate to ensure that stations broadcast in the public interest. In the exercise of this responsibility, it has promulgated regulations to guarantee program diversity that would serve the needs of various groups within the community. However, despite the FCC's recognition that "the broadcaster's public service obligation includes a responsibility to provide diversified programming designed to meet the varied needs and interests of the child audience," it has not sought to guarantee meaningful compliance. Similarly, the FCC had declined to regulate the amount of advertising on children's television even though it has recognized its authority to do so.

Acknowledging its responsibility not to subordinate the "public interest" to commercial interests, the FCC determined that elimination of all advertising could damage the amount and quality of children's programming. In the areas of programming and advertising, it has chosen to rely on the self-regulation of broadcasters. This reliance has not been justified.

Advertising, although reduced, is still frequent; and on the weekdays, it is particularly excessive. In a 1974 study prepared for the FCC at its request, Dr. Alan Pearce, an economist, concluded that all three networks and their affiliates could reduce the sold commercial content of their children's programs to 7 minutes, 30 seconds, with "minimal overall network financial hardship, especially in light of the recent profit levels."[8] This conclusion was buttressed with the argument that reduction to this level might lead to a healthier year-round demand for advertising time, instead

of the current Christmas-time concentration. Regarding the issue
of network profits from individual shows, Dr. Pearce stated: "It
has never been contended that every segment of network programming
should be profitable in and of itself; for example, many network
documentary programs lose money and perhaps some segments of
children's programming ought to be treated this way, especially
since children's programming is profitable overall."[9]

These conclusions are reinforced by Les Brown, writing in the
New York Times: "The networks and stations have thrived despite
the elimination of more than $200 million a year in cigarette adver-
tising in 1971 and the code-mandated reduction in the number of
commercials on children's shows. They have also weathered without
financial hardship, the prime-time access rule, which reduces network time by half an hour a night. . . ."[10] It also is significant to
note that the Group W stations have a self-imposed limit of only
six minutes of commercials per hour in their children's programming.
Similarly, in January 1976 the Post-Newsweek stations reduced
the commercial time on their children's programs from eight to
six minutes. Additionally, under the new Post-Newsweek policies,
commercials are clustered into two five-minute groups at the
beginning and end of the hour, with no interruptions in programming.

The commercial practices of the Group W and Post-Newsweek
stations, plus the observations of Brown and Pearce, testify to the
economic feasibility of reducing advertising time on network television. The industry's code maximum of 9.5 minutes on weekends
and 12 minutes during the week is clearly in excess of what is
necessary to sustain children's programming. In light of the FCC's
obligation to balance public and commercial interest, its refusal to
limit commercial time through regulation is indefensible.

Although commercial independent stations would experience
more economic difficulty in reducing commercial time on children's
programs, Pearce determined that independent stations could,
through a phased reduction, minimize economic loss. Therefore,
the FCC could fairly regulate the amount of commercial time on
independent stations' children's programs.

The frequency of commercial announcements on children's
programming—a maximum of four interruptions per half hour—
exacerbates each of the advertising problems outlined above. This
practice takes advantage of what the FCC described in its report
as the inability of the child "to understand that advertising is not
just another form of informational programming." Last, commercial interruption harms the program's integrity and is likely to
increase a child's difficulty in following plot development.

The amount of advertising time on children's television and the
frequency of commercial interruptions violate the directive of the

FCC 1960 Policy Statement, which cautioned licensees to "avoid abuses with respect to advertising continuity as well as the frequency with which regular programs are interrupted for advertising messages."[11] The FCC has a responsibility to ensure that this directive is followed.

The amount of advertising on television has operated to increase broadcaster and network profits, but has not led to improved programming. Despite the FCC's assertion that broadcasters have a "special responsibility" to design programs specifically for children that will serve their unique needs, such programs are shown only infrequently. There has been no commitment to provide nonanimated children's programs on a regular basis. Age-specific programs likewise are limited. The adherence to an entertainment-dominated program format saturated with animation is motivated by the broadcasters' desire to maintain profits through the economic security of the status quo.

There are two major vehicles for change in the area of programming: federal regulation and public concern. Federal regulation can guarantee that broadcasters allocate a certain percentage of time for diverse children's programs, and public concern can provide pressure to improve the quality of the programming produced.

Television should amuse and delight, but it should be sufficiently diverse to educate and stimulate as well. Broadcasters have a legal obligation to provide the public with program diversity. The Supreme Court wrote in the landmark case Red Lion Broadcasting Co. v. FCC, "[i]t is the right of the public to receive suitable access to social, political, esthetic, moral and other ideas and experiences which is crucial here. That right may not constitutionally be abridged either by Congress or by the FCC."[12] The FCC, in its policy statement Children's Television Programs, observed in response: "This language in our judgment clearly points to a wide range of programming responsibilities on the part of the broadcaster."[13] Specifically, the FCC refused to establish regulations requiring that broadcasters devote a certain percentage of program time to children's programming; create age-specific programming to guarantee that all children have access to suitable programming; and produce educational programming for children.

The FCC has ample authority to regulate in this manner. In the past it has required licensees to serve the needs of minority groups, and it has cautioned broadcasters to schedule public service programming at reasonable times. Since this type of regulation is content-neutral (not affecting the content of programming), it does not violate the First Amendment. Moreover, in this First Amendment area, the Supreme Court in the Red Lion case determined that "[i]t is the right of the viewers and listeners, not the right of the

broadcasters which is paramount." Clearly, part of the child
audience's right includes the right of access to programs that are
designed for children and are diverse in nature.

Since federal regulation can require broadcasters to program
for children, public concern can encourage broadcasters to produce
programs of artistic value. Only the public can demand that program
content be thoughtful, aesthetic, and creative. First Amendment
proscriptions forbid the FCC and Congress from intruding into this
area.

There are various ways for the public to express its concern and
to change current programming. One of the most effective ways is
writing letters. Local stations, networks, sponsors, the FCC, and
the press are important targets for citizen concern. Local stations
have an obligation to program in the public interest and often are
responsive to public input. Networks and sponsors can use public
input to gauge the popularity of current programs and thus affect
future program seasons. The FCC maintains a file on every licensed
station and can use program comments in its decision to renew a
station's license. General comments regarding children's television
can motivate the FCC to promulgate regulation. The 100,000 letters
and comments the FCC received in its last inquiry on children's
television were an important factor in its decision to continue its
investigation. Writing to the press aids the local television critic's
evaluation of children's programming. A published letter can
stimulate community awareness and concern. Letters are effective
because there is the assumption that the writer is expressing not
just his own concern, but that of other citizens. Both positive and
critical letters help—in fact, letters of praise may be more important
than critical ones because they indicate what the public wants and
provide incentive for future programming efforts.

Community action is another way the public can effectively
influence children's programs. Every area has special needs that
local television stations are obliged to ascertain and serve. A local
group can provide a sounding board for community interests and can
act as a source of information. Citizen dialogue with stations has
become an effective tool for change. Also, groups can challenge
license renewals if the local station is not responsive to the community's needs. Very often, the mere presence of concerned
citizen groups can heighten the awareness of local stations and result
in improved programming.

Institutions and corporations, as part of the public sector, have
a unique opportunity to promote children's television. Their financial
resources permit them to sponsor or underwrite programming that
is educational and artistic. Commitment to quality programming
on the part of these institutions can demonstrate how creative talent,

applied thoughtfully to children's programs, can make television an exciting and informative media form for young viewers.

One of the purposes of this study is to provide an objective basis for assessing the present quality of children's television. The facts strongly suggest that change is needed and that the industry and the public must question the failure of television to live up to its potential. It is hoped that the data and observations provided in this study will aid in the continuing inquiry into children's television and will help the reader to determine the right questions to ask.

NOTES

1. William Melody, Children's TV: The Economics of Exploitation (New Haven: Yale University Press, 1973), p. 118.

2. Lewis A. Engman, address delivered before the Young Lawyers' Section of the American Bar Association, Washington, D.C., August 6, 1973.

3. Daniel Yankelovich, Inc., Mothers' Attitudes Towards Children's Programs and Commercials (Newtonville, Mass.: Action for Children's Television, 1970).

4. Richard I. Feinbloom, "Impact of Advertising on Consumers" (Letter submitted by Action for Children's Television to Federal Trade Commission for hearing, November 1971).

5. Federal Trade Commission Act, sec. 5.

6. Mattel, Inc. 3 Trade Regulation Reporter 19,850 at 21,869, FTC November 1, 1971, consent order accepted.

7. Engman, op. cit., p. 12.

8. Alan Pearce, "The Economics of Children's Television Programming" (Report to Federal Communications Commission, Washington, D.C., 1974), p. 26.

9. Ibid, p. 27.

10. Les Brown, "Television Becomes the 'Failure-Proof Business,'" New York Times, March 15, 1976.

11. Federal Communications Commission, "Report and Statement of Policy Re: Programming," 20 Pike and Fisher Radio Reports 1901, 1912-13 (1960).

12. Red Lion Broadcasting Co. v. FCC, 395 U.S. 367, 393 (1969).

13. Federal Communications Commission, Children's Television Programs, Report and Policy Statement, Federal Register, 39, no. 215 at 39397.

I. PROGRAM SEGMENT ANALYSIS

A. Program Title. Write in complete title of entire program.

B. Program Segment or Subtitle. For instance, title of cartoon subsegment.

C. Program Summary. Brief summary of action, plot, character roles.

D. List of Characters. List up to five major characters in the segment (to be coded later).

E. Segment ID No. Write in the number of the segment, as found on the screening sheet.

F. Screening Sheet No. Write in the number of the screening sheet on which the program segment appears.

G. Station Code.
   06–WNEW, 5, New York   11–WDRB, 41, Louisville
   07–WDCA, 20, Washington   12–WYAH, 27, Norfolk
   08–WUTV, 29, Buffalo   13–WTCG, 17, Atlanta
   09–WKBD, 50, Detroit   14–KSTW, 11, Seattle
   10–WVTV, 18, Milwaukee   15–KTXL, 40, Sacramento.

H. Day.
   1–Monday   4–Thursday   7–Sunday.
   2–Tuesday   5–Friday
   3–Wednesday   6–Saturday

I. Program Number. See separate list of program titles. Write in number.

J. Time on. Code actual time the segment started–for instance, 11:02.

K. Length. Code in minutes and fraction–for instance, 11.25, 03.67.

L. Type.
   1–Cel animation (traditional cartoon technique)
   2–3-D animation (photographs of puppets, clay figures, other)
   3–Nonanimated (regular film or tape programs with live humans or animals)
   4–Mixed (part animation, part nonanimated).

M. Format.
   01–Situation comedy (I Love Lucy, Gilligan's Island, Addams Family)

02—Family drama (Partridge Family, Father Knows Best, Leave It to Beaver)

03—Social situation drama (Room 222)

04—Cartoon comedy (Bugs Bunny, Casper, Flintstones, Popeye)

05—Other comedy drama (Three Stooges, Little Rascals)

06—Animal adventure drama (Lassie, Run Joe Run, Lassie's Rescue Rangers)

07—Crime/mystery/detective drama (Mod Squad, Alfred Hitchcock)

08—Action/adventure drama (without element of crime) (Emergency Plus Four, Devlin, Shazam, Robin Hood, Valley of the Dinosaurs)

09—Western drama (Lone Ranger, Cisco Kid, Big Valley)

10—Fantasy/science fiction (Star Trek, Lost in Space, Land of the Lost)

11—Other drama (Davey and Goliath)

12—Movies

13—Variety (music, circus acts, dance, jokes, chatter) (Hudson Brothers, Harlem Globe Trotters, Mickey Mouse Club)

14—Quiz/games/stunts/contests

15—Sports events

16—Other entertainment formats

21—Children's news (In the News)

22—Documentary/travel (What's the Senate All About)

23—Animal/nature films

24—Interview/panel formats (For Kids Only)

25—Discussion/debate formats

26—Music and fine arts programs

27—Foreign-language programs

28—General news, weather, sports

29—Other information programs (Vision on, Make a Wish, Jabberwocky, Captain Bob).

N. Subject Matter Codes. Subject matter is what the program is "about," not the type or format of the program. For example, a program may have animal characters, but not be about animals. A program is not about "history" or "historical events" just because it has a historical setting. Choose at least one, but no more than two, of the subject-matter categories below and code them accordingly.

01—Domestic subjects: marriage and the family, the home, parent-child relations, divorce

02—Crime: corruption, rackets, crime detection, murder, robbery, outlaws, police, detectives

03—Historical: association with historical events or activities
04—Religion: the church, religious customs, the Bible, clergy
05—Love and romance: intimate relations between the sexes
06—Supernatural: superstition, occult, mystical, magic, mythical, gods
07—Nature and animals: jungle, mountains, forces of nature, camping out, fishing, exploration, the elements
08—Race and nationality: ethnic status, foreign lands, foreign peoples, minority or foreign groups, immigrants, American Indians
09—Education: schools, teachers, pupils, instruction, training
10—Business and industry: labor, corporations, private business
11—Government and public affairs: law, the courts, prisons, legislation, politics
12—Science and scientists: medicine, social sciences, technology
13—Entertainment world: amusements, professional sports, "show business," mass media, television, movie stars
14—Armed forces and war
15—Literature and the fine arts: music, classics, poetry, dance
16—Interpersonal rivalry: jealousy, conflict (but not about crime and similar subjects)
17—Crafts and hobbies
18—Language: words, spelling (Grammar Rock)
19—Other: explain under "special notes."

O. Origin.
1—Local, live
2—Recorded (film, video syndication)
3—Network (direct or delayed).

P. Place Setting.
U.S. settings—city
11—Home or around house (yard, house, other)
12—Outside (street, highway, field, open air)
13—Place of work or profession (office, store)
14—Public place (restaurant, cab, theater, hotel)
15—Uncertain
U.S. settings—rural
21—Home
22—Outside
23—Place of work
24—Public place
25—Uncertain

Foreign settings—city
    31—Home
    32—Outside
    33—Place of work
    34—Public place
    35—Uncertain
Foreign settings—rural
    41—Home
    42—Outside
    43—Place of work
    44—Public place
    45—Uncertain.

Q. Time Setting.
    1—Distant past
    2—Recent past
    3—Current, modern, contemporary
    4—Future
    5—Uncertain.

R. Extent of Violence.
    1—No violence
    2—Saturated with violence
    3—Violence subordinate
    4—Violence incidental.

S. Character Codes. Code up to five major characters according to codes below.

Male child
    11—White
    12—Black
    13—Other (Indian, Oriental, other)
    14—Unknown
    15—Animal
    16—Other (monster, robot, other)

Female child
    51—White
    52—Black
    53—Other
    54—Unknown
    55—Animal
    56—Other

Male teen
    21—White
    22—Black
    23—Other
    24—Unknown
    25—Animal
    26—Other

Female teen
    61—White
    62—Black
    63—Other
    64—Unknown
    65—Animal
    66—Other

Male adult
    31—White
    32—Black
    33—Other
    34—Unknown
    35—Animal
    36—Other

Female adult
    71—White
    72—Black
    73—Other
    74—Unknown
    75—Animal
    76—Other

Male other
  40—No age group (animals, robots with male character-
        istics)
Female other:
  80—No age group (animals, robots with female character-
        istics)
Other characters, sex and race unknown
  95—Animal
  96—Other.

T. Questions. Code 0 = no; 1 = yes for each of the following
   questions.
   1. Chase? Was there one or more "chase scenes" in the
      program? If yes, describe the scene briefly and tell
      how the chase ends: (for instance, "police chase crimi-
      nals in car, car crashes into tree, criminals die").
   2. Death? Was there one or more deaths in the program?
      Explain who died and how.
   3. Injuries? Treat same as deaths.
   4. With weapon? This and question 5 refer to any acts of
      violence committed by humans (or characters acting
      as humans). "With weapon" means violence employing
      any traditional weapon (gun, knife, club, other), as well
      as more sophisticated mechanical and electrical tech-
      nology (bombs, ray guns, cannons). Include here any
      mechanical violence caused by the character (for instance,
      driving a car over someone, pushing a button to destroy
      a city).
   5. Without weapon? Traditional violence using fists, hands,
      elbows, feet, other.
   6. Natural violence? Were there storms, volcanoes, floods,
      wind, as well as "acts of god"—accidents not caused by
      humans?
   7. Violent results? Did the violence result in the death
      or injury of anyone?
   8. Violence to humans? Was the violence directed at
      humans, in contrast, for example, with blowing up a
      bridge.
   9. CA tie? Refers to instances in which the host, guests,
      or characters appearing in the program give commercial
      announcements, appear in commercials, or "plug"
      sponsors or products. Include introductory statements
      such as "now for a word from Pepsi-Cola, the drink
      for those who think young," but not simply "now a word
      from our sponsor."

10. Laugh track? Was a laugh track used? Describe or give examples—for instance, "laughter dubbed in after main character is thrown in the lake."
11. Interruption? If the program segment was interrupted for any CA before the story or scene or segment was concluded, mark "1."
12. Situation? Did the program contain any frightening, dangerous, or suspenseful situation? Describe. If the whole program is built on such situations, give one or two examples. Examples: "Man clinging to cliff about to fall," "parachute doesn't open," "held captive by unfriendly natives."

U. Rating. Fill in the rating provided for that program.
V. Percent child audience. Fill in figure provided for that program.

II. COMMERCIAL ANNOUNCEMENTS

A. Product Name. Fill in complete name as given in the commercial.
B. Manufacturer (or company).
C. Description of CA. Write a brief description of the format, characters, plot, and other significant features of the commercial.
D. Product Claims, Assertions, and Slogans. Quote visual and oral claims—such as "best buy," "gives you go power," "runs like the real thing," "for those who think young."
E. ID Number. Write in number assigned on the screening sheet.
F. Duplicate ID No. Refer to list of CAs for duplicating commercials.
G. Screening Sheet Number. See sec. I, F.
H. Station. See sec. I, G.
I. Day. See sec. I, H.
J. Time on.
   1— 7:00- 8:00 am
   2— 8:00- 9:00 am
   3— 9:00-10:00 am
   4—10:00-11:00 am
   5—11:00 am-12 noon
   6—12 noon- 1:00 pm
   7— 1:00- 2:00 pm
   8— 3:00- 4:00 pm
   9— 4:00- 5:00 pm
   0— 5:00- 6:00 pm

K. Length. Code decimally (such as 0.50, 0.67, 1.50).

L. Themes. Classify sec. D above into the following categories. Choose at least one and up to three themes.

00—None: No major or discernible claims or assertions made

01—Appearance of product: Beautiful, shiny, gleaming, rugged appearance, style

02—Quantity/size/amount: Super size, loaded with . . .

03—Convenience/ease of use

04—Taste/flavor/smell: Yummy, delicious, tastes great, fruitiful smell

05—Texture: Thick, rich, crunchy, creamy, light, puffy, stays crisp

06—Fun/happiness: Fun taste, fun to eat, lots of laughs, cup of happiness

07—Health/nutrition/well-being: Low fat, good for you, balanced breakfast, look thinner

08—Peer status/popularity

09—Action/strength/speed/power

10—Adventure: An adventure in every bite

11—Comparative/associative claim: Tastes as good as gold

12—Economy/price

13—Uniqueness: The one and only lollipop with a hole

14—Quality of manufacture, materials or preparation: Quality-controlled, pure

15—Newness

16—General superiority: Fantastic, a miracle, you won't believe your eyes, best.

M. Product Type.

Toys

    01—Cars, planes, trains

    02—Dolls (including G.I. Joe) and doll play sets

    03—Indoor games, puzzles, toys (yoyo)

    04—Outdoor games and toys (frisbee)

    05—Toy stores

    09—Other toys, hobbies, crafts

Cereals

    10—General

    11—Sugared

    12—Not sugared

Candies/sweets

    21—Candy (bars and packaged candies, mints, Lifesavers)

    22—Chewing gum (sugarless)

    23—Chewing gum (regular)

    24—Cakes and cookies

25—Ice cream, puddings, desserts, frozen ice, Tastee
    Freeze, Nestle's Quik
26—Soft drinks (carbonated)
27—Fruit-flavored drinks and ices (Kool Aid, Kool Pops)
28—Juice drinks (orange juice, grape juice)
29—Other

Snack foods
31—Potato chips, corn chips
32—Peanut butter (Koogle)
39—Other snack foods

Other foods
41—Canned, packaged prepared foods
42—Fruits
43—Vegetables
44—Meats
45—Bread
46—Milk, dairy products
49—Other foods

Restaurants, meals, grocery stores, supermarkets
51—Restaurants, meals
52—Groceries, supermarkets
59—Other

Vitamins/medicines/drugs
61—Vitamins
62—Analgesics (aspirin, Bufferin)
69—Other

Household products
71—Cleansers, detergents, bleaches
72—Furniture and appliances (washer, dryer, mattresses)
73—Tools, hardware (power mower, vinyl repair kit)
79—Other household products (Dixie Cups)

Personal care products
81—Shampoos, deodorants, soaps
82—Health items (sauna suit, body shaper, rotary
    massage)
83—Clothing
89—Other personal products

Other products
91—Motion pictures
92—Recreation/amusement (sporting events, county
    fair, racing, wrestling)
93—Books, magazines (TV Guide, TV Facts, Time-Life
    books)
94—Record offers
95—Automobiles (auto repair, auto parts)

        96—Airlines, travel offers (Disneyland)

        97—Schools (CDI, Evelyn Woods, Lafayette Academy)

        98—Hi-fi and stereo stores (television sets, tape recorders)

        99—Other (swimming pool, insurance).

N. Use of Animation.
    1—Animated
    2—Nonanimated
    3—Mixed.

O. Format.
    1—Off-stage voice explaining virtues of the product or commenting on the action in the CA
    2—On-stage announcer
    3—Musical structure (songs, jingles, musical message)
    4—Short dramatic skit
    5—"Talking product"
    9—Other.

P. Style of Product Display.
    1—Product displayed (sitting on stands, tables)
    2—Product illustrated in use (playing with toys, eating cereals)
    3—Product name only (product itself not shown)
    9—Other.

Q. Duration of Display.
    1—Product on screen continually
    2—Product on screen intermittently
    3—Product on screen only briefly
    4—Product not shown.

R. Place Settings.
    1—Home or around home (yard, inside house)
    2—Outside (street, highway, field, open air, playground)
    3—Place of work or profession (office, store)
    4—Public place (restaurant, club, theater, hotel, lobby)
    5—Other
    6—Uncertain.

S. Time Setting.
    1—Historical past
    2—Recent past
    3—Contemporary
    4—Future
    5—Undeterminable.

T. Who "Speaks for" the Product?
    1—Adult male or male voice
    2—Adult female or female voice
    3—Male child

       4—Female child
       5—Other (animal or other male voice)
       6—Other (animal or other female voice)
       9—Undeterminable.

U. Audience Appeal.
       1—Children
       2—Adults
       3—General audience
       4—Parents.

V. Sex and Age Group of Characters. Code the number of each type that has a major or minor role in the commercial—speaking part or acting part. Ignore crowd scenes.
       33—Male child (2-11)
       34—Male teen
       35—Male adult
       36—Female child
       37—Female teen
       38—Female adult
       39—Animals with male qualities (voice, dress)
       40—Animals with female qualities (voice, dress)
       41—Other major characters (monsters, robots, cars with human characteristics, dolls).

W. Ethnic Status.
       42—White
       43—Black
       44—Other minorities (Chinese, Indian, other)
       45—Undeterminable (animals, monsters).

X. General Questions. All CAs. Code 0 = no; 1 = yes. Explain in space provided.
       46—Personality tie-in: Is any program personality, sports figure, figure in the news, or primary cartoon character used in the CA?
       47—Program tie-in: Does host give or participate in announcement, or do characters from the adjacent program give, or are they included in, the CA?
       48—Endorsement-testimonial: Is there product endorsement or testimonial by a celebrity or famous person? Include sports or entertainment personalities, figures in the news.
       49—Qualifier—audio: Are there any limiting or qualifying phrases given verbally (such as "motors and cars sold separately")?
       50—Qualifier—visual: Limiting or qualifying phrases given visually. Words such as "batteries not included" flashed on screen?
       51—Qualifier—both: Is visual qualifier given simultaneously with audio disclosure?

52—Special effects: Are there any special animation, visual
or sound effects, or photography that might tend to
mislead a child viewer? For instance, close-ups without people or other objects to judge the size of the
product, speeded-up photography to illustrate speed,
"worm's eye" views and special lenses to increase size
effects, psychedelic effects, animation or sparkle on
cereals.

53—Price: Is the price of the product itself given either
visually or verbally?

54—Premium: Is there a premium offer along with purchase
of the product?

55—Contest: Is there an offer to participate in a contest
along with the purchase of the product?

56—Use: Is child or other character shown using the product?

57—Product description: Is size, weight, quantity, ounces,
dimensions, materials, or other information given as
description of the product?

58—Warnings: Are any warnings, cautions about overuse,
or hazards of product given?

59—Selling: Is child urged to ask parent to buy product?

60—Comparative claim: Is there a comparative claim—using
another brand-name product for comparison?

Y. Special Questions.

Toys

61—Is toy shown in other than normal child environment?

62—Is sound of real-life objects attributed to the toy
(for instance, real jet engines)?

63—Are items shown that are not included with the toy
being sold? For instance, trucks shown with little
buildings, streets, and other items, even if all being
sold is the truck?

64—Is more than one item in the CA offered for sale?

Cereals/candies/other foods

61—Any reference to nutritional value ("fortified with
protein," "full of vitamins") or health claims?

62—Is "sweetness" mentioned as a selling point?

63—Is food referred to as a "snack" (for instance, cereals
also advertised as snacks)?

64—Is food product shown or represented as part of a
balanced meal?

65—Is food product shown as a substitute for a balanced
meal?

66—Is "taste" or "flavor" (other than sweetness) used
as a selling point?

67—Is taste or flavor ingredient identified as either
natural or artificial?

68—Is caloric value stated?

Medicines/drugs/vitamins

61—Are pills, bottles, or other product elements shaped
or colored in a special way, or is mention made of
how "appealing" they are in shape or color?

62—Is "medicine" or any similar word used?

63—Are doctors or other medical persons involved in
describing, giving medicine, or otherwise endorsing
the product?

64—Any mention of taste of the pill or medicine such as
"candy-flavored"?

65—Are active ingredients specified?

66—Any reference to, or visual or verbal indication of,
"mood change" as a result of taking medicine?

Movies

61—Is movie other than "G" rated?

III. PROGRAM PROMOTIONAL ANNOUNCEMENTS (PROMOS)

A. Promo. Give correct title of program, station, or other
item that promo is advertising.

B. Description. Give brief but detailed description of promo,
quoting important phrases, characters, other items.

C. ID Number.

D. Duplicate ID Number.

E. Screening Sheet Number. See sec. II, 6.

F. Station. See sec. II, H.

G. Day. Day the promo is aired. See sec. II, I.

H. Time on. See sec. II, J.

I. Length. Code decimal length—0.50, 0.67, 1.50, and so on.

J. Program Number. Code the number of the program that
the promo is advertising according to the program list.

K. Program Format. Code program format of program that
promo is advertising according to program format code
(see sec. I, M).

L. Promo for
1—Next week's program, guests, other items
2—Following program ("Stay tuned for . . .")
3—Another program on the station
4—Station promo (or promo for several programs on the
station).

M. Time of Promoted Program. What time is the advertised
program to be aired?

1—Weekdays 7:00 am to 12 noon
2—Weekdays 12 noon to 6:00 pm
3—Weekdays 6:00 to 9:00 pm
4—Weekdays after 9:00 pm
5—Saturday-Sunday 7:00 am to 12 noon
6—Saturday-Sunday 12 noon to 6:00 pm
7—Saturday-Sunday 6:00 to 9:00 pm
8—Saturday-Sunday after 9:00 pm
9—Unknown, uncertain.

IV. NONCOMMERCIAL (PUBLIC SERVICE) ANNOUNCEMENTS (NCAs)

   A. NCA Title.
   B. Organization/Cause. Who sponsored the NCA (may be stated
       in the NCA or flashed as graphic)?
   C. Description. Brief but detailed summary of chain of events,
       quotations.
   D. ID Number (001-   ).
   E. Duplicate ID Number.
   F. Screening Sheet Number (001-   ).
   G. Station Code. See sec. II, H.
   H. Day. See sec. II, I.
   I. Time on. Code actual time according to "Time on" listing,
       sec. II, J.
   J. Length. Code decimal length, such as 0.50, 0.67, 1.50.
   K. Type.
       1—Animated
       2—Nonanimated
       3—Mixed.
   L. Format.
       1—Off-stage voice giving the message or commenting on the
          action in the NCA
       2—On-stage announcer
       3—Musical structure
       4—Short dramatic skit
       5—Talking product
       9—Other.
   M. Who "Speaks for" the Product, Organization, Cause?
       1—Adult male or male voice
       2—Adult female or female voice
       3—Male child
       4—Female child
       5—Other; animal with male voice
       6—Other; animal with female voice
       9—Other; general.

N. Audience.
   1—Children
   2—Adults
   3—General audience
   4—Parents.

O. Number and Type of Characters in NCA. Code number of each type that has a major or minor role in the NCA.
   21—Male child (2-11)
   22—Male teen
   23—Male adult
   24—Female child
   25—Female teen
   26—Female adult
   27—Animals and others with male qualities (voice, dress)
   28—Animals and others with female qualities (voice, dress)
   29—Other major characters (monsters, robots, dolls).

P. Ethnic Status of Characters. Code number, as above.
   30—White
   31—Black
   32—Other minorities
   33—Undeterminable (animals, monsters)
   34—Crowd scene (quick cuts, nondistinguishable groups of characters).

Q. Cause.
   01—Animal care: MSPCA, Humane Society
   02—Anti-discrimination: brotherhood, H.E.W., Campaign for Human Development, equal rights
   03—Athletics: good sports competition, AAU Jr. Olympics, Olympics
   04—Boston Bicentennial: Boston 200
   05—Consumerism: Better Business Bureau, Junior Consumer Tip
   06—Ecology/anti-pollution/anti-litter: Keep America Beautiful, recycling, Give a Hoot, Don't Pollute, USDA, Forestry Service
   07—Government organizations: IRS, Postal Service, Massachusetts Department of Commerce, Division of Tourism
   08—Health: anti-smoking, Lung Association, exercise, dental care, American Dental Association
   09—Museums/science and the arts: Museum of Science, Museum of Fine Arts, Worcester Science Center, Boston Children's Theater
   10—Nutrition: nutrition labeling, eat a good breakfast, eat fresh fruits, Dairy Council

11—Reading/education: Smithsonian Institution, RIF

12—Religious and pro-social announcements: sharing, reputation, kindness, growing up

13—Safety: seat belts, National Safety Council, toy safety, bike safety, Red Cross

14—UNICEF/CARE

15—Voluntary help programs: Big Sisters, Foster Parents, Women's ORT, Voluntary Action Center

16—Youth organizations; Girls Clubs, Boys Clubs, Girl Scouts, Boy Scouts, Cub Scouts, Camp Fire Girls, YMCA.

Market Number	Market	Station	Channel
1	New York	WNEW	5
		WOR	9
		WPIX	11
		WXTV	41
		WNJV	47
		WSNL	67
2	Los Angeles	KTLA	5
		KHJ	9
		KTTV	11
		KCOP	13
		KWHY	22
		KMEX	34
		KXLA	40
3	Chicago	WGN	9
		WCIU	26
		WFLD	32
		WSNS	44
4	Philadelphia	WPHL	17
		WTAF	29
		WKBS	48
5	Boston	WSBK	38
		WLVI	56
6	San Francisco	KEMO	20
		KGSC	36
		KBHK	44
		KTVU	2
7	Detroit	WXON	20
		WKBD	50
8	Washington, D.C.	WTTG	5
		WDCA	20
9	Cleveland	WUAB	43
		WKBF	61
10	Pittsburgh	WPGH	53
11	Dallas-Ft. Worth	KTVT	11
		KXTX	3

Market Number	Market	Station	Channel
12	St. Louis	KPLR	11
		KDNL	30
13	Minneapolis-St. Paul	WCTN	11
14	Houston	KVRL	26
		KHTV	39
15	Miami	WCIX	6
		WLTV	23
16	Atlanta	WTCG	17
		WHAE	46
17	Tampa-St. Petersburg	WTOG	44
18	Seattle-Tacoma	KSTW	11
19	Baltimore	WBFF	45
20	Indianapolis	WHMB	40
		WTTV	4
21	Hartford-New Haven	WHCT	18
22	Cincinnati	WXIX	19
23	Kansas City, Mo.	KBMA	41
24	Milwaukee	WVTV	18
25	Portland, Ore.	KPTV	12
26	Sacramento-Stockton	KTXL	40
27	Denver	KWGN	2
28	Buffalo	WUTV	29
31	San Diego	XETV	Tijuana
34	Charlotte, N.C.	WRET	36
35	Phoenix	KPHO	5
36	New Orleans	WGNO	26
37	Louisville	WDRB	41
39	Greenville-Spartenburg, S.C.	WGGS	16
44	Orlando-Daytona Beach, Fla.	WSWB	35
47	San Antonio, Tex.	KWEX	41
49	Norfolk-Portsmouth, Va.	WYAH	27
71	Paducah, Ky.-Cape Girardeau, Mo.	WDXR	29
73	Fresno, Calif.	KFTV	21
		KAIL	53
76	Chattanooga, Tenn.	WRIP	61
86	South Bend-Elkhart, Ind.	WMSH	46
95	Tucson, Ariz.	KZAZ	11
140	Las Vegas	KVVU	5

BOSTON WEEKEND PROGRAMS

WBZ, Channel 4 (NBC)

Time on	Program Title/Segment
Saturday, April 12, 1975	
7:00 am	For Kids Only
7:30 am	Run Joe Run
8:00 am	Addams Family
8:30 am	Wheelie and the Chopper Bunch
9:00 am	Emergency Plus 4
9:30 am	Something Else
10:00 am	Land of the Lost
10:30 am	Sigmund
11:00 am	Pink Panther
11:30 am	(News—not recorded)
12:00 noon	Jetsons
12:30 pm	Go
1:00 pm	Star Trek
Sunday, April 27, 1975	
10:30 am	For Kids Only

WCVB, Channel 5 (ABC)

Saturday, April 12, 1975	
7:00 am	Jabberwockey
7:30 am	Vision on
8:00 am	Yogi Bear
8:26 am	Grammar Book (adverbs)
8:30 am	Bugs Bunny
8:32	"Shish-Ka-Bugs"
8:41	"Who's Kitten Who?"
8:49	"Bewitched Bunny"
9:00 am	Hong Kong Phooey
9:26 am	Grammar Rock (Mayflower)
9:30 am	Gilligan
10:00 am	Devlin
10:30 am	Lassie's Rescue Rangers
10:55 am	Grammar Rock (nouns)
11:00 am	Leave It to Beaver

Time on	Program Title/Segment

Sunday, April 27, 1975
  7:00 am   Make a Wish
  7:26 am   Grammar Rock
  7:30 am   Davey and Goliath
  8:00 am   Nature World of Captain Bob
  8:30 am   Goober
  9:00 am   Jabberwockey

WNAC, Channel 7 (CBS)
  Saturday, April 12, 1975
    7:00 am   U.S. of Archie (Fulton's Folly)
    7:26 am   In the News (Crumbling Cathedrals)
    7:30 am   Bailey's Comets
      7:31   "Heading Home"
      7:44   "Kenya Catch That Clue"
    7:56 am   In the News (Work Time)
    8:00 am   My Favorite Martian
    8:26 am   In the News (Lady Umpire)
    8:30 am   Speed Buggy
    8:57 am   In the News (Bell Ringer)
    9:00 am   I Dream of Jeannie
    9:26 am   In the News (Wildlife Letters)
    9:30 am   Pebbles and Bamm Bamm (Frog for a Day)
    9:56 am   In the News (Sea Otter)
  10:00 am   Scooby Doo Where Are You? (What a Night for a Knight)
  10:26 am   In the News (Victorian Man)
  10:30 am   Shazam
  10:56 am   In the News (Studying Marriage)
  11:00 am   Valley of the Dinosaurs
  11:26 am   In the News (Party Host)
  11:30 am   Hudson Brothers Razzle Dazzle Show
  11:56 am   In the News (Ch!ang Kai-shek Dies)
  12:00 noon Harlem Globe Trotters Popcorn Machine
  12:26 pm   In the News (Baby Lift)
  12:30 pm   Fat Albert and the Cosby Kids
  12:56 pm   In the News (Americans Escape from Cambodia)
   1:00 pm   What's the Senate All About?

WSBK, Channel 38 (Independent)
  Sunday, April 27, 1975
    8:00 am   Nutty Squirrels
      8:01   "A Horse for Dinner"
      8:07   "The Soccer Game"

Time on	Program Title/Segment
8:15	"Sheepy Wolf"–Ricochet Rabbit
8:23	"The Foxy Wolf
8:30 am	Mr. Magoo and Friends
8:31	"Hamlet on Rye"
8:35	"Tycoon Land"
8:39	"Night Fright"
8:46	"Lippy the Lion"–Hoots and Saddles
8:53	"Raw Raw Rooster"
9:00 am	Wally Gator and Friends
9:01	"Bachelor Buttons"
9:05	"Rapid Romance"–Ricochet Rabbit and Droop-a-long
9:14	"Royal Rhubarb"–Yippee Yappee and Ya Hooey
9:22	"Steal Wool"
9:30 am	Mel-O-Tunes
9:31	"Miguel the Mighty Matador"
9:35	"Ugly Ducklings"
9:39	"Daniel Boone"
9:46	"Laugh a Loaf"–Lippy the Lion and Hardy Har Har
9:53	"Gasomer Wump"
10:00 am	Porky Pig and Friends
10:01	"Porky's Price Horse"
10:07	"Hook, Line and Stinker"
10:15	"Like Wild Man"–Touché Turtle and Dum Dum
10:22	"Porky's Romance
10:30 am	Bugs Bunny and Friends
10:32	"Southern Fried Rabbit"
10:37	"Zipping Along"
10:46	"Zero Hero"–Touché Turtle and Dum Dum
10:53	"Gone Batty"
11:00 am	Rocky and His Friends
11:05	"Fractured Fairy Tales"
11:12	"5, 4, 3, 2, 1 or the Quick Launch Counter"
11:19	"Dudley Do-Right of the Mounties"

WLVI, Channel 56 (Independent)
Sunday, April 27, 1975

10:00 am	Flintstones
10:30 am	Little Rascals
10:31	"Our Gang in Farm Hands"
10:39	"Hook and Ladder"
11:00 am	Gilligan's Island
11:30 am	I Love Lucy

INDEPENDENT STATION PROGRAMS

WNEW, Channel 5, New York City
<u>Time on</u>   <u>Program Title/Segment</u>
Friday, June 13, 1975

3:00 pm	Casper and Friends
3:01	"To Boo or not to Boo"
3:12	"Miners Forty-Niners"
3:21	"The Crackpot Quail"
3:30 pm	Huckleberry Hound and Friends
3:30	"Rustler Hustler Huck"
3:42	"Locomotive Loco"—Quick Draw McGraw
3:50	"The Egg Collector"
4:00 pm	The Hilarious House of Frightenstein
4:30 pm	The Bugs Bunny Show
4:31	"Hare Tonic"
4:43	"Bug Parade"
4:52	"The Grey Hounded Hare"
5:00 pm	The Mickey Mouse Club
5:01	Rodeo Talent Roundup
5:15	"Mystery of the Applegate Treasure"—Hardy Boys
5:30 pm	The Flintstones

WDCA, Channel 20, Washington, D.C.
Monday, June 16, 1975

3:00 pm	Banana Splits (The Conquistador's Curse)
3:30 pm	Marine Boy
4:00 pm	Speed Racer (Girl Daredevil)
4:30 pm	Bugs Bunny and Friends
4:30	"Bowery Bugs"
4:39	"Daffy Duck Hunt"—Porky Pig
4:48	"Sunny Italy"—Mighty Mouse
4:55 pm	Three Stooges
5:15	"The Stowaways"—Heckle and Jeckle
5:23	"A Bone for a Bone"
5:30 pm	Gilligan's Island

WUTV, Channel 29, Buffalo
Monday, June 16, 1975

3:00 pm	Kid Komix
3:00	"Little Ceasarie"
3:08	"Pied Piper Pipe"—Pixie and Dixie
3:16	"Barney Bear's Victory Garden"
3:27	"It's a Worm Day"—Augie Doggie and Doggie Daddy
3:36	"Superboy's Super Dilemma"—Superboy

Time on	Program Title/Segment
3:42	"Innertube Antics"
3:51	"Six Gun Spook"—Quick Draw McGraw
4:00 pm	Kid Komix
4:00	"Sky Princess"—Madcap Models
4:10	"The Cage of Glass"—Superman
4:16	"Brainiac's Bubbles"—Superman
4:24	"Teacher's Pest"—Novelteen
4:30 pm	The Mickey Mouse Club
5:00 pm	Star Trek (The Alternative Factor)
5:58 pm	News Capsule for the Deaf

WKBD, Channel 50, Detroit
Tuesday, June 17, 1975

3:00 pm	Pat O'Brien-Bill Kennedy Movie, "Riff Raff"
3:30 pm	Banana Splits and Friends (The Adventures of Gulliver)
4:00 pm	Addams Family
4:30 pm	Munsters
5:00 pm	Lost in Space (The Raft)

WVTV, Channel 18, Milwaukee
Wednesday, June 18, 1975

3:00 pm	Popeye the Sailor
3:00	"Oil's Well That Ends Well"
3:08	"Meter Knocks"
3:13	"Amusement Park"
3:20	"Duel to the Finish"
3:30 pm	Mickey Mouse Club
3:30	"A Pirate's Chest"—Hardy Boys
3:49	"Toby Tortoise Returns"
4:00 pm	The Flintstones
4:30 pm	The Munsters (My Fair Munster)
5:00 pm	I love Lucy
5:30 pm	The Dick Van Dyke Show (The Life and Love of Joe Coogan)

WDRB, Channel 41, Louisville
Thursday, June 19, 1975

3:00 pm	Presto the Clown
3:00	"Johnny Smith and Poker Hunto"
3:30	"Dog Pounded"—Yankee Doodle
3:40	"Katnip Kollege"
4:00 pm	Three Stooges
4:00	"Hold That Lion"
4:23	"I'm a Big Shot Now"

Time on	Program Title/Segment
4:30 pm	Leave It to Beaver
5:00 pm	Batman Hour
5:30	"While Gotham City Burns"

WYAH, Channel 27, Norfolk/Portsmouth
Tuesday, June 17, 1975

3:00 pm	Timmy and Lassie
3:30 pm	Little Rascals
3:30	"For Pete's Sake"
3:47	"Washee Ironee"
4:00 pm	Flintstones
4:30 pm	Room 222
5:00 pm	Leave It to Beaver
5:30 pm	Hazel

WTCG, Channel 17, Atlanta
Wednesday, June 18, 1975

3:00 pm	Baseball game—Atlanta vs. Cincinnati
3:10 pm	Felix the Cat
3:20 pm	Popeye the Sailor (The Ghost Host)
3:33 pm	Mickey Mouse Club
3:52	"Father Noah's Ark"
4:03 pm	Munsters
4:31 pm	Leave It to Beaver (Kite Day)
5:01 pm	I Love Lucy
5:31 pm	Hazel

KSTW, Channel 11, Tacoma-Seattle
Thursday, June 19, 1975

3:00 pm	Casper and Friends
3:00	"Casper's Spree Under the Sea"
3:09	"Barbecue Magoo"—Mr. Magoo
3:14	"Aladdin's Lampoon"—Touché Turtle and Dum Dum
3:21	"Scaredy Cat"
3:30 pm	Flintstones
4:00 pm	Mickey Mouse Club (Circus Day)
4:24 pm	Munsters
5:01 pm	Leave It to Beaver
5:31 pm	Bewitched

KXTL, Channel 40, Sacramento
Tuesday, July 1, 1975

3:00 pm	Captain Mitch
3:03	"Cactus Makes Perfect"—Three Stooges

Time on	Program Title/Segment
3:23	"Napoleon Bunny Part"—Bugs Bunny
3:31 pm	Batman
4:00 pm	Mickey Mouse Club
4:02	Tuesday, guest star day
4:13	"Mickey's Mechanical Man"
4:30 pm	Partridge Family
5:00 pm	Mod Squad

HUMAN VIOLENCE WITH WEAPONS

Humorous Contexts (Comedy Drama)

"Shish-ka-Bugs" (Bugs Bunny)—Cook threatens Bugs Bunny with a
meat cleaver (cook is human).

"Bewitched Bunny" (Bugs Bunny)—Witch chases Bugs Bunny with a
cleaver (witch is human).

"Rapid Romance" (Ricochet Rabbit)—Guns are fired; their bullets
turn into mallets that hit Rabbit over the head.

"Royal Rhubarb" (Yippee Yappee and Ya Hooey)—Spears hurled at
king, swords thrown at knight, bombs thrown, knight and guards
shot out of cannon, king shot with slingshot and sent underwater
with dynamite.

"Steal Wool" (Looney Tunes)—Cannon, lever, and slingshot used by
Ralph, who is injured by slingshot.

"Southern Fried Rabbit" (Bugs Bunny)—Yosemite Sam shoots at Bugs,
Sam is blasted with a cannon.

"Gone Batty" (Merry Melodies)—Catcher breaks bat over runner's
head. Players are hit with the ball, causing four bumps on the
head.

"Zipping Along" (Roadrunner)—Bird and coyote considered animals,
since they don't speak or exhibit human characteristics. Hand
grenade explodes in coyote's mouth, coyote is caught in mouse
trap he set for roadrunner, coyote launches himself with kite
and bomb, exploding when he hits ground. TNT explodes, rifles
fire at coyote, wrecker ball intended for bird falls on coyote.

"Zero Hero" (Touché Turtle and Dum Dum)—Touché stabs gorilla
with sword.

"Hook, Line and Stinker" (Roadrunner)—Sledgehammer's loose head
hits coyote, dynamite trap intended for bird explodes on coyote,
cannonball lands on coyote's head.

"Like Wild Man" (Touché Turtle and Dum Dum)—Saturday is hit
over head with club and gun is stolen. Saturday shoots at Crusoe.
Wild man threatened with sword, turtle is machine-gunned.

"Porky's Romance" (Porky Pig)—Petunia hits Porky over head with
a rolling pin.

"Genie with the Light Pink Fur" (New Pink Panther Show)—PP is hit
with hockey stick by kid on skate board.

Addams Family—Addams Family goes to Indianapolis Speedway. In
car race between Count Evil and Flash Jorden, the Count uses
a high-powered arrow to puncture the gas tank of his competitor.
Violence intended to foil Flash's chance of winning the race.
No bodily injury was inflicted.

"Ugly Duckling" (Mel-O-Tunes)—Shotguns shoot at ducks (represented
as animals).

"Daniel Boone" (Mel-O-Tunes)—Daniel Boone shoots in a hunting
scene and throws a knife.

"Laugh-a-Loaf" (Lippy the Lion)—Hardy hits Lippy over the head
with a club.

"Heading Nome" (Bailey's Comets)—Clues of bones are shot by
opponents of Comets. Ray gun is used to destroy the temple
clue—violence is used to destroy clues rather than to harm
people.

"Kenya Catch That Clue" (Bailey's Comets)—Giant brick used to
crash car, elevator crashes, glue is used to coat team and
slow them up. Much of the violence is implied rather than
shown, and it is directed at foiling the Comet's chances of
winning, not at the members themselves.

Wheelie and the Chopper Bunch—Motorcycle gang erects roadblock
to stop Wheelie and prevent him from passing road test; Chopper
Bunch is smashed at police roadblock.

Rocky and His Friends—Boris uses a "goof gas" gun on guard.

"5, 4, 3, 2, 1, or the Quick Launch Counter" (Rocky and His Friends)—
Boris uses "goof gas" gun, missiles drop on Potsylvania. Rocky
loses his fur as a result of "goof gas" and scientists become
goofy.

"Dudley Do-Right of the Mounties" (Rocky and His Friends)—Nasty
Noogle uses a gun, bomb, and axe. Violence is directed at
Inspector Fenwick.

Flintstones—Wilma bangs Fred over head with frying pan and hits
Hot Lips on head with her pocketbook.

"Hamlet on Rye" (Mr. Magoo)—Plane crashes, cat is caught in a
trap and vase falls on its head. Magoo beats cat on head with
broom for causing damage.

"Tycoon Land" (Mr. Magoo)—Magoo hits walrus over the head with
wrench.

"Night Fright" (Mr. Magoo)—Cicero is spun through a washing
machine, hit over the head with a bat, slips on a banana peel,
and is shot by Magoo when he is mistaken for a prowler.

"Hoots and Saddles" (Lippy the Lion)—Lippy tries to capture an
escaping horse that is to perform in a contest. He tries to rope
him, fails, and crashes; tries a jet-powered pogo stick, drills
himself into the ground, and blows himself up with dynamite
(horse is animal).

"Raw Raw Rooster" (Merry Melodies)—Foghorn tries to avoid contact with old school chum, Rodh Island. Foghorn squirts him, sets up a punching camera, shooting camera, exploding casava melon, and exploding golf ball—which all backfire and blow up in Foghorn's face.

"The Foxy Wolf" (Nutty Squirrel)—Barnyard animals shoot at foxy wolf.

"Sheepy Wolf" (Nutty Squirrel)—Ricochet and Chavez shoot guns.

"A Horse for Dinner" (Nutty Squirrel)—Horse reroutes banister, which propels blacksmith through roof.

Gilligan's Island—Imposter hits Howell over head with coconut and knocks him out.

Action-Adventure Drama

Lassie's Rescue Rangers—Building is dynamited in bank robbery. Science lab is dynamited and robots killed.

Speed Buggy—Freeze ray and snowball shooter are used to capture car and crew; robots melt.

VIOLENCE WITHOUT WEAPONS

Humorous Context (Comedy Drama)

"Who's Kitten Who?" (Bugs Bunny)—Baby Kangaroo is delivered to Sylvester's house in crate—it uses its fists and feet to kick its way out. (Kangaroo depicted as animal.) Sylvester and kangaroo fight each other. Sylvester is beaten up.

Hong Kong Phooey—"In-nose" man attempts to drown brothers of mystery man.

"Bachelor Buttons" (Wally Gator)—Ella Gator punches Wally, grabs his tail and smashes him, then does the same to a lion.

"Porky's Prize Horse" (Porky Pig)—Clumsy horse crashes through window while jumping.

"Piccadilly Circus" (Pink Panther Show)—Wife slips on items on floor and falls with her bundles.

"Science Friction" (Pink Panther Show)—Anteater is thrown out of laboratory, against tree, and nose is battered. Anteater is kicked (anteater is animal).

Goober—Captain Ahoy captures smugglers.

Sigmund and the Sea Monsters—Sea monsters drag off Sigmund with their tentacles.

"What a Night for a Knight" (Scooby Doo, Where Are You?)—Knight
   attempts to punch, damages picture.
"Rapid Romance" (Ricochet Rabbit)—Slap Jack Rabbit makes punching
   bag out of Rabbit; twists his foot and hits him.
"Royal Rhubarb" (Yippee Yappee and Ya Hooey)—Kings hits tower.
   Knight smashes guard and kings.
"Steal Wool" (Looney Tunes)—Sam punches Ralph every time he tries
   to steal a sheep.
"Gone Batty" (Merry Melodies)—Goon punches umpire.
"Zero Hero" (Touché Turtle and Dum Dum)—Bong is gorilla who
   escaped from circus. Touché Turtle in attempt to capture Bong
   is smashed in his hands.
"Like Wild Man" (Touché Turtle)—Woman jumps from burning build-
   ing and crashes turtle into ground.
"Genie with the Light Pink Fur" (New Pink Panther Show)—PP is
   kicked while he is in Aladdin's lamp becoming a genie. PP is
   burned with hot water and thrown in a city dump.
"Heading Nome" (Bailey's Comets)—Tail of whale hits entire Comets
   team.
"Kenya Catch That Clue" (Bailey's Comets)—Lion attacks hero (not
   actually seen). Bees attack bears.
"Foxy Wolf" (Nutty Squirrel)—Clara is carried in jaws of foxy wolf.
"Our Gang in Farm Hands" (Little Rascals)—Froggy thrown off horse,
   falls on ground.
I Love Lucy—Boy for whom Lucy is baby-sitting kicks her in the shins
   several times.

Action-Adventure Drama

"Else When" (Land of the Lost)—Monsters try to strangle Dad and
   Will, then tie them up.

NATURAL VIOLENCE

Humorous Context

Fat Albert and the Cosby Kids—Thurin falls off things by accident
   and hurts himself.
"Heading Nome" (Bailey's Comets)—A waterfall pours over the team,
   which is trapped in a snowball.
My Favorite Martian—Brennan gets an electric shock. Glider plane
   crashes through window, into door and rain barrel.

"Fulton's Folly" (U.S. of Archie)—Two explosions in science lab, several ships sink.

"Hook, Line and Stinker" (Roadrunner)—Coyote is struck by lightning.

"5, 4, 3, 2, 1, or the Quick Launch Counter" (Rocky and His Friends)— Hot air singes Rocky's fur.

"Hook and Ladder" (Little Rascals)—Fire in barn. Dynamite is thrown out window and explodes.

Action Adventure Drama

"The Magics of Megas-Tu" (Star Trek)—Winds and lightning rock the Enterprise, slightly injuring crew; Kirk falls and hurts his head.

Run Joe Run—Fire results in child being burned.

Emergency Plus Four—Tornado whips through town. Old man's arm injured while he is escaping from the shack that fell because of the storm.

Shazam—Rattlesnake poisons Danny and he is trapped by falling rock slide.

BOSTON WEEKEND TELEVISION

Company	Product	Number of Times Broadcast
Toys		
Cars, planes, other		
Amsco	Sky-Ace	1
Amsco	Skywinder	1
Ideal	Evel Knievel stunt stadium	2
Kenner	Blazin' SSP with ultra chrome and ultra sonic sound	7
Kenner	TTP tower and car	2
Kenner	TTP wild riders	1
Lesney Prod.	Match Box cars	3
Marx	Big Wheel	3
Dolls		
Hasbro	G.I. Joe with Kung Fu grip	3
Hasbro	G.I. Joe adventure sets	5
Kenner	Dusty doll (1)	6
Kenner	Dusty doll (2)	2
Marx	Best of the West collection	2
Mattel	Barbie's World	1
Mattel	Dr. Steele doll	2
Mattel	Gold Medal PJ doll	2
Mego	Wizard of Oz dolls and sets of Emerald City	3
Romper Room	Mr. Potato Head	1
Indoor games		
Topps	Topps baseball cards	2
Outdoor games		
Fonas	Johnny Bench Batter-up	5
?	Puffer kite	1
Other toys and hobbies		
Huffy	Thunder Road bike	2
Kenner	Ice Bird	3
Living World	Habitrail hamster home	3
Living World	Habitrail	1
Sears	Free Spirit ten-speed bike	3

Company	Product	Number of Times Broadcast
U.S. Postal Service	stamp kit	3
U.S. Postal Service	mint set (1974)	1
Wham-O	Super Elastic bubble plastic	1
?	gumball bank	1
Breakfast cereals		
General cereal commercial		
Kellogg's	"Break the fast with a good breakfast"	1
Nonsugared cereals		
General Mills	Cheerios (1)	3
General Mills	Cheerios (2)	2
General Mills	Cheerios (3)	2
General Mills	Cheerios (4)	3
Kellogg's	Raisin Bran (1)	2
Kellogg's	Raisin Bran (2)	1
Kellogg's	Rice Krispies (1)	3
Kellogg's	Rice Krispies (2)	3
Kellogg's	Rice Krispies (3)	1
Kellogg's	Rice Krispies (4)	4
Sugared cereals		
General Mills	Lucky Charms (1)	2
General Mills	Lucky Charms (2)	2
General Mills	Trix (1)	1
General Mills	Trix (2)	4
General Mills	Cocoa Puffs	7
General Mills	Fruit Brute (1)	5
General Mills	Fruit Brute (2)	1
Kellogg's	Sugar Pops (1)	1
Kellogg's	Sugar Pops (2)	1
Kellogg's	Sugar Frosted Flakes (1)	3
Kellogg's	Sugar Frosted Flakes (2)	3
Kellogg's	Sugar Frosted Flakes (3)	2
Kellogg's	Froot Loops (1)	1
Kellogg's	Froot Loops (2)	2
Kellogg's	Apple Jacks	1
Kellogg's	Cocoa Krispies	1
Nabisco	Klondike Pete's Crunchy Nuggets (1)	1
Nabisco	Klondike Pete's Crunchy Nuggets (2)	2
Post	Super Sugar Crisp	8

Company	Product	Number of Times Broadcast
Post	Honeycombs	3
Post	Alpha-Bits (1)	4
Post	Alpha-Bits (2)	4
Post	Cocoa Pebbles and Fruity Pebbles	8
Ralston Purina	Freakies (1)	4
Ralston Purina	Freakies (2)	4
Candy and sweets		
Candy		
Hershey's	Hershey's milk chocolate bar (1)	2
Hershey's	Hershey's milk chocolate bar (2)	4
Lifesavers	Lifesaver lollipops	4
Lifesavers	Lifesaver rolls	5
Nestle's	Chocolite	8
Nestle's	Nestle's Crunch	1
Reese's	Reese's peanut butter cups (1)	5
Reese's	Reese's peanut butter cups (2)	3
Tootsie Roll	Tootsie Roll sweepstakes	4
?	Razzles candy (candy and gum)	2
Mars	Snickers chocolate peanut bar (1)	1
Mars	Snickers chocolate peanut bar (2)	2
?	M & Ms	1
Mars	Three Musketeers	3
Mars	Milky Way	2
Chewing gum (regular)		
Beechnut	Fruit Stripe gum	1
Beechnut	Fruit Stripe gum/Sour Bites	1
Cakes and cookies		
Hostess	Hostess fruit pies	1
Keebler	Fudge Stripes, Fudge Sticks Fudge Grahams (cookies)	2
Kellogg's	Pop Tarts toasted pastries (1)	2
Kellogg's	Pop Tarts toasted pastries (2)	1
Nabisco	Chips Ahoy cookies	3
Nabisco	'Nilla Wafers	1
Nabisco	Nutter Butter cookies	3
Nabisco	Oreo cookies	4

Company	Product	Number of Times Broadcast
Pillsbury	Chocolate chip cookies (slice and bake)	4
Fruit-flavored drinks and ices		
Kool Aid	Kool Aid soft drink mix (1)	6
Kool Aid	Kool Aid soft drink mix (2)	9
?	Tang (1)	1
?	Tang (2)	1
?	Tang (3)	3
Ice cream, puddings, desserts		
Hood	Hoodwinks ice cream	3
Hunt-Wesson	Snack Pak pudding	1
Nestle's	Quik (drink mix)	5
Snack foods		
Frito-Lay	Cheetos (1)	1
Frito-Lay	Cheetos (2)	1
Frito-Lay	Cheetos (3)	2
Frito-Lay	Fritos corn chips	1
Kraft	Koogle chocolate peanut spread	6
Kraft	Koogle peanut spread	5
Other foods		
Canned and packaged prepared foods		
Chef Boyardee	Mini-ravioli	1
Chef Boyardee	Rollercoasters/spaghetti and meatballs	2
Fruits		
Sunkist	navel oranges (1)	3
Sunkist	navel oranges (2)	2
Bread		
Sunbeam	Sunbeam bread (1)	1
Sunbeam	Sunbeam bread (2)	1
Dairy products		
Kraft	Philadelphia imitation cream cheese	1
Hood	Firm and Fruity yogurt	4
Restaurants, Supermarkets		
Restaurants		
Arby's	Arby's roast beef sandwich sale	2
Brigham's	Brigham's birthday party	7
Burger King	Burger King french fries	9
Dairy Queen	Dairy Queen (1)	1

Company	Product	Number of Times Broadcast
Dairy Queen	Dairy Queen ice cream cones (2)	1
Dairy Queen	Dairy Queen (3)	1
Ground Round	Ground Round clown with games	2
Ground Round	Ground Round clown drawing contest	2
McDonald's	McDonald's restaurant (1)	2
McDonald's	McDonald's (2)	3
McDonald's	McDonald's (3)	1
McDonald's	McDonald's fillet of fish (4)	1
McDonald's	McDonald's (5)	1
Papa Gino's	Pizza restaurants and flying pizza frisbee dish	7
Supermarkets		
Stop and Shop	Stop and Shop canned pears (1)	1
Stop and Shop	Stop and Shop canned pears (2)	1
Household Products		
Cleansers and detergents		
Cascade	Cascade dishwasher detergent	1
Other household products		
Dixie	Knock Knock Dixie Cups	4
Personal care products		
Clothing		
?	Buster Brown shoes	4
?	Levi's pants	2
Other personal products		
?	Crazy Foam	1
?	Mr. Bubble	5
Kenner	Snoopy soaper	1
Other miscellaneous products		
Motion pictures		
Paramont Pictures	Charlotte's Web	4
Walt Disney	Escape to Witch Mountain (1)	5
Walt Disney	Escape to Witch Mountain (2)	2
Walt Disney	Escape to Witch Mountain (3)	1
Walt Disney	Superbug	17
Walt Disney	Bambi	1
Travel offers		
Crimson Travel	Disney World and Cypress Gardens, Florida, family package	2

Company	Product	Number of Times Broadcast
Crimson Travel	Weekends to Montreal	1
Crimson Travel	Martinique week	1
Record offers		
Warners	Heavy Metal	1
MGM	MGM records and tapes	1
Recreation		
?	Antique, flea, and craft show	1
Books		
U.S. Postal Service	Stamps and Stories (stamp book)	1

INDEPENDENT STATIONS

Company	Product	Number of Times Broadcast
Toys		
Dolls		
Hasbro	G.I. Joe Sky Hawk	12
Ideal	Evel Knievel	6
Ideal	Evel Knievel trail bike and chopper	1
Ideal	Baby Dreams	2
Ideal	Tiffany Taylor	10
Mattel	Barbie's dream boat	7
Mattel	Growing up Skipper	2
Mattel	Sunshine Family van	3
Meego	Planet of the Apes toys	1
Meego	Star Trek figures	4
Romper Room	Weeble tree house	12
Indoor games		
Remco	Magic Hat	1
Duncan	Duncan yoyo	1
?	Pachinko Palace games	1
Outdoor games and toys		
Chemtoy	Bubble Bee bubbles	3
Marx	Prop Shots	3
Romper Room	Inch Worm	4
Wham-O	Super Pro frisbee	3
Wham-O	Water Wiennie, Monster Bubbles, Zillion Bubbles	2

Company	Product	Number of Times Broadcast
Wham-O	Water Wiggle	4
Wham-O	Mickey Mouse bicycle safety flag	2
Other toys, hobbies, and crafts		
Hasbro	Snowman sno cones	2
Hot Items	Press and Blow Bubbles– Flintstones, Planet of the Apes	2
Mattel	Spin Welder aeroplane factory	1
?	Krazy Straws	1
Breakfast cereals		
Sugared cereals		
General Mills	Lucky Charms (1)	1
General Mills	Lucky Charms (2)	7
General Mills	Trix (1)	3
General Mills	Trix (2)	1
General Mills	Trix (3)	5
General Mills	Fruit Brute	10
General Mills	Boo Berry	2
General Mills	Cocoa Puffs	6
Kelloggs	Froot Loops	1
Kelloggs	Sugar Frosted Flakes (1)	3
Kelloggs	Sugar Frosted Flakes (2)	1
Kelloggs	Sugar Frosted Flakes (3)	3
Kelloggs	Sugar Smacks (1)	1
Kelloggs	Sugar Smacks (2)	1
Kelloggs	Sugar Smacks (3)	1
Kelloggs	Sugar Pops (1)	1
Kelloggs	Sugar Pops (2)	1
Post	Alphabits	1
Post	Honeycombs	4
Post	Super Sugar Crisp (1)	1
Post	Super Sugar Crisp (2)	4
Post	Cocoa Pebbles/Fruity Pebbles	2
Post	Captain Crunch/Crunchberry	2
Nonsugared cereals		
General Mills	Cheerios	14
Kelloggs	Raisin Bran	3
Kelloggs	Rice Krispies (1)	2
Kelloggs	Rice Krispies (2)	1

Company	Product	Number of Times Broadcast
Kelloggs	Rice Krispies (3)	3
Candy and sweets		
Candy bars and packaged candy		
Certs	Certs breath mints (1)	2
Certs	Certs breath mints (2)	1
Charms	Charms Big Pops (1)	6
Charms	Charms Big Pops (2)	1
Dentyne	Dynamints (1)	4
Dentyne	Dynamints (2)	5
Rothchild	Rothchild's candies	1
?	Marathon candy bar	1
?	Skittles Fruit Chews	1
?	Charleston Chews	2
?	Good and Plenty	1
Chewing gum (sugarless)		
Trident	Trident sugarless gum	1
Chewing gum (regular)		
Wrigley's	Wrigley's spearmint gum (1)	5
Wrigley's	Wrigley's spearmint gum (2)	2
Cakes and cookies		
Hostess	Twinkies	1
Kelloggs	Chocolate-peppermint Pop Tarts	6
Nabisco	Fig Newtons	1
Nabisco	Oreo cookies	1
Nabisco	'Nilla Wafers	2
Sunshine	Chiperoos	2
Sunshine	Hydrox cookies	3
Ice cream, puddings, desserts		
Nestle's	Quik	1
Crystal	Crystal ice cream	1
Soft drinks (carbonated)		
Coca Cola	Sprite	1
Coca Cola	Coke	2
Coca Cola	Tab	1
7-Up	7-Up (bicentennial bottle) (1)	1
7-Up	7-Up (2)	1
7-Up	7-Up (3)	1
?	Frostie root beer	1
?	Mr. Pibb	1
?	Dr. Pepper	1
Pepsi Cola	Pepsi	1

Company	Product	Number of Times Broadcast
Fruit-flavored drinks		
?	Country Time lemonade mix	1
Kool Aid	Kool Aid (lemonade mix) (1)	1
Kool Aid	Kool Aid (2)	2
Kool Aid	Kool Aid (3)	3
Kool Aid	Kool Aid (4)	1
Kool Aid	Kool Aid (5)	1
Other		
Pabst	Pabst Blue Ribbon beer	1
Snack foods		
Potato Chips		
?	Golden Flake potato chips	1
Other snack foods		
Kraft	Cracker Barrel cheese spread	1
Other foods		
Canned and packaged prepared foods		
Campbell's	chicken and noodles/stars/ rice (1)	1
Campbell's	chicken and noodles/stars/ rice (2)	2
Hunt-Wesson	tomato ketchup	1
Franco American	spaghetti and meatballs	1
Fruits		
Sunkist	lemons	1
Meats		
Ball Park	Ball Park hot dogs	1
Milk and Dairy products		
?	milk	1
Other foods		
Henri	Henri's salad dressing	1
Restaurants, groceries, meals		
A & W	A & W root beer stands	1
?	Big T family restaurant– Tastee Freeze	1
Burger Chef	Burger Chef (1)	5
Burger Chef	Burger Chef (2)	2
Burger Queen	Burger Queen restaurant	1
Burger King	Burger King (1)	3
Burger King	Burger King (2)	1
Burger King	Burger King french fries (3)	3

Company	Product	Number of Times Broadcast
Burger King	Burger King double meat hamburgers (4)	5
Cape Codder	Cape Codder restaurant	1
Frishe's	Frishe's restaurant	1
Hardee's	Hardee's (1)	2
Hardee's	Hardee's (2)	1
Hardee's	Hardee's (3)	1
Holly Farms	Holly Farms fried chicken	1
McDonald's	McDonald's (1)	2
McDonald's	McDonald's (2)	2
McDonald's	McDonald's (3)	1
McDonald's	McDonald's (4)	1
McDonald's	McDonald's (5)	2
McDonald's	McDonald's McChicken (6)	1
McDonald's	McDonald's cookies (7)	1
McDonald's	McDonald's Arctic Orange shake (8)	1
Mr. Steak	Mr. Steak restaurant	1
Red Barn	Red Barn restaurant	2
Shakey's	Shakey's Pizza Parlor	1
Spoon and Straw	Spoon and Straw restaurant	1
Straw Hat	Straw Hat Pizza Palace	1
Winchell's	Winchell's Donut House	2
A & P	A & P sale on Bar-B-Que	1
Safeway	Safeway Stores (supermarket)	1
Sentury	Sentury Supermarket	1
Tops	Tops Markets	1
Other		
Bruce Wholesale	Bruce Wholesale frozen foods	1
Household products		
Cleansers and detergents		
?	20-Mule Power bathroom cleaner	1
?	Ever Clear glass cleaner	1
Furniture and appliances		
Hoover	Hoover spin drier	1
Kapecky	Kapecky Mattress Company	1
Maytag	Maytag dishwasher	1
Federal Way	Federal Way furniture store	1
Culligan	Culligan water softener	1
Marsh's	Marsh's carpets	1

Company	Product	Number of Times Broadcast
Tools/hardware		
?	EZ Dun vinyl repair kit	2
?	Famous upholstering	1
K-TEL	Fishing Magician	2
Meridian	Meridian waterproofing	1
?	Port-a-Dolly	1
Western Auto	Total Trim power mower	1
?	Stylette stud setter (1)	1
?	Stylette stud setter (2)	1
Personal care products		
Shampoos and deodorants		
?	Head and Shoulders shampoo	1
Noxell	Noxzema	1
Mennen Co.	Protein 21 shampoo	2
House of Style	Musk Dust deodorant	1
?	Irish Spring soap	1
Health items		
?	Rain Jet rotary massage	1
?	Dyna Gym	1
?	Weider total body shaper	1
?	Sauna Slim suit	4
Clothing		
?	Braves hat offer (tennis hat)	2
?	Braves belt offer	1
?	Braves T-shirt	1
Other personal products		
?	Silken Doll cosmetics	1
Johnson & Johnson	Band-Aids	1
Other miscellaneous products		
Movies		
Walt Disney	Bambi	3
Walt Disney	Benji (1)	1
Walt Disney	Benji (2)	6
Walt Disney	Benji (3)	2
Walt Disney	Aloha Bobby and Rose	1
Walt Disney	New York summer film festival	1
Recreation		
?	Northgate Country Fair	1
?	Falsom Rodeo	1

Company	Product	Number of Times Broadcast
?	California Expo Playland (1)	1
?	California Expo Playland (2)	1
?	America on Parade—Disneyland	2
?	Pollardville Ghost Town	1
?	Sonshine Concert	2
?	Motocross Champion	1
?	Beech Bend International Raceway—super track drag racing	2
?	Beech Bend Park	1
?	River Glen Park	2
?	Fairgrounds Speedway—Joey Chitwood Daredevil Show	3
?	Santa Clausland, Indiana	4
Athletic Matchmakers, Inc.	Wrestling at the Milwaukee Arena	2
?	Big "V" Drum and Bugle Corps Championships, Milwaukee South Statium	1
?	Edgewater Park	2
?	Golden Coach, Detroit, Home of Freddy Bowers Show	1
?	Timber Shores resorts	1
?	harness racing/Buffalo Raceway	1
?	Art Park (1)	1
?	Art Park (2)	1
?	Hershey Park	1
?	N.Y. Cosmos soccer team at Downing Stadium	1
?	Channel 50, Jerseyvision	1
?	Elvis Wade at the Driftwood	1
Books/magazines		
?	TV Guide (1)	1
?	TV Guide (2)	1
Disney Co.	Disney's Wonderful World of Reading	1
?	TV Facts Magazine	2
Time-Life	Old West—Time-Life Books	2
?	War Between the Tates—book	1
?	History's Greatest Headlines	1

Company	Product	Number of Times Broadcast
Record offers		
A & E Enterprises	Basketball record—NBA championships	1
Columbia House	Johnny Mathis record offer	1
GRT Corp.	Wake up Again with the Everly Brothers	1
K-TEL	Sound Spectacular	4
K-TEL	K-TEL record offer	2
Longines Sympho-nette	Greatest Hits of Frankie Valle and the Fabulous Four Seasons	
Longines Sympho-nette	40 Funky Hits	1
Mercury Records	Four-Wheel-Drive Album	1
Motown Records	Motown's Greatest Hits	1
RCA	Elvis Presley record offer	1
Sessions	Freedom Album	1
TV Piko	Music Power	1
Telehouse	Al Jolson record offer	1
Warner's Special Products	Rockin' Easy	1
?	English Cats record offer	1
?	Chubby Checker Rock and Roll	1
?	Great Country Gospel Songs	1
?	At the Hop	3
?	Frankie Laine	2
Automobiles and repairs		
Dodge	Austin Marina—Tysinger Dodge	1
AM	American Motors	1
Chevrolet	Bell Air Chevrolet (trucks)	1
Dodge	Tidewater Dodge car service and tune-up	2
Castillo Chevrolet	Castillo Chevrolet	1
Datsun	Datsun Little Hustler pickup truck	1
Dodge	Dodge	1
Dick Balch	Dick Balch Chevrolet	1
?	Ferry Auto Supplies	1
Goodyear	Goodyear auto service	1
Ford	Harrold Ford	1
Ford	Motorcraft auto parts	1

Company	Product	Number of Times Broadcast
?	J & G Motors	2
Volkswagon	Rabbit	1
Travel offers		
Delta	Delta Airlines	1
Schools		
Sawyer	Sawyer Secretarial School	2
Standard	Standard Technical Institute	1
Lafayette	Lafayette Technical Academy	4
MBTI	MBTI Data Processing School	1
Control Data	Control Data Institute	1
Evelyn Wood	Evelyn Wood Reading Dynamics	4
Hi-fi		
?	Music and Sound, Inc.—equipment	2
Panasonic	Panasonic tape and Dynamite 8	2
Tech Hi-Fi	Tech Hi-Fi	1
?	George's Television and Radio	1
RCA	X-100 television	1
Other		
Sears	Sears department store— 4th of July sale	3
?	Red Horse chewing tobacco	1
?	World Book insurance (for children)	1
?	Mr. Insurance—auto insurance	1
?	Sun's chlorine feeder (for pools)	1
Gimbel's	Gimbel's jade sale	1
?	Computer Date Match	1
?	Sweet Kleen laundry and dry cleaners	1
?	WEAM Radio	1
?	Harrow's swimming pools (1)	1
?	Harrow's swimming pools (2)	1
Speidel	Hang-ups bracelets and pendants	1

BOSTON WEEKEND TELEVISION

	Name of Program	Channel	Number of Promos
Cartoon comedy			
Weekdays 12 noon–6:00pm	Cartoon Carnival	38	1
	Flintstones/Little Rascals	56	1
Sat.–Sun. 7:00am–12 noon	U.S. of Archie	7	1
	New Adventures of Gilligan	5	2
	Hong Kong Phooey	5	2
	Bugs Bunny Show	5	3
Sat.–Sun. 12 noon–6:00pm	Flintstones	56	1
Other comedy drama			
Weekdays 12 noon–6:00pm	I Dream of Jeannie	38	2
	Gilligan's Island	56	1
Weekdays 6:00–9:00pm	Andy Griffith Show	38	1
	Hogan's Heroes	38	2
	Beverly Hillbillies	38	2
	Bewitched	38	1
	Dick Van Dyke Show	38	2
	I Love Lucy	56	1
Sat.–Sun. 7:00am–12 noon	Leave It to Beaver	5	3
	Little Rascals	56	1
Sat.–Sun. 12 noon–6:00pm	Gilligan's Island	56	1
Action-adventure			
Sat.–Sun. 7:00am–12 noon	Devlin	5	1
	Lassie's Rescue Rangers	5	1
	Bailey's Comets	7	1
Variety and quiz			
Weekdays 7:00am–12 noon	Truth or Consequences	7	2
	Password	5	1
Weekdays 12 noon–6:00pm	Merv Griffin Show	7	3
	Mickey Mouse Club	38	3
Weekdays 6:00–9:00pm	What's My Line	7	1
	Tony Orlando and Dawn	7	3

	Name of Program	Channel	Number of Promos
Sat.-Sun. 6:00-9:00pm	Cher	7	8
Other entertainment formats			
Weekdays 12 noon-6:00pm	Candlepins for Cash	7	1
Weekdays 6:00-9:00pm	Swiss Family Robinson	5	6
Sat.-Sun. 7:00am-12 noon	Funshine Saturday	5	1
Sat.-Sun. 12 noon-6:00pm	"None but the Brave"	56	1
	NBA playoffs	7	3
	major league baseball (NBC)	4	7
	Masters' Tournament	7	2
	Great Entertainment (movies)	5	2
Sat.-Sun. 6:00-9:00pm	Super Bowl	5	1
Sat.-Sun. after 9:00pm	Great Entertainment (movies)	5	2
Information			
Weekdays 7:00am-12 noon	Good Morning	5	1
	A.M. America	5	1
	Romper Room	5	5
	news highlights (CBS)	7	1
Weekdays 6:00-9:00pm	The People, Cause, Promise	7	1
Sat.-Sun. 7:00am-12 noon	Nature World of Captain Bob	5	3
	Jabberwocky	5	1
	Midday News	5	2
	For Kids Only	4	2
	Eyewitness News	4	1
Sat.-Sun. 12 noon-6:00pm	Farewell to Winter	4	4
	Go	4	1
	What's the Senate All About	7	7
	Sound off	5	1
	Homework Special	5	1
Sat.-Sun. 6:00-9:00pm	Boston 7 Newsroom	7	2
	News 5	5	1
	Big Battles	5	2
Unknown time	Boston Legacy	5	2
Other promos			
	Television Code	38	1
	Better UHF reception	38	2

INDEPENDENT STATIONS

	Name of Program	City	Number of Promos
Cartoon comedy			
Weekdays 7:00am–12 noon	Porky Pig and Friends	Seattle	1
Weekdays 12 noon–6:00pm	Flintstones	Seattle	2
	Flintstones	Norfolk	1
	Flintstones	New York	1
	Bugs Bunny and Friends	Washington	3
	Bugs Bunny and Friends	New York	1
	Huckleberry Hound	New York	1
	Casper and Friends	Seattle	1
Other comedy drama			
Weekdays 7:00am–12 noon	My Favorite Martian	Seattle	1
	Dennis the Menace	Sacramento	1
Weekdays 12 noon–6:00pm	Bewitched	Seattle	2
	Bewitched	New York	1
	Leave It to Beaver	Seattle	4
	Leave It to Beaver	Louisville	1
	Leave It to Beaver	Norfolk	2
	Partridge Family	Sacramento	1
	I Love Lucy	Milwaukee	1
	The Munsters	Detroit	3
	The Munsters	Milwaukee	1
	The Munsters	Seattle	2
	The Addams Family	Detroit	1
	Gilligan's Island	Washington	1
	Dick Van Dyke Show	Washington	1

	Name of Program	City	Number of Promos
	Hazel	Norfolk	1
	Hazel	Atlanta	1
Weekdays 6:00-9:00pm	Andy Griffith	Atlanta	1
	Father Knows Best	Norfolk	1
	Hogan's Heroes	Washington	1
	Hogan's Heroes	Buffalo	1
	Hogan's Heroes	Detroit	3
	Hogan's Heroes	Norfolk	1
	Dick Van Dyke Show	Norfolk	1
	Gilligan's Island	Louisville and Washington	2
	That Girl	Milwaukee	1
	Beverly Hillbillies	Milwaukee	1
	Gomer Pyle	Milwaukee	1
	I Dream of Jeannie	Milwaukee	1
Sat.-Sun. 7:00am-12 noon	Abbott and Costello	Washington	1
	Three Stooges/ Little Rascals/ Addams Family	Atlanta	1
Sat.-Sun. 12 noon-6:00pm	Bewitched	Washington	1
Action-adventure			
Weekdays 7:00am-12 noon	Spiderman	Washington	1
Weekdays 12 noon-6:00pm	Speed Racer	Washington	2
	Marine Boy	Washington	2
	Star Trek	Buffalo	1
	Lost in Space	Detroit	4
	Mod Squad	Sacramento	2
	Batman	Louisville	4
Weekdays 6:00-9:00pm	Untouchables	Detroit	1
	Dragnet	Buffalo	1
	Tarzan	Washington	2
	FBI	Sacramento	1
Weekdays after 9:00pm	Bonanza	Milwaukee	3
	Police Surgeon	Milwaukee	1
Sat.-Sun. 7:00am-12 noon	The Champions	Louisville	1
Sat.-Sun 12 noon-6:00pm	Tarzan	Louisville	1

	Name of Program	City	Number of Promos
Sat.-Sun. 6:00-9:00pm	The Bronx Is Burning	New York	5
Variety and quiz			
Weekdays 12 noon-6:00pm	Hilarious House of Frightenstein	New York	2
	Mickey Mouse Club	New York	3
	Mickey Mouse Club	Milwaukee	1
	Mickey Mouse Club	Seattle	2
	Mickey Mouse Club	Buffalo	1
	Funsville (Presto, 3 Stooges)	Louisville	1
Weekdays 6:00-9:00pm	Dealer's Choice	Atlanta	1
	Diamond Head Game	Atlanta	1
Weekdays after 9:00pm	Dinah	Detroit	1
Sat.-Sun. 7:00am-12 noon	Wonderama	New York	1
Sat.-Sun. 6:00-9:00pm	Hee Haw	Milwaukee	1
Other entertainment formats			
Weekdays 6:00-9:00pm	"Captain from Castile" (movie)	Milwaukee	6
	movies	Washington	1
	movies	Sacramento	1
	movies	Milwaukee	1
	sports— Baltimore Orioles	Washington	1
Weekdays after 9:00pm	movies	Seattle	1
	movies	New York	1
	movies	Detroit	1

APPENDIX G
LIST OF NONCOMMERCIAL
ANNOUNCEMENTS

BOSTON WEEKEND TELEVISION

		Channel	Number of NCAs
Health/safety			
Athletics	AAU Junior Olympics	38	1
	Olympic coins	56	1
	good sports competition—WBZ Radio and Massachusetts JCs	4	1
Health care	Puff 'n Stuff—Overweight caused by overeating	4	1
	anti-smoking—American Heart Association	4	1
	anti-smoking—American Lung Association	4	2
	anti-smoking—American Lung Association	4	1
	good diet to prevent heart disease— American Heart Association	4	1
	diet and exercise to prevent heart disease—American Heart Association	4	1
	oral cancer—American Dental Association	5	1
	dental care—Group W	4	1
	dental care—American Dental Association	38	1
Nutrition	UCLA School of Public Health/ABC	5	3
	President's Consumer Advisor	5	1
	Puff 'n Stuff Goodtime Club	4	1
	Dairy Council—nutrition labeling	5	1
	Cereal Institute, Inc.	38	1
	Group W—PSA	4	2
Safety	Puff 'n Stuff Goodtime Club— seat belts	4	1
	Highway Users Federation—bike safety	38	1
	Red Cross	7	1
	Green Cross-National Safety Council	5	1

206

		Channel	Number of NCAs
	Green Cross, toy safety	38	1
	Green Cross	4	1
	U.S. Consumer Product Safety Commission	5	1
	U.S. Consumer Protection Agency	5	2
	National Safety Council	5	1
Ecology/environment			
Animal care	MSPCA	4	1
	Humane Society of United States	4	1
Anti-pollution/ anti-litter	Southern Baptist—anti-litter	4	1
	Puff 'n Stuff Goodtime Club—recycling	4	1
	Puff 'n Stuff Goodtime Club—clean play areas	4	1
	USDA and Forest Service—don't pollute	38	1
	USDA and Forest Service	5	1
	Advertising Council—babes in the woods	4	2
	Audubon sanctuary	56	1
	Keep America Beautiful	4	2
	State Forester and U.S. Forest Service	4	1
Youth organizations			
	Girl Scouts of America—leaders	38	1
	Girl Scouts of America—leaders	5	2
	Girl Scouts of America	4	1
	Girl Scouts of America	38	1
	Girls Clubs of America	4	1
	Boy Scouts of America	5	3
	United Way-Boys Clubs of America	38	1
	Camp Fire Girls	38	1
	Boys Clubs	38	1
	YMCA	38	1
Other voluntary and nonprofit organizations			
Voluntary help programs	Foster Parents	5	1
	Voluntary Action Center of Met. Boston	7	1
	Women's American ORT	4	1
	Big Sisters	5	1
UNICEF/CARE	United Nations Children's Fund	5	1

		Channel	Number of NCAs
Reading	Smithsonian Institution—RIF	7	1
Museums	Museum of Science	5	1
	Museum of Science—business membership	4	1
	Museum of Science	38	1
	Boston Children's Theater	5	1
	Worcester Science Center	4	1
Prosocial announcements			
Anti-discrimination	Campaign for Human Development/ U.S. Catholic Conference	56	1
	Dept. of Health, Education and Welfare	5	3
	Puff 'n Stuff Goodtime Club	4	1
Religious organization messages	Methodist Church (sharing)	4	1
	Franciscan Communication Center	5	1
	Puff 'n Stuff (sports)	4	1
	Puff 'n Stuff (growing up)	4	1
	Puff 'n Stuff (reputation)	4	1
Miscellaneous/other causes			
Bicentennial	Boston 200	5	1
	Boston 200	4	1
	Boston 200	4	1
	Boston 200	5	1
	ARBA, Washington—Bicentennial	4	1
	Museum of Fine Arts	5	1
Consumerism	Better Business Bureau (Jr. Consumer Tips)	4	2
Government organizations	U.S. Postal Service	38	1
	Massachusetts Dept. of Commerce and Development, Div. of Tourism	56	1
	Department of Treasury	5	1

INDEPENDENT STATIONS

		City	Number of NCAs
Health/safety			
Athletics	N.Y. Association for Health, Physical Education and Physical Fitness	New York	1
Health care	Tidewater Hospitals Council	Norfolk	1

		City	Number of NCAs
	President's Council on Physical Fitness	Atlanta	1
	President's Council on Physical Fitness	Louisville	1
	Society to Prevent Blindness	Louisville	1
	Schick Center for Non-Smoking	Sacramento	1
	backyard fairs for Leukemia	Milwaukee	1
	St. Jude's Hospital—cancer	Washington	1
	American Association of Orthodontists	Washington	1
	Public Service Announcement—child's health	Detroit	1
Nutrition	Ad Council—cookie monster	Milwaukee	1
Safety	Safety in the subway	New York	2
	Fire Dept.—how to report a fire	New York	1
	American Red Cross	Washington	1
	U.S. Consumer Product Safety Commission	New York	1
	California Highway Patrol	Sacramento	1
Ecology/environment			
Animal care	Dept. of Fish and Wildlife	Louisville	1
	National Audubon Society	New York	1
Anti-pollution/ anti-litter	South Coast Botanical Garden	New York	1
	Ad Council—prevent forest fires	Louisville	2
	USDA-Forest Service	Norfolk	1
	EPA—clean up	New York	1
	forest fire prevention	New York	1
Youth organizations			
	Boy Scouts of America	New York	1
	Boy Scouts of America	Buffalo	1
	Boys Clubs of America	Milwaukee	1
	Girl Scouts of America	Detroit	1
	Camp Fire Girls	Buffalo	1
	Milwaukee YMCA	Milwaukee	1
Voluntary and nonprofit organizations			
Voluntary help programs	Seattle Urban League	Seattle	1
	Goodwill	Atlanta	1

		City	Number of NCAs
	CARE World Hunger Fund	Norfolk	1
	United Negro College Fund	Milwaukee	1
	Christian Children's Fund	Washington	1
UNICEF	UNICEF	Atlanta	1
Reading	Smithsonian Institution—RIF	Milwaukee	1
	Project Shape—funded through CETA	New York	1
Museums	Leddon Aquarium	Buffalo	1
	Crafts Museum—Niagara Falls	Buffalo	1
	Metropolitan Museum of Art	New York	1
	Afro-American Cultural Center	Buffalo	1
	Hudson River Museum	New York	1
Prosocial announcements			
Religious messages, other	PCU—God's Love	Norfolk	1
	School for the Deaf—let people be friends	Washington	1
	Dept. of HEW—be yourself	Washington	1
	Catholic archdiocese—gossip	New York	1
Miscellaneous			
Government organization	Social Security	Washington	1
	U.S. Savings Bonds	Louisville	1
	Upward Bound	Washington	1

Product Type/ Company	Product Name	Number of Times Aired
Toys (cars, planes, other)		
Ideal	Evel Knievel stunt cycle	1
Ideal	Evel Knievel Formula 1 dragster	1
Ideal	Evel Knievel stunt and crash car	1
Ideal	Derry Daring and her motorcycle	1
Ideal	Mighty Mo dump truck	2
Ideal	Tiny Mighty Mo	1
Kenner	SSP Smash-up Derby	2
Kenner	SSP Tournament of Thrills	1
Kenner	TTP tower and car	1
Marx	Pit Change Charger	1
Mattel	Putt-Putt Railroad	2
Mattel	Thundershift 500	4
Mattel	Sunshine Family van	2
Mattel	Spinwelder race car factory	1
Mattel	Spinwelder airplane factory	5
Meco	Mobile Bat Lab/Jokermobile	1
Dolls and doll play sets		
Aurora	Kar-a-a-ate Men	3
Hasbro	G.I. Joe secret mountain outpost	2
Hasbro	Fantastic Seawolf	2
Ideal	Rub-a-Dub Dolly	1
Ideal	Baby Dreams	3
Ideal	Live-in Train	3
Kenner	Dusty gymnastic set	1
Kenner	Six Million Dollar Man and bionic transport and repair station	5
Marx	safari adventure set (1)	2
Marx	safari adventure set (2)	1
Mattel	Baby Tender Love	3
Mattel	Baby Thataway	5
Mattel	Quick Curl Barbie beauty center	3
Mattel	Barbie's dream boat	5
Mattel	Barbie's townhouse	1
Mattel	free-moving Barbie	1

Product Type/ Company	Product Name	Number of Times Aired
Meco	Planet of the Apes fortress/catapult	1
Meco	Waltons' farmhouse gift set	1
Romper Room	Weebles West, Weebles tree house	1
Indoor games and play		
Child Guidance	Push and Play/Schroeder's piano	1
Child Guidance	Kentucky Fried Chicken	2
Child Guidance	Brunswick bowling center	2
G.A.F.	GAF Viewmaster gift pack	1
G.A.F.	GAF Viewmaster rear screen projector	1
Hasbro	Lite Brite	2
Ideal	Mousetrap game	2
Kenner	Spirograph	2
Kenner	girder and panel building set	2
Kenner	Snoopy Drive-in Movie/movie viewer (1)	1
Kenner	Snoopy Drive-in Movie/movie viewer (2)	1
Lego	Lego building system 190	2
Lego	Lego building set 145	1
Marx	Electra Hockey	2
Marx	Rock 'em Sock 'em Robots	1
Marx	Barnstormer	1
Marx	Magic Shot shooting gallery	2
Mego	Star Trek U.S.S. Enterprise gift set	1
Milton Bradley	Pitch-a-Roo	1
Parker Brothers	Nerf gliders	2
Parker Brothers	Lost Gold	3
Remco	Magic Hat	1
Romper Room	Weebles treasure island	2
Schaper	Ants in Pants	1
?	TV magic cards	2
Outdoor games and toys		
Cox	Cox Sure Flyer Piper Comanche	3
Honda	Kick 'n Go	6
Marx	Big Wheel	3
Sears Roebuck	Free Spirit 10-speed bike	1
Toy stores		
Child World	Child World	1
Other toys, hobbies, crafts		
Gabriel	Potterycraft	1
Kenner	Betty Crocker Easy Bake potato chip maker	1
Mattel	Jewel Magic	5
U.S. Post Office	U.S. stamp kit	1

Product Type/ Company	Product Name	Number of Times Aired
?	Mr. Bubble bank	3
Breakfast cereals		
Sugared cereals		
General Mills	Trix	4
General Mills	Lucky Charms	2
Kellogg's	Apple Jacks	1
Kellogg's	Frosted Flakes (1)	2
Kellogg's	Frosted Flakes (2)	1
Kellogg's	Frosted Flakes (3)	1
Kellogg's	Sugar Smacks	1
Kellogg's	Sugar Pops (1)	3
Kellogg's	Sugar Pops (2)	1
Kellogg's	Cocoa Krispies	3
Kellogg's	Frosted Mini-Wheats (1)	2
Kellogg's	Frosted Mini-Wheats (2)	1
Post	Honeycombs (1)	1
Post	Honeycombs (2)	1
Post	Super Sugar Crisp	3
Post	Alpha Bits	1
Quaker	Captain Crunch Punch Crunch	5
Ralston Purina	Freakies (1)	5
Ralston Purina	Freakies (2)	5
Nonsugared cereals		
General Mills	Cheerios (1)	2
General Mills	Cheerios (2)	2
Kellogg's	Raisin Bran (1)	1
Kellogg's	Raisin Bran (2)	2
Kellogg's	Rice Krispies	5
Candies and sweets		
Candies		
Mars	Milky Way	1
Mars	3 Musketeers	1
?	Kit Kat	1
?	M & Ms	1
Reese	Reese's peanut butter cup (1)	2
Reese	Reese's peanut butter cup (2)	1
Hershey	Hershey's milk chocolate with almonds (1)	1
Hershey	Hershey's milk chocolate with almonds (2)	1
Hershey	Rally	1

Product Type/ Company	Product Name	Number of Times Aired
Hershey	Mr. Goodbar	9
Life Saver	Lifesaver rolls/lollipops	2
Nestle's	Nestle's Crunch	2
Nestle's	Chocolite	5
Nestle's	$100,000 candy bar (1)	1
Nestle's	$100,000 candy bar (2)	1
Cakes and cookies		
Keebler	Rich 'n Chips	1
Kellogg's	chocolate-peppermint frosted Pop Tarts	1
McDonald's	McDonaldland cookies (1)	1
McDonald's	McDonaldland cookies (2)	1
Nabisco	Chips Ahoy	3
Nabisco	Oreo cookies (1)	2
Nabisco	Oreo cookies (2)	1
Nabisco	Fig Newtons	1
Pillsbury	chocolate chip cookies	4
Sunshine	Hydrox cookies	1
Ice cream, desserts		
Hunt-Wesson	Snack Pak	1
Nestle's	Nestle's Quik	4
Fruit-flavored drinks and ices		
Kool Aid	Kool Aid soft drink mix	2
Other candies, sweets		
Durkee-Mower	Marshmallow Fluff	3
Snack foods		
Pringle's	potato chips	1
Other foods		
Canned and packaged prepared foods		
Chef Boyardee	mini-ravioli	1
Chef Boyardee	Rollercoasters/spaghetti and meatballs	1
Chef Boyardee	ravioli	1
Dairy products		
Hood	Firm 'n Fruity yogurt	2
Restaurants and supermarkets		
Brigham's	birthday party	3
Burger King	hamburger (1)	2
Burger King	hamburger (2)	3
McDonald's	cheeseburgers (1)	2
McDonald's	burgers/fries/shakes/cookies (2)	1
McDonald's	McDonald's (3)	2
McDonald's	McDonald's (4)	1
McDonald's	McDonald's (5)	1

Product Type/ Company	Product Name	Number of Times Aired
Vitamins and medicine		
?	Appedrine	1
Household products		
Janex	Batman and Robin talking alarm clock	1
Kenner	Snoopy pencil sharpener	2
Personal care products		
?	Crazy Foam soap	1
Kenner	Snoopy toothbrush	2
Miscellaneous products		
Motion pictures		
Paramount	The Snow Queen	2
Walt Disney Prod.	Snow White and the Seven Dwarfs (1)	1
Walt Disney Prod.	Snow White and the Seven Dwarfs (2)	1
Walt Disney Prod.	Treasure Island/Dr. Syn Alias the Scarecrow (1)	1
Walt Disney Prod.	Treasure Island/Dr. Syn Alias the Scarecrow (2)	2
Recreation and travel		
Edaville Railroad	Edaville Railroad	1
Crimson Travel	California trip	1

APPENDIX I
LIST OF TOY PRICES

Company	Basic Item(s) Advertised	Basic Price	Other Components—Sold Separately	Add'l. Price	Total Price
		Cars, Planes, Other			
Ideal	Evel Knievel stunt cycle (incl. motorcycle, starter)	$ 9.96	Evel Knievel figure	$ 3.87	$11.99*
Ideal	Derry Daring and her motor-cycle (incl. figure, cycle, winder)	12.99			12.99
Ideal	Tiny Mighty Mo (incl. fire engine, tank, dump truck, $3.99 each)	11.97			11.97
Ideal	Evel Knievel stunt and crash car (incl. car, ramp, figure, winder)	10.92			10.92
Ideal	Mighty Mo dump truck	10.88			10.88
Ideal	Evel Knievel Formula 1 dragster (incl. winder, parachute, figure)	14.99			14.99
Mattel	Sunshine Family van (incl. Piggyback Shack, craft book)	9.99	Sunshine Family (three figures and book)	6.99	16.98
Mattel	Putt-Putt Railroad (gas station, truck, depot, engine, two cars)	10.86			10.86
Mattel	Spinwelder airplane factory (incl. welder, airplane parts)	7.87	six-volt lantern battery	2.18	10.05
Mattel	Spinwelder race car factory (incl. welder, parts for two cars)	7.87	six-volt lantern battery	2.18	10.05
Mattel	Thundershift 500 (two hot wheels, Flying Thunder cars, track)	11.87			11.87
Marx	Pit Change Charger (power wrench, battery box, jack, spare tire)	11.99	two batteries	.59	12.58
Kenner	SSP Smash-up Derby (incl. car, truck, two ramps)	7.88			7.88
Kenner	SSP Tournament of Thrills (car, removable figure)	7.88			7.88
Kenner	TTP tower and car (car, winder, ramp) (four cars shown, $6.54 ea.)	26.16			26.16
Hasbro	Fantastic Sea Wolf (giant squid, scope)	13.99	G.I. Joe figure	3.99	17.98
Meco	Mobile Bat Lab (Batbasket and Bat-hook, $12.97); Jokermobile (incl. squirt-ing daisy, Batbumper, $4.97)	17.94	22 posable figures, $3.49 ea.; 4 fighting superheroes, $2.69 ea.; 16 bendable heroes, $.99 ea.	103.38	121.32
Parker Bros.	Nerf Gliders: Jumbo Jet, Delta Wing, Splash Plane, Fabulous Plane, $1.69 ea.	6.76			6.76

*Total price includes basic item and other components purchased together.

Company	Basic Item(s) Advertised	Basic Price	Other Components— Sold Separately	Add'l. Price	Total Price
		Dolls and Doll Play Sets			
Ideal	Baby Dreams	$11.99			$11.99
Ideal	Rub-a-Dub Dolly (with shawl)	10.88			10.88
Ideal	Live-in Train (incl. four dolls, locomotive, two cars, luggage)	14.99			14.99
Aurora	Kar-a-a-ate Men (two action figures)	13.92			13.92
Hasbro	G.I. Joe secret mountain outpost	9.97	Mike Powers (Atomic Man)	$ 4.99	14.96
Kenner	Dusty gymnastic set (two outfits, trampoline, swings, other equipment)	8.87	Dusty doll	4.99	13.86
Kenner	Six Million Dollar Man ($6.87) and bionic transport repair station ($9.87)	16.74			16.74
Marx	safari action set (crocodile, $3.79; elephant, $8.99; buck hunter, $3.99; Kim, $3.99)	20.76			20.76
Marx	safari adventure set (lion, $4.99; buck hunter, $3.99; tiger, $4.99; gorilla, $4.99)	18.96			18.96
Meco	Planet of the Apes fortress (incl. weapons and weapons bench, $12.97) and Planet of the Apes catapult (with six boulders, $9.97)	22.94	10 action figures, $2.99 ea.; 5 bendable figures, $4.95 (Planet of the Apes collections)	34.85	57.79
Meco	Waltons' farmhouse (six Waltons, chair, bed, couch, radio)	17.89			17.89
Mattel	Baby Tender Love (bottle, Kleenex)	10.99			10.99
Mattel	Baby Thataway	9.87	batteries	.59	10.46
Mattel	Barbie's dream boat (flags, plates, other equipment)	9.87	Barbie doll	4.84	14.71
Mattel	Barbie's townhouse (couch, end table, two easy chairs, table, others)	16.96	Barbie Sweet Sixteen doll	5.99	22.95
Mattel	free-moving Barbie (shorts, shirt, gown, tennis racket, ball, golf club)	4.84	other Barbie fashion clothes	7.05	11.89
Mattel	Quick Curl Barbie beauty center (makeup, hair-styling equipment)	10.87			10.87
Mego	Star Trek U.S.S. Enterprise gift set (with command chair, console, three telespeed cards)	11.99	5 Star Trek action figures, $2.66 ea.	13.30	24.99*
Romper Room	Weebles treasure island (ship, longboat, hammock, islands, four Weebles)	10.88			10.88
Romper Room	Weebles West (incl. fort, house, Indians, $11.88) and Weebles tree house (tree house, two figures, table, chair, tricycle, $9.88)	21.76			21.76

*Total price includes basic item and other components purchased together.

Company	Basic Item(s) Advertised	Basic Price	Other Components— Sold Separately	Add'l. Price	Total Price
			Indoor Games and Toys		
Kenner	Snoopy drive-in movie (with cassettes, $12.99) and Snoopy movie viewer (with cassettes, $7.99)	$20.98	three D-type batteries	$ .89	$21.87
Kenner	Spirograph (incl. various disks)	4.97			4.97
?	TV Magic Cards	2.49	TV Mystery Cards	1.99	4.48
Lego Systems	Lego building set 145 (incl. wheels, shutters, windows, doors, bricks)	23.89			23.89
Lego Systems	Lego Building Set 190	28.89			28.89
Parker Bros.	Lost Gold (treasure finder, comic book, map)	5.97			5.97
Remco	Magic Hat (hat, wand)	9.99			9.99
Marx	Magic Shot shooting gallery (with gun)	7.99			7.99
Ideal	Mousetrap game (four mice, dice)	7.87			7.87
Milton Bradley	Pitch-a-Roo (four sets of cards, scorecards, target)	10.88			10.88
Child Guidance	Push and Play/Schroeder's piano	7.97			7.97
Marx	Rock 'em Sock 'em Robots	11.99			11.99
Hasbro	Lite-Brite (board, pegs)	7.97	refills: Bugs Bunny and Bozo, $1.99 ea.; light bulb, $.39	4.37	12.34
Schaper	Ants-in-Pants (complete)	3.97			3.97
Marx	Barnstormer (airplane, landing field, blocks for towers)	5.99			5.99
Child Guidance	Brunswick bowling center	11.87			11.87
Marx	Electro Hockey (auto scoring, point bell)	29.88	three batteries	.89	30.77
GAF	GAF Viewmaster gift pack (Viewmaster, five slides)	5.99			5.99
GAF	GAF Viewmaster rear screen projector	18.99	reels: Casper, Flint- stones, $1.75 ea.	3.50	22.49
Kenner	girder and panel building set	12.97			12.97
Child Guidance	Kentucky Fried Chicken (food, motorcycle, cars)	8.88			8.88
			Outdoor Toys		
Marx	Big Wheel (saddlebag, racing brake)	13.88			13.88
Cox	Cox Sure Flyer Piper Comanche (plane, fuel, battery included)	11.97	starter	2.99	14.96
Sears	Free Spirit ten-speed bike	129.95			129.95
Honda	Kick 'n Go	29.95			29.95
			Other Toys, Crafts, Hobbies		
Gabriel	Potterycraft (wheel, tools, paints)	12.99	batteries	.89	13.88
U.S. Post Office	U.S. stamp kit	2.00	Five other stamp kits shown, $2.00 ea.	10.00	12.00
Mattel	Jewel Magic (beads)	9.87			9.87
Kenner	Betty Crocker Easy Bake potato chip maker (two pans, bowls, squeezer, mix)	4.99	Easy Bake oven	12.87	17.86

F. EARLE BARCUS, professor of communication research at the School of Public Communication of Boston University, has spent the past several years studying the content of modern mass communication in addition to teaching communication theory, broadcast research, and the social effects of mass communication.

Prior to recent studies of children's television, supported by grants from Action for Children's Television, his research included analyses of nonprescription drug advertising on television, the social content of newspaper comics, and parental influences on children's media exposure.

Professor Barcus received his Ph.D. in communication from the University of Illinois in 1959. He is the author of a book, Alumni Administration, and has contributed chapters on communication and health education, drug advertising, and content analysis techniques. Articles have appeared in Annals of the American Academy of Political and Social Science, Journalism Quarterly, Journal of Broadcasting, and The Progressive.

RACHEL WOLKIN is general counsel to Action for Children's Television. She received her J.D. degree from Villanova Law School, where she was an associate editor of the Villanova Law Review.

Before attending law school, Ms. Wolkin studied various aspects of children's television at the Annenberg School of Communications of the University of Pennsylvania. She also holds a Master's of Arts in teaching from Johns Hopkins University.

CARRASCOLENDAS: Bilingual Education Through
Television

Frederick Williams and
Geraldine Van Wart

CITIZENS' GROUPS AND BROADCASTING

Donald L. Guimary

GETTING TO SESAME STREET: Origins of the
Children's Television Workshop

Richard M. Polsky

TELEVISION AS A CULTURAL FORCE

edited by Richard Adler and
Douglass Cater

POLITICS IN PUBLIC SERVICE ADVERTISING
ON TELEVISION

David L. Paletz, Roberta E.
Pearson, and Donald L. Willis